Joseph Cowen

# Speeches delivered by Joseph Cowen

As Candidate for Newcastle-upon-Tyne, at the General Election, 1885

Joseph Cowen

**Speeches delivered by Joseph Cowen**
*As Candidate for Newcastle-upon-Tyne, at the General Election, 1885*

ISBN/EAN: 9783337176761

Printed in Europe, USA, Canada, Australia, Japan

Cover: Foto ©ninafisch / pixelio.de

More available books at **www.hansebooks.com**

# SPEECHES

DELIVERED BY

# JOSEPH COWEN,

AS

CANDIDATE FOR NEWCASTLE-UPON-TYNE,

AT THE

GENERAL ELECTION, 1885.

Newcastle-upon-Tyne:
ANDREW REID, PRINTING COURT BUILDINGS, AND 12, COLLINGWOOD STREET.

1885.

# INTRODUCTION.

In compliance with a desire, which has found extensive expression, not only in the immediate district, but even in remote parts of the country, the Election Speeches of Mr. Joseph Cowen are issued in the form of the present volume. A pressure of work, occasioned by the official requirements of the General Election, has slightly delayed the completion of the undertaking beyond the contemplated date; but serving, as the collection is chiefly meant to do, the purposes of future perusal and consultation, no inconvenience is likely to arise from this cause.

The circumstances and conditions of the campaign which has been so recently brought to a close have been unique in the history of local, if not of national, electioneering. Determined to carry out, in his own person, alike the letter and spirit of the Corrupt Practices Act, now for the first time brought to a general test, Mr. Cowen, from the outset, dispensed with all organized assistance, whether voluntary or hired, save that of his legal agent, Mr. T. J. Forster; and through the medium of public meetings, which he freely held and addressed, he appealed to the intelligence and sense of justice inherent in the community with which he had been so long identified, and which he had hitherto so faithfully served. Although conscious of the great disadvantage at which he was placed by the systematic and methodical machinery brought to bear in the interests of his rivals, Mr. Cowen steadily adhered to this course to the end; and his triumphant return, for the fourth time, as one of the members for Newcastle, fully vindicates the soundness and wisdom of the policy which he has pursued.

With the view of rendering the book useful as a permanent source of reference, there has been added a copious and carefully compiled index of subjects at the close; and a glance at this section of the work will at once reveal the wide and comprehensive field of political questions, of past, present, and prospective interest, which the addresses have traversed. If they may not obtain universal assent, it will be generally conceded that the speaker has placed his opinions, and the arguments upon which they are based, with sun-clearness before the public; and the information elicited through the channel of question and answer will be valuable to many classes of readers. The speeches, even in the fugitive journalistic form, in which alone they have yet appeared, have been pronounced to be "a compendium of political science unmatched in our literature;" and, as such, it is hoped they may prove not unacceptable in the more convenient and accessible shape in which they are now presented.

*Newcastle-upon-Tyne*,
*December*, 1885.

# CONTENTS.

# ELECTION SPEECHES, 1885.

## THE PERSONAL ASPECTS OF THE ELECTION.

DELIVERED IN THE CIRCUS, NEWCASTLE-UPON-TYNE, ON SATURDAY EVENING, NOVEMBER 14TH, 1885.

CHAIRMAN—DR. RUTHERFORD.

MR. COWEN, M.P., who was received with loud cheering, which was renewed again and again, said :—Political controversy cannot be conducted with mathematical precision or metaphysical abstraction. It seldom evolves the best side of human nature, and often gives play to the most conflicting passions. Electioneering brings its angriest and most splenetic features to the surface. People go into it with all their rivalries newly ground and pointed—with the caulkers of their animosities sharpened, as smiths sharpen horses' shoes in a frost. (Loud laughter and cheers.) Such is the alchemy of faction, that it extracts scandal out of circumstances the most innocent and laudable. A candidate is forced, whether he likes it or not, to be egotistical. Self is his theme, and it is an awkward and embarrassing one. Mr. Cobbett, when censured for his self-laudation, justified it on the ground that, as he could not get any one else to praise him, he must needs praise himself (Laughter.) It is easy to be as overweening as Mr. Cobbett, but difficult to be as eloquent or as entertaining. (Hear, hear.) I am not placed in such a position, as I get more applause than I am entitled to. (Cries of "No, no.") But my abnormal relations with a section of Newcastle Liberals, impose on me to-night a less impersonal method of discourse than is to my taste. I will, however, put all I have to say on this subject into the shortest space compatible with clearness, and have it out and over at once and finally. (Loud cheers.) Let us go to the genesis of the differences. (Laughter.) I will attempt to define the requisite qualifications, and delineate the reciprocal duties, of electors and members of Parliament. What is the primary requirement for a representative? Character! (Cheers.) Errors in men, occupying private stations, harm only those who commit them; but a man, placed in a position of responsibility, owes much to himself and more to the crowd. When a watch goes wrong, it misleads only its owner; but when the town-clock gets out of gear, it misleads the public. (Loud laughter and cheers.) A man who tries to set society the right time should keep his clock in order. If he is to reform the world, he should render his life worthy of his principles. Ability is not in every man's power, but probity is. Talents are an adornment, but honesty alone is strength. (Cheers.) I do not stipulate that public men should be either saints or martyrs—that they should display the self-abnegation of General Gordon or the stoicism of Antoninus—but I do stipulate that they should be equal to the mean virtue of their generation, and that they should, at least, attempt some commerce in good actions. This is not an impossible ideal, and constituencies are entitled to exact it of their members. What is the second qualification? Knowledge! (Cheers.) If the science of legislation is to be learnt, it must be cultivated. No man can do this in a day. It must be the labour of years. And, to that labour, he must bring the powers of a mind prepared by previous training, and strengthened by preliminary discipline. He will find in history the hidden springs of human conduct. From the similarities and analogies which he will discover between what has been and what is, he will be able to draw guidance and inspiration.

Causes and events are linked, one with another, by an invincible fatality. They are founded on a train of occurrences seemingly without connection, but still all connected. It is an immense machine in which all is wheel and pulley, chain and spring. The genius and creative principle of each era is explicable only by a survey of the entire series. (Cheers.) A man is expected to serve an apprenticeship, or to pass a competitive examination, for every profession save criticism and government. (Laughter and cheers.) Legislators, like censors, are ready made. (Hear, hear.) Politics, however, are not personalities; yet, a man who can rattle off a list of names and measures, with the chronological exactness of a sporting prophet recounting the pedigree of a horse, is deemed a politician. (Laughter.) These authorities will tell you when such a member made a certain speech, or lost or won a given division, with the same minuteness that a tipster can tell you when "Hermit" won the Derby in a snowstorm, or how much weight "Barcaldine" carried when it won the Northumberland Plate over a weltering course. (Great laughter and cheers.) These personal data may be entertaining enough for gossip; but they are a trumpery contribution to the philosophy of government. (Hear.) It is no more politics than the gearing of an engine is its motive power. (Hear, hear.) What is the third qualification? Adaptability! (Hear, hear.) The House of Commons was once counted the best club in London. It is not so now. Caucuses have to be surmounted to enter it, and conciliated or beaten to stay in it. (Laughter.) Friction has risen there, as elsewhere; and energies are absorbed in interminable and often profitless debates. A medical certificate is as necessary for a legislator as for a soldier. (Loud laughter.) Men with weak digestions, or feeble hearts, may write books and start theories, but you want men with thick necks and deep chests to face, fight with, control, or keep abreast of, the fierce and eager natures to be met with in the Parliamentary *melee.*

(Renewed laughter and cheers.) When the mighty metropolis is putting its pulses to rest, the House of Commons is pumping away the sustaining blood of the nation. It is said to be the best night-house in London; but that is for the audience, not for the performers. (Laughter.) Only a strong enduring man is equal to the wearying strain requisite to win his way to the front. There are men who survive this effort, and discover in it material for a comfortable existence. They form the working strength of Parliament. There is a House of Commons' character, and a House of Commons' intellect. Their gifts are not of an exalted order. They neither imply greatness, nor are they altogether incompatible with it. Really great men seldom succeed in Parliament. (Hear, hear.) Burke was a dinner-bell; and Gibbon, Jeffrey, and Macintosh were without influence in the House, although they were in their own spheres unrivalled. Even Sir George Lewis, the most learned Parliament man of our generation, was overshadowed by noisy mediocrities. Now, how far do I fulfil these conditions? That is the touchstone. (Loud cheers.) Well, I am neither a Solon nor a Thomas-a-Kempis; neither am I a Tartufe nor a Bœotian. (Laughter.) Compared with my ideal, I fail egregiously. But, perhaps, without any pharisaical pretence to an austerity of excellence above the composite of good and evil in ordinary mortals, I may compare with the average. (Cries of "Above it," "Far above it," and loud cheers.) Nothing more. I may, too, without incurring the accusation of vanity, urge that I know something of the local life of the community. (Hear, hear.) This is not an indispensable, although it is not an unimportant, qualification. But the same candour that leads me to confess my defective attainments and capacity, permits me to claim to have laboured for the constituency—faultily it may be, but faithfully and fearlessly I am sure. (Great cheering.) I would count myself an arrant coward if I had placed the desire of pleasing before the duty of serving you. (Hear, hear.) Plato expelled professional politicians from his Republic, and I suspect he was right in doing so. (Laughter and cheers.) Politics with me are a creed, and not a profession. (Renewed cheers.) I have espoused them as a duty, and not as the surest road to notoriety, or as an ultimate way to gain it. My tree of life is too firmly set for the bias of its stem to swerve in any new direction; and my convictions are too deeply rooted to be shaken by the blast of party displeasure. (Hear, hear.) They are the result of study, and have not been caught by contagion. (Laughter and cheers.) They may separate me from the party, but they unite me more closely to the nation. (Hear, hear.) About the third qualification, I am uncertain. I doubt whether I have the vigour, the vehemence, or the strong volition necessary to impress spoken thought on an independent audience; but as I neither dine out, dance, play whist, nor indulge in any of the exhausting excitements of the dinner-giving world of London—(loud laughter, and a voice: "Nor drink champagne")—I am able to fight through a session better than many who are much more robust. (Cheers.) I am sure, however, that I cannot get up the enthusiasm about details that many manifest. Some members will squabble for bare life over a word. Yet, their bills at best are but memoranda. The only vitality they have is in the character of the people who give them force. The only laws that last are those built on ideas; and the only stable form of rule is that in which the laws express the ideas of the population. This much for the duty of a member to his constituency. Now, as to the duty of the constituency to a member. (Hear, hear.) It is to be summed up in one word—confidence; watchful but not captious confidence. (Hear, hear, and cheers.) Obtain from him an explicit exposition of his principles. If he violate them, dismiss him. If he hold by them, trust him. Scrutinise him as closely as you like, but not cantankerously. (Cheers.) Insist on a vigorous fidelity to principle, but allow reasonable latitude in detail. Remember that, although elected by a section, he is member for the whole. He is a trustee for the country as well as the constituency. (Hear, hear.) His local knowledge may give colour to his thought, and enable him, with more effect than a stranger, to plead its interests when assailed ; yet, he should no more narrow his patriotism to his locality, than his services to a faction. (Cheers.) He is a representative, and not a delegate. There is nothing derogatory in being a delegate. They are often necessary ; but in Parliament delegation is impracticable. Every session emergencies arise when a decision must be given impromptu. But even if a reference were requisite, to whom is the member to refer ? (A cry of "Spence Watson," and loud laughter.) To the entire body of electors ? Then, there would have to be a vote of the constituency, before there could be a vote in Parliament. To state the proposal is to answer it If not to the electors, to what section of them ; how selected ; and how controlled ? Will the people thus duplicate their mandate ? I do not think so. If a member is to be a mere marionette—only to move when the strings are pulled—(loud laughter)—why not save the elections and the labour of direct representation ? The decisions of the constituencies, or the caucus, could be more easily transmitted by post or telegraph. This would answer as well, if making enactments summed up the whole duty of a representative. But there is something more to be done, in Parliament, than law-making and tax-levying. Popular liberty has to be guarded, justice has to be enforced, and aggression has to be resisted. This cannot be done by machines, however deftly manipulated. (Cheers.) It would be puerile to ignore that my following the line of action thus indicated has led to a local schism. The schismatics have not formulated their indictment, but they have assumed a Dr. Fell-ish attitude. What they dislike in my conduct, and why they dislike it, they do not tell. Perhaps it is too vague for definition. (Laughter.) Their unfriendliness puzzles me. I have tried—honestly tried—to account for it, but have not succeeded in doing so satisfactorily. It probably has various origins. Every man has rivals. But inasmuch as any ambition I have is erratic, and does not run counter to the common current, I do not see why it should excite either enmity or jealousy. Some men have enemies—often for no good reason. The set of a man's gait, or the shape of his head, may be an eyesore, and engender unknown alienation. (Laughter.) This, or something equally petty, may be the unconscious occasion of some of the political ill-will I have provoked. Who knows? But I suspect that the main cause of it is ignorance. (Hear, hear.) Many of my opponents are young men, and others strangers. They are not familiar with the past of Newcastle politics. None of them are men with whom I have been much associated. They talk of me as an old political comrade, and conjure up fanciful conflicts in which they and I have been jointly engaged. This is only a well-meant hallucination. (Laughter.) I never was associated with any of my antagonists until immediately preceding the election of 1874, and I had been active in public affairs for a quarter of a century before then. (Hear, hear.) In the work in which over that period—a long stretch in a man's lifetime—I was engaged, I had them always as critics, often as opponents, but certainly never as colleagues. (Hear, hear.) They misapprehended the bent of my mind, and the purpose of my efforts. (A voice: "That's true.") They took me to be a partizan, who would complacently fetch and carry for the Ministerial Whip. When they discovered their mistake, they were angry. Perhaps not unnaturally. But I cannot take blame to myself. My creed is written in the records of Tyneside in no equivocal language. It has been tainted with no falsehood—polished with no flattery. I acknowledge the right of my opponents to urge any or all their objections. Disappointment, rivalry, jealousy, dislike are, and have been, in all ages—and will be to the end of time—recognised as justifiable incentives to party warfare. I make no complaint if they are made to operate to my detraction. To argue against such mingled sentiments, however, would be as wise as arguing against the east wind. (Laughter.) It might irritate, but could not convince, those who cherish them. Time may wear away this ill-will; controversy won't.

> Things without all remedy
> Should be without regret;
> What's done is done.

The feeling of hostility with some of my antagonists has worked itself into a fanaticism. (Loud laughter.) It reminds me of a tale that is told of the fierce partizanship that once raged in Italy, between the admirers of Dante and of Ariosto. This was carried to such lengths that the champions of the rival poets resorted to duelling. One Danteite, who had often fought for his side, was at last wounded unto death. When dying, his only regret was that he could not live a few months longer, so as to be able to read the poems for whose superiority he had so often risked, and was now about to lose, his life. He had "gone out" twelve times, to uphold the reputation of the author of the "Divina Comedia" against that of the author of "Orlando Furioso," and he had never read the poems he had fought for. (Loud laughter.) Could the force of zealotry further go? Some stubborn controversialists in Newcastle have, I suspect, metaphorically fought numerous wordy duels—during this Liliputian controversy—(roars of laughter)—who are as ill-informed as to the merits of the matter in dispute, as the Italian duellist was of the poems of the man who was sometimes a Guelph and sometimes a Ghibelline. I am sorry for the dispute. There is nothing more noxious than prejudice, and few things more fatal than party spite. It is a species of mental vitriol which men bottle up in their bosoms to discharge against their opponents, but which, in the meantime, irritates, corrodes, and poisons their hearts. (Hear, hear.) I have no feeling of resentment for what is past. After viewing all the circumstances, and making due allowance for what has been accidental, and for what has been intentional, I retain the impression that nothing I have done, or said, justifies the acerbity that has been displayed in some quarters. (Hear, hear, and cheers.) And I know more than the public do. Men are often punished more for scandal than for sin. A lie, if it be killed, can sting sometimes like a dead wasp. But everything in life has its compensation, and if I have had to bear the brunt of party bitterness, I have been treated by the general public with a considerate generosity far beyond my deserts. (Cries of "No, no," and cheers.) I have infinitely more cause to be thankful than to repine. Virtue is the highest end of man's endeavour; but virtue is independent of the popular shout, of the lictor's *Fasces*. "It is the same, whether with or without the laurel crown or the curule chair. Honours do not sully it, and obscurity does not degrade it." The man who does his duty need not exclaim against fortune's fickleness. He can take its buffets and its rewards with equal thanks. But while there are some who, from personal or other reasons, have assumed an attitude of irreconcilable hostility, there are others who, while honestly disapproving of the course I have pursued on some questions, have not made their differences a cause of quarrel. (Hear, hear.) I respect their opposition, I am not dogmatic. I may be wrong (Cries of "No, no," and cheers.) Come, then, let us reason together, without any trace of condescension on the one side, or servility on the other. Let us be candid. Where there is no candour there can be no conciliation. Men are never so likely to settle a question easily, as when they discuss it freely. Discussion is not dissension, any more than denunciation is argument. I do not dislike clamour when there is an abuse. The fire-bell at night disturbs your sleep, but it keeps you from being burnt in bed. (Loud laughter.) Chase all opinion into the field of battle. There error dies—truth alone can live through such an ordeal. We will follow it whithersoever it leads—whether to our defeat or victory. (Cheers.) It is easy for us to satisfy ourselves that our convictions are held, in sacred trust, for the enlightenment of other men's minds. But it is not so easy for us to comprehend that other men's convictions are held in trust for the enlightenment of our minds. Can we be both logical and generous? We will try. I need not rhapsodically descant on points of argument. That is easy enough at any time. I will face the gulf that divides us, and either bridge it or level it up. (Cheers.) We will have no verbal quibbling. For purposes of detraction, there is nothing easier than to pick out sentences in a man's speeches or writings, divorce them from the context and the circumstances, and deduce from them an altogether different meaning from that which was meant. (Hear, hear.) Away with such Pecksniffianism! It is fit only for quibblers. Where, and when, have I differed from the organised Liberals during the last Parliament? On three cardinal questions—Parliamentary procedure, Ireland, and Egypt. (Hear, hear, and cheers.) Take them *seriatim,* listen to the reasons for my dissent, and say whether, or how far, I was or am right. I have always held that Parliamentary regulations needed re-adjusting—tightening in some directions, relaxing in others. They originated in different times, and were devised for different conditions, to those we live in. They were not drafted, off-hand, like a French constitution; but were the outcome of experience—the embodiment of precedent. Rules so devised are safer, stronger, more elastic, and better capable of defeating resistance from without, or controlling disorder within, than a minute code of practice drawn with lawyer-like precision. The object of the authors of the old procedure was to secure liberty of action and speech for members.

Kings formerly deprived them of one, and punished them for the other. But all interference by a single sovereign has long since ceased. A many-headed one, however, is scheming for his place. He will be as exacting as the former, and he brooks criticism as badly. I would jealously guard the power won from the old despotism, so as to be better able to contravene the new. I would have Parliament as free from caucuses, as from the Crown. (Loud cheers.) And to secure that I would resist, to the last, any attempt to tamper with the right and practice of untrammeled discussion. (Renewed cheers.) I am for leading, not driving, men. Comradeship, and not coercion, is my specific for good order. (Hear, hear.) Business can be better advanced, in an assembly of 600 free men, by mutual forbearance and courtesy than by force. The new code was long deliberated upon, and laboriously enacted. It is fair to assume that it was the product of mature Ministerial decision. It has been three sessions in force, and with what result? Practically none. (Hear, hear.) Business does not proceed one whit faster than it did. There has been a change, but no improvement. Debate, blocked up in one direction, has burst out in another. The old constitutional right of demanding redress of grievances, before voting supplies, has been all but abrogated. And what has happened? Members put their grievances into questions, and the "heckling" that goes on every night, and which you hear so much of, is but the water of Parliamentary talk forcing itself to its level. Discussion being stopped, on going into committee, it takes place in committee, with the consequence that the time occupied in voting the estimates has been lengthened, and not lessened, by the restrictions. (Hear, hear.) This much for the muzzling process, which I opposed. (Laughter.) What for the devolution scheme, which I cordially supported? It has not succeeded, though it cannot be said to have entirely failed. The principle is good, but it is fettered in operation. In its due development, I can alone see the machinery by which Parliament can keep abreast of its ever increasing work. Parliamentary arrangements, as they now stand, are a bundle of contraries. Members begin work when other people are leaving it. They live the finest part of the year in London, and the worst part in the country. (Laughter.) Why cannot the House meet in November instead of February? Between then and Christmas the Government could introduce their bills, and submit their estimates. On re-assembling in January, the bills could be discussed and read a second time. That done, the House should divide itself into committees, and proceed with the measures in detail till Easter. Between Easter and Whitsuntide the bills could be considered on report, read a third time, and rejected or passed. (Hear, hear.) This scheme would preserve the rights of debate, lighten the labour of members, and facilitate business. Every proposal tending in that direction I have supported, and will continue to do so. (A Voice: "You will," and cheers.) Every proposal, cloture-wise, I have opposed, and will oppose. What say you—am I right or wrong? (Shouts of "Right, right," and loud cheers.) Now, about Ireland—that thorny topic concerning which I have incurred unceasing censure. I will discuss ulterior projects for the government of that country at a subsequent meeting. Meanwhile, I only charge myself to defend my action in the last Parliament. I start from these premises—that it is the interest of the two countries to remain united, and that union is impossible if one is to coerce the other. (Cheers.) I argued, with what many thought wearying iteration, that coercion would not only fail in its immediate effect, but that it would leave behind a rankling sense of discontent which would be a present weakness, and might be a future danger, to the empire. (Hear, hear.) Is there any informed and unprejudiced man who will deny the truth of my contention, or the correctness of my forecast? The late Government put one thousand men in gaol without accusation or trial. (Cries of "Shame," "Shame.") Is there anyone here who will defend such a high-handed violation of the cherished principle of the Constitution? ("No, no." If there is, he is a bolder man than the authors of the Act. They are ashamed of it, and want it and all its equivocal accessories forgotten. ("Aye, well they may," and cheers.) It took them twelve months to discover what every tyro in statesmanship ought to have known would be the case—that the wholesale imprisonment of unaccused and innocent men could only intensify popular acrimony. When they learnt this, they entered into arrangements with Mr. Parnell for the release of the prisoners. But it was too late. The mischief had been done. The men who had been incarcerated were not "village ruffians," but village leaders. (Hear, hear.) When they were removed from their special spheres of influence, the direction of affairs passed to other and more desperate characters. The movement was driven underground, secret societies succeeded open agitation, and assassins succeeded agitators. (Hear, hear.) The storm had long been gathering. The lightning tarried only for a conductor. It found one in the "Invincibles." (Hear, hear.) Englishmen were startled, and yet there was nothing novel in what took place. The experience had been undergone a hundred times before. It is axiomatic—coercion begets conspiracy, and insurrection and assassination follow as certainly as the night the day. (Cheers.) But such was the unreasoning temper of the English people, that the voice of anyone who dared to repeat this historical truism was drowned in opprobrium. (Hear, hear.) The inevitable terror followed, and, like all other terrors, red or white, it has left a saddening trail behind it which this generation will not see erased. How stands Ireland towards England to-day, after four years of coercion? More gloomily resentful, disaffected, and estranged, than she has been since '98. Liberalism there, as a political force, is extinct. Coercion has killed it. The well-meant

Land Act and the Suffrage Act have failed to erase the chronic resentment engendered not only by repression itself, but by the spirit in which it was enacted, and the manner in which it was applied. I never questioned the motives of Ministers; but I did, and do, their wisdom. (Hear, hear.) It is easy to be wise after the event; but in this matter I was wise before it. (Loud cheers.) Next, about Egypt. In foreign affairs there are, roughly stated, two lines of policy—the national, and the cosmopolitan. I am for the former. (Hear, hear.) It is possible to abandon our dominions, and it is possible to hold them, but it is impossible to hold them and not be ready, if required, to fight for them. A big State is not necessarily a great State. We do not measure nations by their bulk, any more than we measure men by inches.. If we did, China would be our ideal, and not Athens. But while size is not synonomous with worth, I believe the advantages of a big British Empire, to its people and the world, are such as to outweigh all drawbacks. I am prepared to pay the price of its maintenance. The price may often mean war, and it always means preparedness for war. A commercial community cannot accept peace at all hazards, because no commerce would be safe under a flag dishonoured or despised. (Cheers.) But while upholding British interests, I would discharge British duties. I will hereafter explain, with more detail, this doctrine. For the present, it is sufficient, for my purpose, to say that while a policy of abandonment or retention is each logically defensible, there is no defence for the intermediate course which would retain the Empire, and yet refuse to take the necessary steps to do so. (Hear, hear.) We cannot neglect the diplomatic relations of European Powers, and yet assert a prominent interest in questions about which all Europe is interested; we cannot refuse to take precautions against Russia till she is at the very threshold of India, and yet declare that the independence of Afghanistan shall be defended at the cost of any number of English millions; we cannot, consistently, massacre unoffending savages in the name of Christian brotherhood; we cannot, in short, carry out the work of Pitt and Palmerston on the principles of the Peace Society. (Hear, hear.) One or other line we must run on. It is because the late Government tried to run on both that they ran into the gutter. (Loud cheers and laughter.) While I am for keeping what we have—by force of arms if requisite—I am not for aimless extension, or factious meddling in the affairs of other nations. Sancho Panza, administering and defending his island, is a better model than Don Quixote sallying forth to right the wrongs of the universe. (Hear, hear, and laughter.) Just as an individual would become an intolerable plague to his neighbours if he were always interfering with their domestic affairs, so a weak State becomes ridiculous, and a strong State tyrannical, when it seeks to enforce its form of Government upon peoples not subject to its sovereignty. (Cheers.) This is what the late Government tried to do in Egypt. England, as a nation, is interested in that country because we want a right of road through it. Englishmen, as individuals, are interested in it because they are large investors there. But Egypt is as much a part of the Turkish empire, as Canada is of the British empire—(hear, hear)—and it does not concern us what pacha is president, provided the road is kept and order is secured. For some incomprehensible reason, the Liberal Government took an inveterate dislike to Arabi; and the gratification of that dislike has cost the English and Egyptian taxpayers many millions of money, and entailed the loss of many thousands of lives. ("Shame.") The Cabinet were warned, solemnly and earnestly warned, by their agents, of what would follow the bombardment of Alexandria; but buoyed up by the transitory success of their Dulcigno exploit, they heeded not the warning. They fired on the forts, and the fire they then lighted is burning still. It has burnt a hole in many pockets, and not a few reputations. (Hear, hear.) I opposed that policy throughout, and argued that if disorder were imminent in Egypt, and our interests required protection, we should act with, or by, or through the Sultan as the sovereign of the country and the head of its religion. (Cheers.) But the official Liberals were too busy donning their war-paint, and their supporters were too confiding, to listen to warnings from outsiders. (Laughter.) If there be any merit in foreseeing the end from the beginning, I may fairly claim it in this case. (Hear, hear.) I do not pretend that the circumstance proves the possession of any unusual perspicacity. Anyone would have seen it if he had looked with his own eyes, and not through Ministerial spectacles. (Laughter.) The position created by the late Ministry raised the most formidable difficulties, and caused the bitterest disappointments and deceptions. They failed, from the first, to grasp the determining cause of events, and to measure the forces at their disposal or arrayed against them. They rushed into the enterprise without deliberation, and, when its magnitude dawned upon them, they were paralysed. They missed every opportunity, exaggerated every difficulty, provoked all our neighbours, while enforcing the respect of none, and left every problem unsolved to embarrass them in the treatment of the next. (Cheers.) Everything they endeavoured to shirk they were compelled to do; only they always did it too late, and reaped nothing, but added humiliation and renewed disaster. I care not to shelter myself behind great names; but it is a certain satisfaction that the policy I and others advocated, when it had few friends, has been the policy advocated by such competent but contrary authorities as Prince Bismarck and General Gordon, and which, with such modifications as the circumstances would permit, has been adopted by the present Ministry. (Hear, hear.) To judge by the events, therefore, on the three subjects in which I have differed from the late Government—Parliamentary procedure, Ireland, and Egypt—I have been right. (A voice: "So you have," and loud cheers.) But therein lies my offence.

(Laughter.) If I had been wrong, I could have been easily forgiven. But to be opposed to your party, and be right at the same time, is "intolerable and not to be endured." (Renewed laughter and cheers.) Two thousand years ago, Aristotle warned candid friends of the troubles that were in store for them, and Mr. Canning embodied the philosophical hortation in two well-known lines—

> **Of all the plagues, good heaven, thy wrath can send,**
> **Save, oh save me, from a candid friend.**

(Loud laughter.) M. Constance, the French statesman and author, relates that he knew a sailor who was once on board a vessel with a passenger who had freqnently made the same voyage. The passenger pointed out to the captain a rock hidden beneath the waves; but the captain would not listen to him. The man insisted upon it, and his urgency causing some uneasiness amongst the other passengers, the captain, under the plea that the man's presence incited to mutiny, had him thrown into the sea. This energetic measure put an end to all remonstrance; and nothing could be more touching than the unanimity that reigned on board, until suddenly the vessel struck the reef and was lost. They had drowned the giver of the warning; but the rocks remained. (Loud laughter and cheers.) We have not quite reached that point yet. The men who signal a political shoal are not thrown into the sea; but they are thrown out of the party—not, perhaps, that that is always an unsurmountable or unconsolable privation. (Laughter.) Partizans seek victory rather than truth—(hear, hear)—and they do not wish any troublesome stoic to remind them that they are fallible. It is disagreeable and inconvenient. While the late Government stuck to Liberal principles, they succeeded; when they abandoned them, they failed. (Hear, hear.) Witness their success when reforming the representation, and their failure when restricting the right of free discussion in Parliament; when limiting personal liberty in Ireland; and when, under the sophistical euphemism of "a military operation," they made unprovoked war on the Egyptians. (Hear, hear.) In their home policy, I have given them an ungrudging and an unwavering support—(cheers)—but their coercion in Ireland, in Egypt, and in Parliament, I have opposed strenuously and unfalteringly, but not factiously. (Renewed cheers.) I never once moved the adjournment of the House, or of a debate. I never put a question except to elicit information. I never "blocked" a bill, or moved a dilatory resolution. But when the occasion arose, I said, right out, what I thought truth and justice demanded. (Cheers, which were again and again renewed.) Ought that to be displeasing to independent and liberal men? The theory of my censors is, that the late Government should have been supported when they were right, because they were right; and it ought to have been supported when they were wrong, because it was, *a priori*, certain that their successors would be further wrong. (Laughter.) In other words, their cry is—"Your party, right or wrong!" (Hear, hear.) It was not by following such a policy that slavery was abolished, the corn-laws repealed, and the franchise extended. (Loud cheers.) The promoters of these measures put principles before party, and measures before men; and they were successful because they did so. (Hear, hear.) "Eternal vigilance is the price of freedom." Power is ever shifting from the many to the few. The manna of popular liberty must be gathered every morning or it rots. "The living sap of to-day outgrows the dead rind of yesterday." Only by continual oversight, can the democrat in office be prevented from hardening into a despot. (Hear, hear.) Only by unintermittent watching, can you prevent liberty being smothered in material prosperity, or frittered away by trimmers. The moment you begin to solder right and wrong together, your consciences become like Brummagem goods

—specious but counterfeit. (Loud laughter and cheers.) "Trimmer" is not a title of savoury repute. (Laughter.) Trimmers were the spawn of the degenerate Stuart days. A sham may keep its throne a whole age longer if it skulk behind some far-sounding name, so we now call trimming by the French synonym of "Opportunism." (Roars of laughter.) The chief of trimmers, the Marquis of Halifax, justified his trimming by arguing that all good things were trimmers. "Our climate is a trimmer between that part of the world where men are roasted, and the other where men are frozen. (Laughter.) Our Church is a trimmer between the frenzy of Platonic visions, and the lethargic ignorance of religious dreams. Our laws are trimmers between the excess of unbounded power, and the extravagance of liberty. Virtue is a trimmer, as it dwells between two extremes." Very pretty, but sophistical, special pleading—nothing more. (Laughter and hear, hear.) Analogy is not argument. Lord Halifax might have carried his contrasts further, and told us that if a trimmer saw a man drowning, he would trim to keep his place on shore rather than risk his life to save him. (Loud laughter.) A trimmer can never perform great works; can never effect great reforms; never demolish great vices. "He sings where praise and pudding wait his strain." The earnest thought, honest instincts, and fierce passions of the people, start the game which the trimmer bags. He never joins a cause until it is safe, and until its adherents are respectable. (Hear, hear.) He is far removed from the grandeur of Attic virtue, and still further from the sublimity of Christian principle. His effort is to do what is expedient, not what is right. (Loud cheers.) Trimming palsies our faculties. We want more heart in public life. The malady that afflicts us is want of faith. (Hear, hear.) We want the moral electric current that darts through and through the community, kindling each soul with enthusiasm, and each mind with conviction. And that you cannot get from trimmers. Whatever else I am, I am not a trimmer. (Prolonged cheering.) I would rather be "a pagan, suckled in that creed outworn," than subscribe to that baleful article of social faith—worship of success. (Cheers.) I do not play at politics; it is not a gambler's game. A line of action is either right or wrong. (Hear, hear.) It is not another move on the chess-board of Parliamentary hazard. I would be wary, but true; charitable, but not lukewarm; prudent, but not time-serving, cowardly, or compromising. ("Bravo!" and cheers.) I do not seek, nor do I care for, sham successes—the easy victory of the mountebank or the conjurer. Opportunism has eaten like a gangrene into the French Republic, and threatens to kill it. (Hear, hear.) Opportunism was first the bane, and at last the ruin, of the strongest Liberal Government this country has known. (Hear, hear, and cheers.) Such an attitude raises the whole question of party obligation and allegiance. Some persons grossly exaggerate them. They make a fetish of party. To oppose your party is, in their judgment, not only unwise but positively sinful. (Laughter.) I do not share this fanaticism, (Hear, hear.) Party is not an end, but only a means to an end. It was made for man; man was not made for it. You might as well worship the steamship that brings you the riches of the East, or the telegraph that carries you glad tidings, as worship a contrivance that at best is but a sounding board of partizans. (Hear, hear.) Men always gravitate to one of two sides—the progressive or the stationary. The volition of the former is the desire for development, and the latter for conservation. Though conflicting, they are necessary influences. The one imparts movement, and the other stability, to society. Men are usually conservative when they are least vigorous and most luxurious—after dinner, before going to bed, and when they are ailing or aged. (Laughter and cheers.) They are usually radicals when their intellects are stirred, or their consciences aroused. (Hear. hear.) Faith and hope typify the first section; prudence and security the second. This is the broad and natural cleavage which has always divided men, and which holds through the most varying circumstances and conditions of existence. But there are infinite divisions and subdivisions. All constitutional States are ruled mediately or immediately, by the popular will acting through one or other of such divisions. A party is only vital as long as it is vivified by an avowed principle, and dedicated to a defined aim. When that aim is abandoned, and the principle is achieved, the party becomes extinct. No charlatanry can keep it alive after the soul has departed from it. A catching cry may give it momentary excitation; but it is worthless as a basis of combination. The peas in a bushel are in a state of association; but they are kept so by the sides of the measure which hold them. Remove the sides, and the peas slip and slide in all directions. Remove its principles and the party slides also. If an attempt is made to hold it without a principle, it becomes a faction fighting for the personal ambition or aggrandisement of its leading members. Principles are permanent; but in the flux and reflux of our Parliamentary system, party allegiance is temporary. English parties since the succession of the present dynasty, have passed through many stages. For the first half of last century, Whiggism meant the maintenance of the house of Hanover, Toryism meant covert sympathy with the Stuarts. The Whigs had the best cause, and the Tories the best men. When the Hanoverian succession was secured, party lines became blurred. When they again sharply showed themselves, and party became once more an aggressive force, Toryism meant the revival of the power of the Crown, and Whiggism opposition to it. This struggle ended in a compromise, and English parties exhibited for a time a dissolving view. Then came Pitt's victory. Toryism during his ascendency, meant what was called the preservation of the Constitution and the Empire; Whiggism a protest against the burthen of the war with France, and a denial of the dangers that justified it. Peace concluded, this phase of party life passed away too. As new wants became urgent, partizans began to recast themselves; and as the war with France opened up one era, the Reform Bill opened up another. Whiggism meant the remodelling of our fiscal system, and the reduction of the long arrears of legislation which had accumulated during the European struggle. That phase has lasted until now—until the enfranchisement of the urban artizans and rural labourers. We are at the parting of the roads; at the opening of a new era. The present treads on the heels of the past, and the future hurries forward to its place—the footprints of the first making sure foot-grouud for the passage of the next. The hours are never resting. Old dogmas are dying; and old names, by which different tendencies were designated, are rapidly falling into desuetude. They are no longer expressed with distinct and definite conceptions. The ideas on which they were based are no longer the vital forces of political life. New elements have entered actively into our national system, and new creeds, new combinations, are necessary to represent the change. The progressionists are the most powerful; but their power is, by its own nature, self-neutralised. There is only one way of standing still; but there are many ways of going forward. Conservatism is a single idea. It is a unity of itself. Progression involves a multitude of ideas. It is not a unity, but a congeries of designs, including as great a variety of detail as there are phases of human thought. But in the melting of sections into each other—which always takes place on the day of a new departure—there may be some who neither desire, nor are able, to remain with their old associates. The scruples of such dissenters should be treated with tolerance and courtesy. (Hear, hear.) If they cannot follow the flag, let them drop out of the ranks without reproach or without imputation. Liberalism ought not only to be a creed, but a spirit; and in no way can its spirit be better shown than in its liberality to men who differ from its conclusions. (Cheers.) For my part I am for progress—decisive but rational progress; and for liberty—literal and genuine liberty. (Cheers.) I would not undermine the present, nor fling away the past. I would neither ignore tradition nor history; but would retain and build upon the foundations that have been gained for humanity. Whenever a man proclaims himself a democrat, the phantom of 1793 rises before Englishmen. Their conception of democracy has not got beyond the guillotine, surmounted with the red cap. (Laughter.) I am a democrat. (Cheers.) Novalis says that the Christian religion is the root of all democracy—the highest fact in the rights of man. I am not a socialist. (Loud cheers.) I would make the shoe take the form of the foot; not the foot the form of the shoe. (Hear, hear, and laughter.) I would adapt the institutions to the men; and not the men to the institutions. To my mind we are governed too much. (Hear, hear.) I wish fewer laws, less confided power, and greater growth of individual worth and wisdom. I aim at producing a nation of healthy men; not a nation of legislative cripples, who can walk only by the aid of State crutches—(laughter)—a nation of men, not a nation of official automatons who can think only as they are told, and act as they are ordered. (Loud cheers,) As a party without a principle becomes a faction, so a society without a principle becomes a clique. (Hear, hear.) We have had, in this country, illustrious organizations formed to achieve definite reforms. The abolition of slavery, the establishment of free trade, the extension of the franchise, were all accomplished by first educating public opinion, and then focussing it on the legislature. There are kindred societies still labouring around us; and whatever we may say as to the end they seek, no one denies the legitimacy of the means they employ. They are trying to convert the people to their cause, by appeals to reason and sentiment. But we have recently had formed creedless associations which vindicate no right, brand no crime, propose no generous policy, and only aspire to get a given set of men into office, and when in keep them in. (Hear, hear and laughter.) Their ideal is personal, their ends sectional; and the machinery, whatever it is now, must in time become like such machinery in America—corrupt. They tell us that their meetings are open, and their managers are elected. Very likely. But what is the use of an election in which a mere fraction of the population takes part? (Cheers.) Many men, from the urgency of their private affairs—some from a temper adverse to contention, and others from disapprobation of the means pursued—withhold themselves from these combinations. (Hear, hear.) The eager and acrimonious may attend; but those who have no resentments to gratify, or personal purposes to promote, will either be absent, or overborne. (A voice: "That's true," and cheers.) What justification can be advanced for a few persons, thus chosen, assuming to speak in the name of the constituency? They are entitled to be listened to as men, but not as representatives. They learn by rote the shibboleth of a party, and, when any one has the temerity to call in question their leader's wisdom, they, like a certain Demetrius, a silversmith of Ephesus, summon their craftsmen to the Town Hall, and silence all remonstrance with the shout of "Great is Diana of the Ephesians"—(much laughter)—a cry that is as effective now as it was against Paul and his companions in the classic city of Asia Minor. Truth disclaims all alliance with marshalled or tumultuous numbers, in whose midst it is often killed by the slow mistakes of prejudice and the impetuous injustice of passion. The caucus is anti-democratic. (Hear, hear.) It substitutes fugitiveness for patriotism. It reduces politics to personalities, and agitation to a business. (Cheers.) It plants between the representatives and the people an intermediary power, whose endeavours either galvanise them into frenzy, or produce an unreal tranquillity—the tranquillity of galley slaves, who row in cadence and in silence. I have summarised my conception of the common obligations of electors and representatives—what service the one may demand and the other should render. (Cries of "Go on.") I have dwelt on the few points of difference, rather than on the many points of agreement, between us, because I would have counted it pusillanimous to sneak from the consequences of my course. On purely personal grounds, I would gladly escape the ordeal of an electoral contest; but a man is not always his own master. I never coveted a seat in Parliament, I never sought for one, and only took one at your solicitation. (Cheers.) After eleven years' experience, I would willingly betake myself to more congenial and equally useful pursuits. ("No, no," and cheers.) But my conduct has been impugned. I am accused of having been recreant to my principles, and false to my trust. (A voice: "Never," and renewed cheers.) I traverse the indictment, and put myself before my fellow-citizens. (Loud and prolonged cheering.) If they endorse the charge, I will bow without a murmur to their decision, and make my exit, as I made my entrance, in obedience to their verdict. ("No, no.") I will try no electoral legerdemain to cozen them out of their votes. I will win or lose without the aid of meretricious accessories. I set no store by my abilities or attainments; I prefer no request on the score of old services; I make no whine about the past; but I modestly, yet unabashed, insist that I have done my duty, that I have practised no deceit, violated no principle, broken no pledge. (Cheers.) Gentlemen, I surrender you your mandate untarnished. (Loud cheers.) I have not traded with it, nor used it as a key to unlock courtly presence chambers. (Laughter, and "Hear, hear.") I have never prostituted it to purposes of mercenary advantage or personal ambition. (Hear, hear.) The coveted letters which you empowered

me to attach to my name have never been hawked about as a decoy to credulous investors, nor as a peripatetic bait to attract alien audiences. (Renewed laughter and cheers.) I have now pieced out my merits and imperfections, and I appeal—not to the prejudices of partizans, nor the rancour of lynx-eyed censors—but to the judgment, intelligence, liberality, and manliness of the men amongst whom I have lived and laboured for a lifetime, for an answer. (Loud cheers.) My competitors have the adventitious support of organization. I have not. I want none. ("You don't need any," and loud cheers.) I have got no committee; I will have no carriages, and no canvassing. I will do my best to elucidate what may appear to anyone to be abstruse, to explain what may seem ambiguous, to illumine what may look dark in my creed; but, beyond that, I will neither go, nor be driven. (Cheers.) If I am wanted, I will be elected; and if I am not, I will be dismissed. I have faith in the people. It is a libel to say that they seek to be petted and flattered—that they can be "pleased with a rattle, and tickled with a straw." (Loud laughter.) They have been victimised, but not vitiated, by party selfishness. (Hear, hear, and cheers.) They do not require the sheen of official position to lead them to comprehend great principles. They do that intuitively, and they will courageously support those who seek their realization. They want truth proclaimed, liberty defended, justice upheld. (Hear, hear.) I, at least, believe that, and will help to do it with such power as I possess. (Cheers.) One of the greatest dangers of the present day is the general insincerity of politics. I will not travel in disguise, and by circuitous paths. All equivocation is effeminating and corrupting. I will knowingly offend no one. I mean, however, to mince nothing, to conceal nothing, to evade nothing. (Loud cheers.) But while not sparing doctrines, I will be mindful of men. I will attack errors, not persons. Truth can be told without bitterness. (Hear, hear.) If my advocacy is strong, I hope it will be without sting. I may be driven out into the political prairie, but I would prefer to be a poor trapper beyond the frontiers, rather than barter my independence for all the small grandeurs of place and of power—

> The reward is in the race we run,
> Not the prize.

(Loud cheers, the audience rising *en masse* and continuing the applause for some minutes.)

# POLITICAL PRINCIPLES.

---

DELIVERED IN WESTMORLAND ROAD BOARD SCHOOL, ON MONDAY, NOVEMBER 16TH, 1885.

---

CHAIRMAN—MR. HEDLEY CHAPMAN.

---

Mr. COWEN on rising to address the meeting, was received with prolonged cheering. He said :—Mr. Chairman, ladies, and gentlemen, I am indifferent about party ; but I try to be true to principles. (Hear, hear.) If you will follow me, I will endeavour to define what I mean. I cannot think for anyone. I would not if I could. (Laughter.) But it is permissible for any person to attempt to throw open the path of thought for others. (Hear, hear.) There is no sacrifice of independence in accepting information, or instruction, by whomsoever given, but there is in accepting tutelage. I speak without shuffling, shirking, evasion, or reticence—as an equal, not as a tutor. (Hear, hear.) Liberalism ! I don't like the word. It is too vague. It may mean much or little—anything or nothing. (Hear, hear.) Some Liberals are very faint types of freedom. (Laughter.) Radicalism, which was once a voice, and is now only an echo, is better. Democracy, whose adherents hold that all power originates with, and should be exercised for, the people, is better still. (Cheers.) But we won't cavil over the nomenclature. A Liberal is supposed to be a person who places principle before prescription. Principle—what is it ? It is not opinion. Principle is immutable. It is antecedent to experience, and surpasses and regulates it. Opinion is mobile, desultory, and various as the minds of men. One is fixed; the other is vibratory. Opinions are parts of ourselves—principles are truths independent of us. In matters of principle, there should be no latitude. (Hear, hear.) In matters of opinion, there should be the fullest. We want unity of principle, but diversity of opinion. (Cheers.) A man may be erratic concerning immaterial matters, but immovable concerning vital ones. He may not estimate highly all professing Christians, but that does not make him a pagan if he believes in, and lives up to, the principles of Christianity. (Cheers.) So a Liberal may be opposed to his *confreres* on some subjects, but that does not constitute him an apostate, if he professes and practises the cardinal articles of their faith. (Cheers.) Principles should govern party, and party should not govern principles. (Cheers.) Liberal principles—what are they? The first is equality. I do not mean equality of social condition. That is a speculative chimera that never can be realised. One man owns his clothes, and another owns a county. (Laughter.) If they were made equal to-day, they would be unequal to-morrow. I mean equality of opportunity—a clear and equal course, and victory to the wisest and the best. (Cheers.) That is practicable. Our social forces tend to destroy equality. I would have them tend to create and maintain it. I would remove all artificial impediments and restraints that make the path of progress tedious and painful. To live in a society of equals quickens a man's spirit, and expands his faculties. (Hear, hear.) Equality is really a question of human reverence. He who denies the manhood of the lowest, denies the divinity of man, and degrades himself by making his manhood dependent upon exceptional causes or special endowments. (Hear, hear.) Mr. Matthew Arnold says that our inequality materialises our upper, vulgarises our middle, and brutalises our poorer classes. (Cheers.) The only distinctions which should be recognised are those of integrity, incorruptibility, usefulness, cultivated intellect, and fidelity to truth. (Hear, hear.) Carry the principle of equality to its conclusions. Try by it, as a tally, our institutions. What ensues? Every man is made equal and independent before the law—equal as to the protection from positive wrong which it affords, as well as to the benefit it confers. Poverty would inflict no disqualification, and wealth and station confer no advantage. No man should be arbitrarily fined or punished, or have his property or liberty impaired, except after lawful trial. This is the primeval principle, not of Liberals alone, but of all Englishmen. It is on everyone's lips, but not always in everyone's mind. It was violated when Irish peasants were arrested, under *lettres de cachet*, and kept in gaol on mere suspicion. (Hear, hear.) But the principle of equality goes much farther than the prohibition of arbitrary imprisonment and taxation. It provides that anyone may rise to power who can, by desert, attain it. It erases all exclusive privileges, all caste prerogatives, and establishes complete civil, ecclesiastical, and political co-ordination. Equality is the antithesis of heredity. There is not a problem in Euclid more mathematically true, than that hereditary government is theoretically indefensible. It is the product of the feudal, as the feudal was the product of the patriarchal system. A limited number of persons owned the soil and ruled the inhabitants. Their right to rule descended with their right of inheritance. Force was the readiest means of ruling, and landed property was the sole source of power. This was the origin of hereditary law-making. It can only be defended on two hypotheses—either that a privileged class is born to govern, and all others have to obey, or that it constitutes a barrier between the infirmity of the one and the rashness of many. This latter position is debatable; the former is not. But I dispute the one, and deny the other. (Hear, hear.) The wrong which began a thousand years ago is as much a wrong as if it began yesterday. (Hear, hear.) The right which originates to-day is as much a right as if it had the sanction of a thousand years. (Hear, hear.) However mild it may be, a class-government can never be good. Even if the soil, which territorial legislators inherit, grew thoughts instead of turnips; if, instead of wheat, it realised every year a harvest of information, if every acre that belonged to them were a wiseacre—(loud laughter)—still their rule would not be comparable to one based on the principle of civil equality. (Hear, hear.) By its inherent tendency to progress, by the instruction that every failure produces, and by the conscious dignity felt by each citizen being a part of the system of society in which he lived, the most erring form of self-government is better than the most benign despotism that ever existed, or can be conceived. (Loud cheers.) Time has no influence on principles. It cannot change their nature or their quality. We have long since settled that man can have no property in man; and neither ought one generation to have property in the generations that are to follow. (Hear.) But our Peerage is founded upon public opinion as much as upon law. It is not a cause; it is an effect. It is the sequence of a condition of the national mind. We are illogical. We avow a belief in equality, but it is only from the teeth outwards. (Laughter.) Inwardly and secretly, we dearly love a lord. Faith in aristocracy is a living, active, life-giving power, and an apparently inseparable element in our character. All classes are imbued with it. It is found everywhere—in the poor man who struggles along bent beneath his accumulated burthens as well as in the lord whose horses bespatter him in passing. If any one here doubt it, let them witness the Oriental servility, and the carnivalesque pomp, exhibited at a Royal drawing-room or levée. (Loud laughter and cheers.) Liberals opposed to the House of Lords! (Laughter.) Yes, when they are talking to Buncombe. (Renewed laughter.) If they are really so opposed, they take effective means of dissembling their opposition. They have made since 1830, 150 Peers; and the Tories have made 53. (Loud laughter.) The late Prime Minister made one-third of the total number himself. (Laughter.) This may be meant to indicate distrust and dislike. There is no tracking the sinuosities of partizanship, or fathoming the depth of statecraft. Making Peers may be a clandestine method of destroying them, but it is too subtle for my comprehension. (Much laughter and cheers.) Our practice likewise belies the theory in other and less defensible ways. The country is busy electing a new Parliament. Theoretically, the men to be chosen should be notable for sagacity, experience, foresight, knowledge, and abnegation of self. Now, candidly, is that the case? How many are there who will be elected for these qualifications? Will not wealth often outweigh culture—(hear, hear),—intelligence, and noble sentiments? Run over the list of candidates, and say—Will not the Plutocrat with few qualifications often beat the poor man with many?

'Tis true, 'tis pity, and pity 'tis 'tis true.

(Cheers.) The same disposition is displayed when workmen, with low wages, are looked down upon by those who are better paid; when the skilled artisan counts himself the social superior of the labourer. This exclusiveness used to be shown in Birmingham, where the public-houses had two parlours—one for the button-makers, and the other for the gentlemen button-makers. (Laughter.) The sentiment that sanctions such distinctions would re-create another aristocratic class if the present one were extinguished. (Hear, hear.) The root is there. It would only want room and verge enough to flower into a full-blown Peerage of wealth or race, if not of birth. (Hear, hear.) It is the idea we should attack, if we wish to kill the institution. The first Liberal principle, then, is equality, and the way to incorporate it in law is for its professors to practise it in their lives—not to substitute the barren proclamation of Liberal formulas for the equalising spirit. Equality without liberty is a deception, and responsibility without liberty is an anachronism. (Hear, hear.) Liberty, then, is the second Liberal principle. By liberty I mean much more than liberty of locomotion, or liberty to buy in the cheapest, and sell in the dearest, market. I mean liberty of thought, speech, and development. Physical liberty constitutes us free agents; intellectual liberty gives us the power of acting up to our sense of right and wrong; religious liberty enables us to make the decisions of our consciences our rule of conduct; and civil liberty gives us the unchecked opportunity of growth. (Loud cheers.) The idea running through these definitions is that of self-sovereignty. If our volitions do not originate with ourselves, we have not personal freedom; if our convictions are controlled by our prejudices, and our consciences controlled by our passions, we have neither mental nor moral freedom; if we have to practise or pay for modes of worship imposed by others, we have not religious freedom; and if any power assert the right to inflict upon us laws or taxes without our leave, we have not civil freedom. (Cheers.) In all these cases, there is a force opposed to our will, and, as far as it operates, it implies or produces servitude. Without physical liberty, a man is a machine; without moral liberty, he is the victim of his appetites—(cheers)—without mental liberty, he is a slave; and without political liberty, he is a serf. (Hear.) Every human being has an organization peculiar to himself. He has his own life to live, his own work to do, and no one can live the one, or do the other, for him. It is with man as with nature. Each plant grows by itself in the sunshine or the shade. The thistle gives no laws to the convolvulus. The oak and the willow have their different growths; the rose and the daisy their different forms and hues. But each has its separate function, and each its distinctive beauty. In humanity, there is the same unbounded diversity. So all men, however different their capacity, should have equal liberty of germination. (Loud cheers.) The same sun warms them, and the same wind breathes to them melodiously. The "storm frowns not less darkly on the monarch—the flower gives not less fragrance to the slave." One man is born with a faculty for sculpture, and another for mechanics. Let each have the space and the culture most fitted for the unchecked unfolding of his powers. One man is a heretic; another is orthodox. Give both equal liberty to preach their doctrines. (Hear, hear.) Truth is militant, and can best establish itself by conflict. (Loud cheers.) It is only possible to ascertain which side is right, after comparing what each has to say for or against the other. (Hear, hear.) Don't secretly assassinate error by calumny, but help it openly to its destruction by inviting it into the arena of free debate. (Renewed cheers.) Legal penalties, or social ostracism, may scotch it; but they cannot kill it. Argument alone can do that. If a man assert a falsehood, confront him with the truth. (Hear, hear.) If he bewilder you with sophistry, throw the light of reason on his deceptions. (Hear, hear.) I plead for unfettered liberty of speech as well as of thought. To put men under a ban for their opinion, is, of all kinds of violence, the most reprehensible—(hear, hear)—and of all kinds of illiberality the most cowardly. (Cheers.) Personal liberty developes individual energy, and raises the level of human dignity, by inspiring in it sentiments of self-reliance. A nation is but an assemblage of units; and in a free State that unit is a man. Individual liberty, pushed even to license made little Athens a giant; while individual restraint reduced the colossal empire of Charles the Fifth to a decrepit dwarf. (Cheers.) The history of the past and the present reads the same lesson. It is not the institutions of a country, but the spirit of its people, that protects its liberty and sustains its greatness. (Cheers.) I am for liberty, therefore, for each man to develop his characteristic nature in the entireness of his attributes. (Cheers.) Everyone has qualities which are peculiar to himself alone, and which distinguish him from every human being that has been, that is, or that will be. These qualities constitute his life, and I am opposed to all laws, customs, and restraints that fetter their exercise. (Hear, hear.) Apply the principle of liberty thus defined to current politics, and what does it secure? Complete suffrage has its public recognition and legal guarantee. Complete suffrage includes women as well as men. (Cheers.) It embraces, too, not only the right of election, but the right of selection. It does not recognise the interjection of a force between the candidate and the constituency—(laughter)—and it repudiates both compulsory and chance combinations for that purpose, though they may be designed by philosophers and regulated by patriarchs. But liberty of choice for all, and from all, is little better than a mockery, if the roll of candidates is limited by the imposition of conditions that one class only can comply with. (Hear, hear.) What more right has a country to the unremunerated labour of those who work by the intellect, than to the product of the industry of the rest of the community? Pay all election expenses out of the rates, and members of Parliament out of the taxes. (Cheers.) Then, and not till then, will there be a Government freely assented to by all, and acting for all. Control in national, carries with it control in local, affairs. A central authority, springing directly from the people, should utter the national idea, fix the national taxation, hold the national purse, and superintend the maintenance of justice. (Hear, hear, and cheers.) The rule that holds with a State should hold with a district; the whole adult population should be sovereign. The permanent design of all organizations—local and national—should be to cultivate self-depending energy. The surest method of defeating this design, of dwarfing its development, and of circumscribing liberty, is to centralize responsibility, and delegate the exercise of power into the hands of cabals, cliques, or classes. (Loud cheers.) Liberty and equality are rights. There is a political school who deny this. In their view, organized society is the creature of arrangement in which natural rights are surrendered in exchange for the advantage of protection. A citizen, they contend, has no natural rights. But he has political privileges which are granted, or withheld, as it is deemed expedient. This is the utilitarian theory. It is not mine. (Hear, hear, and cheers.) I hold that a man has rights, deeper than society, written in the constitution of his being, and that they are inalienable. No Government gave them, and no Government, without injustice, can deprive him of them. (Cheers.) This inherent law says—"Be a man, and respect your fellow men." This right a man guarantees to others, and others guarantee to him. He has, in addition, legal rights which emanate from the nation, and are an equivalent for liberties surrendered and services rendered. These legal rights are qualified and conditional. When a man enters a conventional State, and partly surrenders his liberty for security, he reserves to himself the right to insist that the conditions of the contract are complied with. The essence of the agreement lies in the right of each party to demand its fulfilment. The State can require allegiance, and enforce obedience. The citizen can de-

mand equity, and insist on freedom. (Hear, hear.) But this is somewhat digressing. It is useful, however, in these compromising days—when success and not truth is the party slogan—(laughter)—to go back to first principles. A bold re-statement of them may act as a tonic to relax political consciences. The possession of these rights entails duties which it is not in any man's option to evade. He has borrowed from the past—succeeded to its stores of strength and knowledge—and he must pay the debt to the future with interest for its use. (Hear, hear.) He cannot isolate himself, or barter his inheritance for an existence of ease and irresponsibility. Everything that ever has been, belongs to him, and he belongs to the future. Tennyson makes Ulysses say—"I am part of all I have seen." The converse would be more correct—what we have seen has become part of us. And we have to transmit the bequest untarnished and amplified to posterity. (Hear, hear.) How? By the discharge of our obligations as men, neighbours, and citizens. Every political theory implies a moral system. The end is not merely to live, but to live nobly. (Cheers.) The initiative of all national reform is to be found in personal reformation. It begins with the individual—with his aboriginal self. Awaken in him the dormant power of thought. Plant in him principles of intellectual independence and moral worth, and let them radiate from him as a centre. Raise his conceptions of life. Elevate his aspirations above what is abject, vicious, distorted, or corrupt. Make him a man of character, and he will become a monitor and a conscience to the circle in which he moves. (Cheers.) That is the basis on which we must build. The first sphere of his beneficent activity is the family. That is the nursery of the State. The next is the city. That is the school. In it men learn the mutual restraints that fit them for greater responsibilities. Identity of occupation, of scene, and of interest, impresses them with a common design; while local action begets a companionship which blossoms into patriotism. (Hear, hear.) As the individual is the initial of the family, and the family is the initial of the city, so the city is the initial of the nation—an enduring community, broad-based on personal character, family sympathies, public spirit, and the harmonious aim of its people. There run through it the same promise, the same memories, and the same hopes. It is a fusion and expansion of a series of units. Local institutions find their beginnings in these units; and national institutions are the instrumentalities which come into existence, because of the aggregation of the units. A nation is thus no mechanism, but the rational life of self-conscious freedom. It stands in the same relation to other nations that the individual does to the family, or the city to the country. It has a diversified but homogeneous unity, stamped with its own physical characteristics, and its own distinctive intellectual and moral traits. Its sovereignty is the manifestation of its power, and the indication of its location in life and its place in history. A nation's mission in the world is as clear and as well defined as a man's in society—to assert its own right, and fulfil its own duties towards others. It is a loyal but vigilant township in the human commonwealth. It cannot act a Cain-like part. It cannot drag on a mere negative existence. It cannot dissolve its brotherhood. It must fulfil the duties that brotherhood imposes upon it, or die; die unhonoured—unhonoured and unwept—of inanition or paralysis. Rights entail duties. Duties fulfilled assure security. Work is a social duty. The man who works has the right, and he alone, to the creation of his work and sacrifice. No confederation, or commonwealth, has any right to trench upon a man's personal possessions, and rob him for the world's benefit. (Cheers.) The things that are produced by him, purchased by him, or given to him by others who fairly own them, are his and no other's. (Hear, hear.) But it may be said he has a superfluity, while others want. Possibly. Still, the State cannot honestly or wisely sequestrate. If it could, what would follow? The man would cease to labour. He would not work if the fruits of his toil were to be confiscated. (Cheers.) He may give of his free will out of his abundance. That may be a moral obligation; but his obligation to give does not entitle the State to take. (Hear, hear.) The institution of property and its security is the basis of civilization and liberty. Instead of there being too much private property, there is too little. (Hear, hear.) I don't grumble at the few having, but at the many not having. (Laughter.) Such reasoning may seem trite and commonplace. But it is requisite to solidify, in the popular mind, the elementary and essential tenets of our social system, as we have had recently put into authoritative currency confused and hazy views which, if pushed logically to their basis, would upset it. Their propagators have either not reasoned these doctrines to the roots, or they have not foreseen their conclusions. (Hear, hear.) When the Mephistopheles of Socialism quickened the inherent conservatism of the French peasant, by propounding the startling axiom that property was robbery, he merely gave epigrammatic point to certain nebulous theories that periodically float over the surface of society. M. Proudhon had remarkable analytical power, and was logical in deducing the consequence from his first proposition. But, then, his first proposition was wrong. He put as the basis of every social function, not the individual, but "the contract"—a theory which has served sometimes as the defence of the most rigid repression, and at other as a summons to revolution. This principle is not the foundation, it is the dissolution, of the organization of society. Our neo-socialists—who are constantly harping on the theory that the political unit is not the man, but a group of men have got hold of the same idea which, when developed, will involve them in a net of inextricable complications. There are few inquiries more fascinating than that into the origin of property--how it has been affected by economic conditions, and the political careers of human societies. But it is too abstract, and not altogether appropriate, for an election address. I am desirous, however, of recording my belief in the inviolability of private property, and my disbelief in any fanciful scheme for the organization of labour. (Loud cheers.) The germs of all these schemes are to be found in Plato, in Campanella, and in More. If poetry and eloquence, learning and devotion, could have established them, they would have been in existence centuries ago. Their projectors began at the wrong end. They busied themselves with society, and forgot the individual—with the house, and not with the living being who had to inhabit it. They overlooked the fact that the social arrangements of the external world are the manifestations of the interior man. When Plato was drawing his magnificent socialistic Republic, his countrymen were administering hemlock to Socrates. Campanella painted the "City of the Sun," and was imprisoned and tortured. More wrote his "Utopia," and was beheaded. Their speculations and devices have left no trace on the modern life of Greece, of Italy, or of England. The ancients had an organization of labour—they called it slavery. (Laughter.) It was forced labour, rewarded according to the pleasure of him who imposed it. Communism is forced labour, rewarded according to the pleasure of the State. The only difference between the old system and the modern scheme, is that of a single master and many. If I had to choose, I should prefer the private master; as there always are, even in a Legree, the distorted remains of humanity. But an abstract, inflexible, insensible organization, is impervious to generous influences. It has neither a body to be kicked nor a soul to be saved. (Great laughter and cheers.) It is an unconscionable task-driver. Society, regulated in detail and petrified in form, as Communism would make it, would reduce man to a cypher or to a machine. His free will, his personal merit, his never-ceasing aspirations towards new modes of progress, would disappear. It would be the serfdom of the middle ages, without the hope of manumission. All that the State can do, all that it is desirable it should do, is to secure to everyone fair ground for equal effort, and leave the rest to the individual—to his application and his aptitudes. Enfranchised labour—master of itself and its products—will soon be master of the world. Land stands on a different footing from other property. It is not a product of human labour. A man's coat is his own. He made it, or he bought it, or had it given to him—(laughter)—and there is no power in the State to deprive him of it, however much it may be to the State's advantage to possess it. But the same man's land, which he values as much as he does his coat, the State can take if it needs it, legally and forcibly. The difference of treatment, in the two classes of property, defines a principle which every English jurist assents to, and which every Parliament acts upon—that the holders of land have only the usufruct—not the absolute, possession of the soil. The suzerainty is so clogged with conditions, that it may not be of much money value. But it unquestionably exists; and the nation can, and does, act upon it as it pleases. When, however, the State takes land, it must compensate the holders of it for their interest in it—(hear, hear)—that is for the labour and capital which they or their predecessors in title have expended. To take the property of a man, without it is for a public advantage, would be tyranny; and to take it without paying its market value, would be theft. (Hear, hear.) It is argued by some that no compensation is due—that as all had equal rights to it, all still have. Admit the contention. What then? The original right was worthless. Land must be enclosed, and cultivated, and drained, to give it value. The man, or men, who did this first, sold their improvements, or gave them to his or their successors—to a tribe or to a person. The land thus improved, passed from one to another; sometimes as the reward of honest toil, at others as the recompense for dishonest service; to this man by fair means, and to that by foul. Some worked for it; others played tricks, or told falsehoods, or cut throats for its possession. (Renewed laughter.) Thus it may be traced back to its origin. Every successive owner did something, little or much, to add to its value, until what was once a rock became a garden; what was once a swamp or forest became a site of a factory or a palace. The magic of ownership turns sand into gold, and the camping-place of savage warriors becomes the scene of industry's peaceful triumphs. (Loud cheers.) Some of these transfers may have come in questionable form, but purchase and possession have ripened them into indefeasible titles, which can only be upset by robbery or revolution. (Cheers.) But it may be said that there is still some common land. There is. And it is as much the duty of the State to prevent it from being appropriated by individuals, as it is the duty of the State to prevent private property being appropriated by the public. (Hear, hear.) While the State should see that every man holds inviolate his right to enjoy and bestow his own, it should strenuously guard the people's right to enjoy their own. But the abstract ownership of land, and the laws that regulate its tenure and transfer, are different questions. These latter need very drastic revision. (Hear, hear.) In primitive times, land in this country was often held in common. Village communities were the proprietors. This antique form of agrarian partnership, which through all our legal intricacies and customs can still be discerned, was supplanted by feudalism, which is the groundwork of our modern English land system. In it the owner of the produce is distinct from the owner of the soil. In France, the very opposite method prevails. There cultivation is the condition of ownership. To both systems there are objections. In France, the multiplication of landowners, which is beneficial, has led to minute subdivision, which is injurious. In England, large farms have led to cheapened cultivation and increased production, which are beneficial. But they have led also to the dependence of the farmer and the degradation of the labourer, which are injurious. Any change in our system, to be both permanent and beneficial, will have to be wrought out in accordance with the natural laws of evolution. We cannot revive the agrarian institutions of our ancestors; nor can we transplant, at once, to a soil choked with the growth of centuries of feudalistic customs and aristocratic law-making, the product of democracy. (Hear, hear.) Every dispassionate observer must detect grave political danger in the locking up of so large a portion of the soil of the country in the hands of a section of the population—relatively small and progressively dwindling—who have profited so enormously, and with so little effort of their own, by the national prosperity. It is not easy to create a peasant proprietary in this age of railways and telegraphs, and in the midst of keen mining, manufacturing, and commercial enterprise. Men will devote themselves to pursuits in which they can realise the greatest profits for their labour and capital—(hear, hear)—and that is certainly not, as things are, in the cultivation of small farms. They may take to that vocation for health or pleasure, but not for money-getting. Agriculture is a game of hazard. Its followers are incessantly throwing handfuls of gold upon an earthly faro-table. They play out a match with the skies, and the skies, like the owners of the gambling banks at Baden-Baden and elsewhere, usually win. (Loud laughter.) I do not expect to witness any rapid or sudden creation of peasant proprietary in England. A busy civic population cannot all at once adapt itself to the slow pursuits of agriculture, even if they were so disposed. (Hear, hear.) But we ought to facilitate their creation, by abrogating the custom of primogeniture, by repealing all laws which make the sale and transfer of land tedious, difficult, uncertain, and expensive. (Cheers.) Our rural economy should ensure two objects—an augmented proprietary, and the greatest production of food with the least expenditure of force. (Cheers.) These broad principles, stated in halting phraseology, and with many faults of style and manner, embrace my political faith. I ask for liberty, without which there can be no responsibility; and for equality, without which liberty would only be a deception—the lifeless equality of despotism. (Hear, hear.) The fruition of these principles is the extinction of all class—civil and religious inequality, and the establishment of unfettered freedom of growth, utterance, and action, for the weakest as well as the strongest, for the individual in the constituency and the representative in the National Council. Equality and liberty are rights to which every man, by nature and by citizenship, is entitled. The possession of these rights entails duties. The sphere in which, and through which, these duties can be most effectively performed, and the human faculties and forces most harmoniously developed, is the world-old organization of family, city, and country. The nation owes like duties to its brother nations that circles of citizens owe to themselves. Its nationality, indicated by consanguinity, tradition, language, homogeneity of interest, and aptitude for associated effort, is the sign of its individuality and the evidence of its mission. National ends are identical, but their means various. The mission of no nation is monopolising and usurping, seeking its own grandeur in the inferiority of others, but it is in securing equal progress for all, and in sustaining against oppression the cause of right and justice. (Cheers.) The fulfilment by the individual of the treble duty of man, citizen, and patriot, entitles him to the unhampered pursuit of his life's ideal, and the security of his property, not because its possession is synonymous with virtue or intelligence, but because it is the sign and fruit of his labour. The fulfilment by the State of its duties guarantees its independence, and assures its status in the family of nations. Individual welfare is thus harmonised with national progress. On these living principles, and to this logical end, I would work. (Hear. hear.) Only a malignant madman would wish to pull about his ears the fabric on which the wisdom and patriotism of centuries have been lavished. (Cheers.) I would preserve, with conservative tenacity, not only all that is necessary, but all that is not injurious, in the old State. (Hear, hear.) I would link past tradition with future hope, and subordinate the interest of party to that of the nation, the interest of classes to that of justice, the interest of sections to that of liberty, and the interest of all to the elevation of man. (Loud cheers.) There is nothing original in this summary of truths. They are but texts from the well-thumbed horn-book of political philosophy. They were theoretically conquered centuries ago; and neither I nor anyone can add a new thought to their general stock, or clothe the old thought in new language. They are the common property of every man who has, however superficially, studied the science of Government, and that branch of ethics which relates to the creation and execution of law. This, then, is my political creed, hallowed by the conviction of my conscience, and espoused by the sympathies of my heart. (Cheers.) In the May-morn of life, it aroused my enthusiasm;

and in manhood's maturity it has ripened into a passionate intuition. Men's reasonings usually mould themselves into apologies or approvals for the course of life they adopt. But I can honestly say that amidst the crowd and jostle, the noise and strife, the splendour and the spleen of an artificial and contentious society, I have kept the faith, and striven to embody it in my actions. (Loud cheers.)

For loyalty is still the same,
Whether it win or lose the game;
True as the dial to the sun,
Although it be not shin'd upon.

(Hear, hear.) My opinions, however, as to the method by which these principles can best be realised have been modified and mellowed by experience. The man who has reached the shady side of fifty, and does not make such an acknowledgment, must either be a bigot or a blockhead. (Hear, hear, and laughter.) Emerson says that a verbal consistency is the hobgoblin of little minds. The wisest of us may be wiser to-day than he was yesterday, and to-morrow than he is to-day. Total freedom from change of opinion would imply total freedom from error, and that is the prerogative of Omniscience alone. (Hear, hear.) Fervid reformers expect too much. I did once. I have been mistaken—not as to the measures, but as to their consequences. I looked for a democracy of principle and virtue. I fear we have not yet got it. A change of the machinery has not made a change in the men. Bettered conditions have not much bettered our conceptions. I have been disappointed—not personally, as I have had more success than I am entitled to—(cries of "No, no")—and much more than I ever looked for—but at the meanness and petty vexations of our politics. (Cheers.) We stand amidst the decay of a perishing political system. The reign of privilege, if not over, is doomed. The people have entered on their heritage. There never was more need for public men with nerve enough to resist the manufactured despotism of an artificial public opinion, to throttle corruption and cowardice in its countless disguises, and to speak the truth and fear not. Yet, we behold them crawling to combinations that they may climb to power. (Cheers, and a Voice : "That's true.") We see public affairs subordinated to a subtle game in which the players are cringing or clamorous, vehement or virulent, only that they may the sooner be hired to be silent. (Laughter.) We are witnessing too many of the newly enfranchised, amidst hurrahing and placarding, hurrying to equip themselves in the prison uniform of party—to speak by their leaders' briefs rather than by undying principles, and to trust perishable names and interests rather than realities. (Cheers.) This abject worship of events, this bustling success, is no test of right. You don't weigh merit by applause, any more than by avoirdupois. (Laughter.) It was never my aim to ride the whirlwind of a keyhole, or direct the storm of a saucer. To do my duty has been my effort. There are times when the highest duty is not to succeed—(hear, hear)—if success is to be secured by adventitious popularity, by intrigue and self-seeking, and by cowardice at the cost of truth, independence, and integrity. (Cheers.) I am concerned about what I do, and not about what people think. (Hear, hear.) I have seen many bright hopes shattered, and many illusions chilled by the ice-breath of delusion and discouragement. The sea of time is restless and encroaching. The wave of each returning hour washes into oblivion some cherished Utopia, and hides in death's dateless night some faithful comrade in the combat for the right. When they pass in memory before us, and we feel the body crumbling beneath the spirit's action, a nameless languor irresistibly steals over our energies, as we strive to hide from ourselves the path they have trodden, and that we have yet to tread. But despondency negatives, and scepticisms slacken, the springs of endeavour, while faith in renovating principles serves it with incessant affirmatives, and sets it beating through the storm. Regret for the past and discontent with the present are useful only so far as they can be transmuted into renewed force for the future. Vice and virtue grow up as naturally amidst each other as corn flowers amidst the corn. In the political as in the moral life, the best stimulus to effort is for man to throw himself, in the full sense of security, upon principles; and then he is safe from being depressed by oppression, scared by uncertainty, or demoralized by defeat. (Loud and continued cheering during which Mr. Cowen resumed his seat.)

# THE BRITISH EMPIRE, FEDERATION, AND FOREIGN AFFAIRS.

DELIVERED ON WEDNESDAY EVENING, NOVEMBER 18TH, 1885, IN THE HENRY STREET SCHOOL-ROOM, SHIELDFIELD.

CHAIRMAN—ALD. HENRY WILLIAM NEWTON.

Mr. COWEN, who was received with rounds of cheers on rising, said: Mr. Chairman, ladies and gentlemen,—the permanent importance of the external business of the British Empire is demonstrated by our having three great officers of State—the Ministers for India, the Colonies, and Foreign Affairs—charged with its administration. Upon the wisdom, moderation, and manliness of its management; upon the delicate but vital shading which is constantly given to, or is withdrawn from, diplomatic doings and correspondence, depend vast issues. A blunder at home may be repaired with no further inconvenience than a display of party acerbity, or the delay of some needed reform; but a blunder abroad may inflict colossal injuries, paralyse industry, convulse trade, plunge the population into penury, and the country into disgrace. (Hear, hear.) Foreign policy may be made an instrument for securing great national advantage and renown, or an instrument for entailing great national injury and degradation. It is the pivot on which the national mechanism revolves. (Hear, hear.) When it is loose, the empire oscillates, and society is shaken. The slightest vibration is felt alike by the fireside of the humblest and in the palaces of the powerful. Yet, the public interest in this department of

State is fitful and fluctuating. It is not sustained by serions attempts to trace events to their origin, or steadied by dispassionate discussion. Amongst the numerous, but not very enlightened, section of the population who regard the Empire as an objectionable excresence—something between a hindrance and a help—a paltry parish squabble, or an insignificant project of domestic improvement, is held of infinitely more importance than the efficiency of our national defences, or the safety of India. (Cheers.) Such persons do not comprehend, when a province is closed to our merchants, that manufacture is stopped somewhere; that money circulates so much less freely; that the wages fund is so much reduced; and that the loss falls, ultimately, not less upon the artizan at the lathe, and the rustic at the plough, than upon the capitalist in his counting house. But indifference is only one evil. Nor is it the worst. (Hear, hear.) Foreign affairs are permitted for years to drift on uncontrolled and unnoticed. Suddenly, a conjuncture occurs which the party managers conceive they can turn to their advantage. Thereupon, the party bellows is blown, and a fire is kindled which scorches all who endeavour to keep it within the furnace. (Loud laughter.) National welfare is subordinated to the shifting and conflicting interests of heated rivals. Grave and delicate deliberations are made dependent upon the caprice of ill-instructed controversialists, and the government of the Empire is left as the prize of a scramble amongst a crowd of eager, contentious, and scheming partisans. (Laughter and cheers.) Can we call a truce to election clamour and recrimination, and bestow unexcited and sober consideration upon a subject in which we are all so deeply affected? We will look at it as Englishmen, and forget, for an hour, the personal bearings of the pending contest. We are seeking identical ends. We want to consolidate the power, and uphold the honour, of our country.

We desire power, not for the display of imperial arrogance or exclusiveness; but for the maintenance of international rights and the fulfilment of international duties. (Hear, hear.) The sentiment of empire is innate in Britons; and we are under obligations to see that it is not played upon for unworthy purposes. (Hear, hear.) Now, what is the British Empire? The words are often used, but not so often understood. There is a tale told of an English statesman who, when unexpectedly called to the presidency of the Colonial Department, asked his secretary to get a map of the world into his room, as he wanted to see where the places were situated that he had to rule. (Laughter.) A decent gazetteer would also, he thought, be serviceable. (Renewed laughter.) I do not vouch for the truth of the story. It is probably told to give point to the popular want of knowledge as to our colonial possessions. Be that as it may, I have acted on the suggestion of the unknown Secretary of State. Here's such a map as he desiderated, and, for the nonce, I will act as the gazetteer. (Cheers.) The British dominions embrace one-seventh of the land surface of the globe, and nearly one-fourth of its population. They cover 3½ millions of square miles in America; over a quarter of a million in Africa; over a million and a half in Asia; and three millions in Australia. The total area is 8,600,000 square miles, or 65 times the extent of the United Kingdom. That is, for every square mile of land we have at home, we have 65 square miles across the seas. The population is estimated at over 310,000,000, and includes men of all colours—white, black, red, and yellow—(laughter)—and all creeds. The Queen rules over nearly one-third more Mussulmans than the Sultan does; she has over one-third more Mahometan than Christian subjects; and as many believers in Brahma as in Mahomet and Christ put together. There is not now, and there never has been, an empire which has equalled it in extent and population, in industrial enterprise and wealth since the world began. (Loud cheers.) There has never been one that approximated to it in self-government. It is that faculty and habit of independence, which has been spun into the staple of our being, that has given such boundless vitality to the English race, and conferred upon them the uttermost parts of the earth as an inheritance. Wherever the tracery of her widely-spread web extends, her responsibility is carried. She is here a citadel, encircled by an admirable line of defence—the ocean. She has not only to mount guard upon it, and all its outworks and dependencies, but she has long and intricate lines of communication to keep open and intact. This involves exceptional responsibilities, and necessitates wariness, energy, and spirit. There are broad distinctions between the British and other empires—ancient and modern. It is more scattered. It has not four, but four thousand frontiers, touching, at one or more points, nearly every civilized State, and innumerable savage tribes. Such expanded and undulating borders, and such varied and uncertain neighbours, involve us in constantly recurring conflicts, which make less figure in our annals than they do in our estimates. Physically, Great Britain is an island; but, strategically, she is a great Continental Power. Other great States are more homogeneous and their frontiers less exposed. This is true of Russia, China, and the United States; and still more so of Germany, France, and Austria. The British Empire combines the trading, colonizing, and military characteristics of the Phœnicians, the Greeks, and the Romans. Its citizens have carried into their struggles with the untried and the unknown, in their distant dependencies, the national gifts and political virtues acquired by a long practice of liberty. To keep free and safe our ocean intercourse, on which the Empire depends for its existence, we require to plant numerous arsenals, garrisons, and coaling stations, along the routes into which trade has settled. (Hear, hear.) There are five such main lines, intersected with naval and military stations. The first, the oldest, and the shortest, but not the least important, route is to Canada. It is 2,000 miles long, between the nearest points in England and Newfoundland. There is one station on it, at Halifax, Nova Scotia, where there is an extensive dockyard and military depot. The second line is to the West Indies. It is 3,000 miles long between the nearest points. On it there are four stations—Bermuda, the Bahamas (the first point discovered by Columbus), Jamaica, and Antigua. There is an iron dry dock at Bermuda, which was made at Liverpool at a cost of £300,000. The British trade passing over these two routes amounts to upwards of 200 million pounds a-year, and it will increase. When the Canadian inter-colonial railway is developed, and the Panama Canal is opened, it will be the best and quickest route to the North Pacific. The third line is to the East, through the Suez Canal. By this it is 4,000 miles to India, and 9,000 to Australia. On it there are seven stations—Gibraltar, a strongly-fortified place; Malta, where we have a naval establishment at least half the size of that of Sheerness; Aden; Cape Comorin; Singapore; Hong Kong; and King George's Sound, in Western Australia. This long chain of stations gives a good idea of the precautions taken to secure the safety of British commerce. Singapore is not only a great naval, but a great commercial emporium, and is destined in time to govern the whole Malayan peninsula, and give it arts and civilization; while Cape Comorin and Trincomalee are the keys to the farther east. The fourth line is to the south and east by the Cape of Good Hope, and on it there are six stations —Sierra Leone and St. Simon's Bay on the African mainland; the islands of Ascension and St. Helena off the coast; the Mauritius; and King George's Sound. British trade, to the value of £300,000,000, annually passes these two routes. The fifth line is round Cape Horn to the Pacific and Australia. It is 10,000 miles long, and £45,000,000 worth of trade passes over it yearly. It utilises two of the Cape line stations—Ascension and Sierra Leone ; and it has three others—the Falkland Islands (over our conquest of which Dr. Johnson lavished so much eloquence and philosophy) ; Sydney ; and Fiji. Besides these stations, we have a number of naval outposts capable of storing considerable supplies of all naval and military requisites. We have also a dockyard at Yokohama ; Esquimault, a land-locked harbour in Vancouver's Island ; Hong Kong ; and Fernando Po, in the Bight of Benin. There never was an empire with more chinks in its armour; and if we were at war with a great Power, it would tax the combined skill and resources of the colonists and the mother-country to prevent it being pierced in a vital part. (Hear, hear.) Our safety is in our fleet. (Cheers.) It is the visible bond which secures the union. But for it we could be denuded of our possessions. England will be the victim of the sea when she shall have ceased to be its queen. It both serves and menaces her. It is the road that will lead our enemies to our hearths when we are unable to patrol it. If our navy dwindled into inefficiency, English workmen would soon find their occupation gone—(hear, hear)—and the price of bread quadrupled at a stroke. The system of defence defined by these routes, fortresses, stations, depôts, and dockyards is the product of ripe experience, and the outcome of generations of observation. It will suffice for ordinary times ; but the aggressive designs that other States have latterly developed necessitate its being strengthened and supplemented. We will require more ships, as well as larger arsenals and shipyards; and it is to provide these that an estimated additional expenditure of nearly £10,000,000 has been sanctioned by

Parliament. (Hear, hear.) It was for that end that Port Hamilton was got, and that a sharp eye is being kept over sundry groups of islands in Polynesia. We will see, in a few years, a naval station, equal to Malta, constructed in the Pacific —possibly at Levuka in the island of Ovaalu. At present, the most important of these highways are those by Suez and the Cape. They lead not only to India and China, but to our Straits Settlements and Australia; and no money is wasted in providing for their security. Whether, and how far, they may be influenced by the construction of the canal across the Isthmus of Panama, which is to be completed in three years' time, is a question on which authorities differ. But though it may divide the current of trade, and revive our rather languishing dependencies in the West Indies, it is scarcely likely to work such a revolution in the means of transit as the Suez Canal did. By a map, any speaker may make his meaning clearer than he can do by a speech. Doubting my capacity of exposition, and wishing you to grasp at once the scope of my contention, I have presumed to illustrate it by having this chart prepared, and by circulating *fac-similes* amongst those interested in the subject. (Cheers.) They give a ready idea of the vastness and variety of the British Empire. It is a noble inheritance; and every Briton should be proud of it. (Hear, hear.) There is a tale told of some Americans who, when celebrating a victory of the Federal arms by a banquet, had proposed to them by the chairman as a toast—"The United States, bounded on the north by British America ; on the south by the Gulf of Mexico ; on the east by the Atlantic ; and on the west by the Pacific Ocean." One of the guests thought this far too limited, and gave as an amendment—"The United States, bounded on the north and south by the two poles ; on the east by the rising, and on the west by the setting sun." (Loud laughter.) Even this capacious sentiment would not satisfy all, and a more ambitious member of the party proposed—"The United States, bounded on the north by the Aurora Borealis; on the south by the procession of the equinoxes; on the east by primeval chaos; and on the west by the Day of Judgment." (Much laughter.) There are Englishmen with high aspirations; but this Yankee sky-scraper outstrips them—(renewed laughter)—although the expansive British Empire bears a closer resemblance to his ideal than the magnificent, but compact territory over which the stars and stripes float in such honoured and uncontested supremacy. Our vast dominions have been acquired by conquest, cession, and colonization. Six million square miles came to us by settlement, and two by war. The whole is the accumulation of not more than two centuries and a half. "Nothing great hath great beginnings." The acquisition of none of this territory dates back beyond 1600. In that year, we had not a solitary colony. The same reign that gave England Shakspeare's poetry, and Bacon's philosophy, gave her the supremacy of the seas, the nucleus of her empire, and pre-figured her subsequent splendour. (Loud cheers.) It was then that the European States mingled fighting for religion and prestige with fighting for trade. It was then the two new worlds were opened up to European industry; the Indian Company's Charter was granted; and the first English settlement across the Atlantic was planted. Our enterprise in the East began in commerce, and ended in an empire which holds in its hands the welfare of millions; while out of that in the West has been evolved a marvellous aggregate of personal enterprise and political courage—the fruition of the struggle for liberty which commenced on the plains of Runnymede, and was crowned at the Appopomax Court House. (Loud cheers.) It took well nigh a thousand years to build up the Roman Empire. In a fourth of that time, "England," to use the words of Mr. Webster, "has dotted over the surface of the whole globe with her possessions and military posts—their morning drum-beat, following the sun, and keeping company with the hours, circles the earth with one continuous and unbroken strain of her martial music." (Loud cheers.) Is the empire worth preserving? (Cries of "Yes," and renewed cheering.) Putting the question first on its lowest level, Do we receive value for our money? (A Voice: "Rather," and cheers.) It is costly, but not so costly as it once was. A quarter of a century ago, the mother-country spent £4,000,000 a-year in providing soldiers for the defence of the colonies. The expenditure on this head is now less than half that amount. The British garrisons have been withdrawn, and their places taken by volunteers raised and paid by the colonists themselves. (Hear, hear.) About £2,000,000 is now our average colonial expenditure in times of peace. The colonies are divided into three classes. The first class comprises colonies possessing responsible government, in which the Crown has the appointment of the governor, and a veto on the legislation, but in which the Home Government has no control. The second class consists of colonies possessed of representative institutions, in which the Crown has a veto on legislation, and the Home Government has the control of public officers. The third class embraces colonies in which the Crown not only appoints all the officers, but has the entire direction both of legislation and administration. All the larger colonies have responsible government; all the medium-sized ones representative institutions; and all the smaller ones, being little more than military and naval stations, are ruled direct from London. Excluding India, there are about 10,000,000 colonists living under responsible government; about 4,000,000 under representative institutions; and 2,000,000 in Crown colonies. But although the direct colonial expenditure is only £2,000,000—(hear, hear)—the sum indirectly expended on the maintenance of this great organization, and for enabling our commerce and capital to circulate safely between Great and Greater Britain, is greatly in excess of that amount. Without her colonies, England would want only a small fleet, and a smaller army. She would only have to defend her shores from invasion, her institutions from attack; and that would not absorb half the money now devoted for defensive purposes. Without calculating the cost of constantly-recurring wars, the average annual outgoing for sustaining our Imperial possessions cannot be assessed at less than from £10,000,000 to £15,000,000 a-year. What do we get in return for this outlay? Much. First, markets for our commerce. Trade, for the last decade, has been a vanishing commodity. (Hear, hear.) In many branches, it has been receding, and, in most, it is stationary. Statistics are not required to prove what has been brought home so forcibly to our businesses and bosoms. We have been hit all round. Our production has increased, the demand has decreased, and the prices have fallen. The home markets are overstocked; the foreign markets are closed; and in neutral markets we are being undersold. We can manufacture for the world. (Hear, hear.) We either require increased consumption by our old customers, or a supply of new ones. We cannot get the former, and where can we find the latter but amongst our colonists? (Hear, hear.) Along with India, they now take fully one-third the goods we export, and one-half as many as all our foreign customers together—£68,000,000 out of £200,000,000. Relatively to population, the colonial consumption of British merchandise is greatly in excess of foreign; and it is regularly and rapidly increasing—(hear, hear)—while the foreign consumption is declining. Some of our colonial populations are proportionately better customers than those at home. Each emigrant, sent to Canada, represents a customer for England's goods to the extent of £2 10s. per annum; if sent to Australia, of £8 per annum; whereas, if sent to the United States, he would not take more than 15s. worth of English goods in the year. Each Australian consumes £3 4s. worth of textile fabrics per annum, as against a home consumption of £2 per head. The colonial are but an extension of our home markets. Their trade is steadier and safer than foreign trade. (Hear, hear.) It is increasing concurrently with the growth of their prosperity, and the development of their almost illimitable resources. It is to the colonies that we must look for purchasers for our capacious and augmenting produce, and for an outlet for our surplus population. We are adding rapidly to our numbers, doubling them in seventy years, but we cannot add to our land, and we are growing no more food. Of the 35,000,000 persons inhabiting these islands, at least 17,000,000 are fed on food which is not produced at home. On an average, each member of the community now consumes to the value of two-and-a-half times as much foreign food as he did twenty years ago. The colonies are an augmentation of the national estate. (Hear, hear.) England has a superabundance, the colonies have a paucity, of population. England is unable to raise her own food; the colonies can raise more than they can consume. England has a plethora of wealth; the colonies need all she can give them to develop their prairies. The necessity is mutual. Both will be gainers by it being met and supplied. It is the privilege of honourable trade that, like mercy, it is twice blessed. "It blesseth him that gives and him that takes." (Hear, hear.) Each of its dealings is a benefit. The increasing trade, and lessened supervision, have sweetened the relations between the mother-country and her off-shoots. (Hear, hear.) A very different sentiment from the one now prevalent formerly obtained. When the Queen came to the throne, in 1837, *Te Deums* were sung in honour of the event in colonial churches. The discontent with England, who acted then as an exacting step-mother, was so strong that, in North America, the congregations walked out. They have since been knit together in a mutual intercourse of good offices, and Canada is now more loyal than Northumberland. (Cheers.) Home-Rule has produced a union, whose strength is in proportion to its elasticity. (Renewed cheers.) The origin and essence of this new feeling are to be found in common descent, speech, and tradition; in unity of social and commercial interests, and in common citizenship. That is the silver braid that has woven, in its heroic loom, the tale divine, and not political restraints and coercion. But it is contended, by some, that if the colonies left us, their trade would not; that they would still welcome our ships, receive our cargoes, and send us their wealth—become generous allies instead of troublesome subjects. This is a theory based upon a hypothesis. There is no warrant for it. All experience is against it. When they declared their independence, the United States had a population of 2,000,000. The total value of our exports then was £16,000,000. Out of these sixteen millions, the two million American colonists purchased £6,000,000 worth. The population of the United States now is 50,000,000, and they take goods to the value of £26,000,000 annually. In other words, they took, when British colonists, £3 a-head of the population, and they now take ten shillings. Of course, the conditions are different; but the figures dispose of the illusion that the States are as good customers, when independent, as when they were colonists. (Hear, hear.) This is our position with the Americans, who are our best foreign customers. A comparison between the colonies and Continental countries shows the colonies in a still more favourable light. There is a positively Protectionist panic raging equally in

Republican and Autocratic States. Whichever way they turn, our merchants are confronted with a barrier of adverse influences and hostile tariffs, which is daily gaining height and strength. History has demonstrated, beyond dispute, that trade follows the flag—(hear, hear)—and that the markets for our industry, the channels of our trade, and the sources of our food supplies, would be closed against us if our determination to defend them declined. (Hear, hear.) All experience is false, if lessened trade does not follow in the footsteps of lessened strength. Sovereignty has often changed its seat, and trade has uniformly followed it. The correctness of this world-old maxim has had recent verification in Central Asia. Twenty years ago, when Professor Vambery—(applause)—was there, Manchester cottons, Birmingham hardware, and Sheffield cutlery, were found at all the fairs, and most of the bazaars. Since then, Russia has penetrated to, or rather over, the borders of Afghanistan; and now Russian goods are sold, and British goods are banished, from all the markets west of the Heri Rud. In other words, English traders have lost, and Russian traders have gained by the transfer of influence from one empire to the other. This is a modern, permit me to adduce an ancient illustration, of how like causes have produced like results. The Portuguese were once lords of the Indian seas. Their navigators were the Crusaders of commerce. Lisbon was the medieval London—the mart of the world. It is difficult to trace a resemblance between the daring men who first doubled the Cape, and discovered and settled energetic colonies in far Cathay, and the lethargic mariners and languishing dominions of the present Portugal. The Spaniards, delirious with the riches of South American El Dorados, aspired to play the part of the Romans after the conquest of Carthage. Their galleons, freighted with the precious products of two worlds, plied the Pacific unchallenged, and Madrid was the focus of imperial magnificence. But Spain shone like the child whose parents, to display their wealth, covered it with gold leaf, which closed the pores of its skin, and stifled it. The Dutch moored an immense commercial empire to the piles on which they built their houses and palaces. Their ships swept the ocean, and the Hague became the centre of the world's diplomacy. But its splendour has departed ; and so, too, has that of the all-potent Hanseatic League, which once commanded the respect, and defied the power, of kings. Venice, who, "throned on her hundred isles," held the gorgeous East in fee ; Florence, who was as famous in trade as in letters ; Genoa the Superb, who shook the thrones of Catacuzen ; those maritime Mahometans, the Moors, the "mildest mannered men who ever scuttled ships or cut a throat"—(laughter)—where are they all now ? I could push the inquiry further back, and gather confirmation for my argument from the mythic annals of decades of centuries and nations, as they "spin for ever down the ringing grooves of change." Phœnicia, the first pilot in the stream of history ; Carthage, to which all lines of wealth bent towards, concentrated in, and then radiated from, lie buried in the dust, without the record of a written line or a chiselled stone. The glory that was Greece, and the power that was Rome, have vanished. And why ? Because, intoxicated with success and insolence, they gave themselves up to the Delilah charms of luxury. "Their garments were all fringes, and their meals all sauces." (Laughter.) Ease, enervation, and cupidity blinded them. They turned too self-assured and self-indulgent to protect their empires. They first crumbled, then tottered, then fell. They teach an identical moral, and it is this. If dominion goes from a people, trade goes. What has been, will be. If England is to keep her commerce, she must keep her empire ; and she can only do that by paying a steady and sufficient premium against all risks ; in other language, by being resolved to enforce her rights, and prepared to defend her interests. (Loud cheers.) And this resolve gives a nation something more precious than gold—it gives it character. Our empire cannot be converted into a joint-stock company, involving limited and isolated liabilities. We have been made, by the irresistible sequence of events, paramount potentates in the Eastern seas. (Loud cheers.) It is the behest of destiny. Our ships swarm in every creek and harbour; our merchants press everywhere, trade everywhere, settle everywhere; and our captains and consuls follow to protect, and, if need be, to control them. (Cheers.) We cannot evade either the dignity or the obligations of the position. These obligations strengthen our national character, prevent us from degenerating into parochialisms, and convert a community of merchants into a race of teachers and rulers. (Hear, hear.) The position involves undoubted difficulties ; but it should be our glory to confront and overcome them. If we wrestle with them, they will strengthen our nerves and sharpen our skill. When the Athenians learnt of the mighty preparations of the Persian King of Athos, and of the shores of the Hellespont being united, Themistocles told them they had only one refuge—their own courage. Out of that self-reliance came forth those miracles of power—Thermopylæ and Salamis. Englishmen have all the courage in war, the sinew in labour, the cunning in workmanship, the daring in seamanship, that are requisite to constitute them the centre of such a vast territorial circumference. They are the inter-penetrating and binding power—the international amalgam that reaches to all, webs each to each, and all to themselves. That position can only be held, that puissant nationality can only be sustained, that sceptre can only be swayed, by a continuous and undaunted display of the imperial characteristics that won them, and by making our multitudinous obstacles occasions for fresh efforts, and converting new dangers into instruments of new triumph. (Cheers.) It is not sufficient, however, to possess the power—it is necessary to have the will and the ingenuity to apply it. Centuries before any modern nation, when Britain was buried in barbarism, and America was undiscovered and undreamt of, the Chinese made gunpowder, discovered the mariner's compass, and invented the printing press. They possessed, in these three instruments, the means for securing military, maritime, and literary supremacy. But they had not the *nous* to utilise them. Gunpowder, in their hands, produced only crackers and fireworks. (Laughter.) Junks, to navigate the seaboard, were all they drew from the mariner's compass; while printing produced nothing but stereotyped editions of Confucius. We have not buried our talents in the earth and hid them; but we have made them agents of our enterprise, furrowed the earth with railways, and given aerial wings to human speech. We have fought and conquered, and sailed and traded, through every zone; foreign skies only uncoiling the strength, and adding to the electric energy, of the race. Character in a nation, as in a man, is strength. (Hear, hear.) And it is cumulative. The consciousness of a train of great achievements behind adds to its present force and dignity, and guarantees them for the future. Courage calls forth emulation. But assuming that the benefits of the Empire were less, can we dissolve the international partnership, and capriciously break up such a gigantic moral and physical apparatus? (Cries of "No," and cheers.) Consider what would happen if we did so. The colonies do not seek separation. They may quarrel with the Colonial Office, but they never quarrel with England. Their loyalty is more than a sentiment; it is a passion. Although strong as a part of a great confederation, they would be weak if alone. The colonies could not stand by themselves; and would either become the victims of civil contention, or the prey of some prowling Power ready to play the part of buccaneer or bully. (Hear, hear.) Our exit from India would mean Russian entrance, and, preparatory to that, a reign of loot and rapine. The native princes, like eels in a jar—(laughter)—would wriggle for ascendency; and, whoever secured it, humanity would suffer and civilization be retarded. (Hear, hear.) South Africa would become the prize of slave-holding Boers, or a hunting-ground for marauding tribes. (Cheers.) The West Indies might be seized by the United States; but, before that was done, we would see a servile war, in which the dominant race-enmities would be revived; the hopes which England has nourished of redeeming the negroes would be blighted; and the sacrifices she has made so ungrudgingly for that purpose would be thrown away. (Hear, hear.) The shock of separation might shake Canada into the American Union, and our large Pacific possessions into a federation; but the smaller ones would fall into the covetous embraces of Germany and France. (Hear, hear.) Colonies, with mixed and aboriginal populations, could not be abandoned without positive cruelty. But this is not all. A desertion of our posts, as mediators or masters, would be followed by a demand for indemnity to those settlers whose position, assumed on our security, would no longer be tenable. It is estimated that the European investments in British dependencies, in loans, land, railways, and public and private works, equal in amount our National Debt. All this large sum would be endangered, and most of it lost, if we severed the connection. Can any colonist anticipate such a sacrifice with equanimity, or any patriot contemplate such a catastrophe with composure? (Cries of "No," and cheers.) No. We cannot, without a dereliction of duty, amounting to a crime, capriciously abandon the obligations of protection and control we have voluntarily assumed. Sympathy with the native races, whom we have rescued from barbarism ; justice to our countrymen, who have staked their property and imperilled their lives on the faith of the imperial connection ; security for the men who have driven the eagle to higher retreats, and the panther to deeper jungles, who have converted swamp, morass, and wilderness into scenes radiant with contentment, and who have lessened the misery at home by creating markets abroad ; devotion to the regenerating civilization, which robes men in the nobler raiment of rectitude and moral principles, calls into exercise the highest capacities of the human soul, and opens up a boundless infinitude of resources—would all combine to brand us as infamous for such a wanton and selfish repudiation of our responsibility, as the demolition of the Empire would involve. (Loud cheers.) I would appeal from Englishmen's interests to their duties ; from their pockets to their consciences—(cheers) —from their Epicurean timidity to their traditions of liberty; from ignoble ease to memories that will not dié, and cannot be destroyed, against such sacrilege and cowardice. As we cannot abandon the Empire, in what manner shall we govern it ? How must we deal with our dependencies ? and how with the nations with whom they bring us always into contact, often in competition, and sometimes in conflict ? First, as to our dependencies. We must have a centre. Sovereignty must reside somewhere, and that sovereignty cannot be elsewhere than in England. (Cheers.) Nationality is not imagination only. It is a powerful bond of action. Like the mainspring of a watch, it sets the whole machinery in motion ; like the heart, it causes the pulse of life to beat in the farthest extremities of the system. It is the soul which animates and exalts the whole brotherhood of associated men. This sentiment should be, and is, the link of life between England and her colonies. The less it is regulated, the more robust it will grow. The fullest freedom, compatible with union, is a specific alike for the relief of the mother-country, the masculine well-being of the dependencies, and the vigorous integrity of the Empire. (Hear, hear.) Along with absolute local liberty, give the colonists their proportionate share of imperial authority. Let them feel that the difference between the colonist and the citizen is a difference of distance, and not of status or influence. England's greatness is their greatness; England's honour their honour; England's glory their glory. (Cheers.) They cannot separate themselves from her past history, nor her future fortunes. The ties of kindred, the instincts of race, and common tradition, are, and ever will be, the motive forces. In such a spirit of liberality, forbearance, and justice, we should rule the colonies; and, if we do, we shall "grapple them to us with hoops of steel." (Cheers.) There is not time, nor is this the occasion, in which to indicate a method of federation. I am only preaching the principle. It is capable of embodiment, in a form that will promote unity, preserve liberty, foster local independence, and give strength and splendour to the British Empire. (Cheers.) Great power means many responsibilities, and a great empire means many wars. Out of the 16,000,000 of people in the colonies, about half are of British descent. In the other half, nearly every known race is represented. Most of this non-European population is in Africa and the West Indies. There are about 100,000 red Indians in Canada, who live partly on their own resources and partly by Government subsidies; and about 40,000 Maoris. The Maoris have the franchise, and send members to the New Zealand Parliament. Both in America and in the Pacific, the natives are inoffensive; but they are rapidly disappearing. In South Africa and the West Indies, on the other hand, they thrive and multiply. One of the most gratifying results of English colonization is the steady rise of the social position of the aborigines. In increasing numbers, they are becoming not only labourers, but skilled agriculturists, merchants, contractors, and professional men. The difficulties with them, and the disputes with those across the border who are allied to them by descent and creed, involve us in interminable embroilments. This is one of the penalties of empire. We have had only one European war since the treaty concluded at Vienna seventy years ago; but we have had thirty colonial wars during that period. It is impossible to calculate the combined cost of all these military operations, big and little, to the mother-country and her dependencies; but it cannot have been less than £200,000,000, or an average of £3,000,000 a-year. We cannot avoid frontier collisions, and we cannot save this outlay. Whenever civilized and savage, or semi-savage people come in contact, friction first, and then fighting, are inevitable. (Hear, hear.) But by respecting native susceptibilities, by honesty in our dealings, and by justice in our treatment of our unlettered neighbours and fellow-subjects, we may minimise the disquietude and trouble. The colonies are not governed for our benefit alone, but for the treble benefit of settlers, aborigines, and the mother-country. No nation has heretofore acted on this principle. Other States have treated their colonies as spoils, and their inhabitants as slaves. Hence their failure. Unredeemed brute force has never led to permanent conquest. No inferior race ever displaced a superior one, except when the superior one had first become demoralised. Inferior races have swept over lands as scavengers—clearing the way for better tenants. They have never held what they won. The ultimate victory has always been for the fittest, and it will be so with England. So long, and so long only, as she shows herself fit and equal to the task, will she hold her own against the wild and warlike clans that converge on her every frontier, and threaten all her outposts. (Loud cheers.) England, up to the reign of Elizabeth, had gone to war only for kingly aggrandisement or renown. She then went for a principle—the solidarity of free States. There has seldom been a time when Europe has not been dominated by an autocrat. Forty years ago, it was Russia; then it was France; now it is Germany. In Elizabeth's days, it was Spain. Conceiving Europe's danger to be her own, England gallantly placed herself between the tyrant and his prey. The achievements of her statesmen, at that era, dwarf the feats of modern diplomatists; while her warriors inspired the awe of her enemies, and won the admiration of all ages. (Cheers.) England then emerged from an insular to an imperial position. The nation was alive in every fibre. Cromwell maintained the position with imperial imperiousness. He intimidated Holland, humiliated Spain, and twisted the supple Mazarin round his fingers. These nations were unfriendly to the rising power of England; but they swerved before the authority of the man who had coerced at once her aristocracy and her factions. (Cheers.) Political debauch succeeded political purity. Charles II. wiped out the record of English fame and influence by shameless dependence and corruption. (Hear, hear.) England's king became a pensioner of France, who had worked her way to the sway Spain had lost, and, in her turn, jeopardised the independence of Europe. Again England stood in the breach. William the Third gave her freedom, and us a National Debt. The historic policy was sustained by his predecessors. Another war trebled our debt, but secured the Hanoverian succession, and our North American colonies. Under the corrupt administration of Walpole, we kept tolerably clear of foreign entanglements; but, while subjected to the inspiring pulsation of the two Pitts,

England became continental arbitress. There was not a cannon fired in Europe that we did not demand to know the reason why. (Cheers.) We fought the battles of foreign sovereigns, subsidised their armies, lavished blood and treasure to keep them on their thrones; and when peace came, we frequently found ourselves abandoned and betrayed, by the men who owed their crowns to our unexampled exertions, unparalleled fortitude, and unprecedented public spirit. (Cheers.) The melancholy outcome of the last war with France was a political system, which mercilessly violated the most sacred rights of humanity, and impiously claimed the Judge of the earth as an accomplice in its tyranny. Europe was held under the heel of autocracy, and the first symptoms of revolt were stamped out, as we stamp out the first symptom of cattle plague. Mr Canning promised that England would make "inharmonious the music of the Holy Alliance;" and, had he lived longer, he would have done more to redeem his pledge. But even despots cannot dethrone human nature. (Cheers.) The struggle for liberty recommenced at the foot of the scaffold. The idea gained strength here with the hammer and the anvil. The blood-stained compact of the tyrannical triumvirate, devised to strangle freedom and national aspirations, has been overturned. A dozen royal dynasties have been engulphed in the abyss of popular fury. Belgium has been separated from Holland; Greece has risen from the tomb; Austria has been driven out of Italy; Germany has been united; Russian preponderance has been destroyed; the Bourbons have been expelled from France, to be succeeded, first, by a Napoleon, and then by a Republic—(cheers);—while forgotten and almost unknown races, Sclavonian and Roumanian, have disinterred their traditionary titles, and secured representation in the congress of nations. And all this in the short space of forty years! (Hear,

hear.) It is a tempting recital, and contains much over which a politician may usefully moralise. Time will only allow me to summarise, in a few sentences, the leading purposes of England's foreign policy. Its object up to the sixteenth century was personal, and not national. It was the offspring of royal emergencies and aristocratic intrigues. The objects sought by the Elizabethan and Cromwellian statesmen were Protestant ascendency, and colonial expansion. The objects sought by King William and Queen Anne were the assuring of the Hanoverian succession, and the establishment of the balance of power—a device of the Italian republics, by which they hoped, through combination, to curb the aggressive designs of the Hapsburgs and the Bourbons. The objects of Chatham were to assert the authority, and sustain the influence of England, as a member of the European family of nations. (Cheers.) The objects of his son were, first, to stop the spread of "French principles"—an impossible task—and afterwards to stop the spread of French conquest. The object of Mr. Canning was to prevent autocratic interference in the internal affairs of other States; and, by encouraging the Spanish colonies in South America to assert their independence, to call a new world into existence to redress the balance of the old. The object of Lord Palmerston—(hear, hear)—was, by representation, advice, and remonstrance, to multiply the number of constitutionally governed States. There runs through all this record the assertion of the right of England to a voice in the councils of Europe, and to use it in every controversy. The method of its exercise has varied according to circumstances; but the principle, which is the developed product of English history, has come down unbroken from Burleigh to Bolingbroke, from Cromwell to Chatham, and from Pitt to Palmerston. (Hear, hear.) We have fought not only for trade and territory, but for forms of faith and modes of government; and we have done so because we could not isolate ourselves from our fellows, or divorce ourselves from the duty that their fellowship imposed. We may often have been in error in interpreting our duty, and still oftener ineffective in its execution ; but the idea of national responsibility has operated throughout. (Cheers.) This policy is being recast, and these principles are being modified. We are neither absolutely off with the old faith, nor entirely on with the new. (Laughter.) We are in that most unsatisfactory of all states—the transition state. It is a witches' Sabbath with our statesmen—(laughter)—who are confusingly inconsistent when they try to reconcile the sentiment which prompted us to assume the attitude of liberators, ready to throw our sword into the scale for freedom, and the utterly conflicting doctrine of non-intervention. This dalliance makes them often Brobdignagian in words, and Liliputian in acts—lays them open to the charge of substituting interest for justice, and cupidity for right. (A voice: "Question.") Question? (Loud laughter and cheers.) If that be not the marrow of the question, I don't know what is. (Renewed cheers.) Non-intervention was originally a protest against the lust of conquest and the appetite for war. As such, it was a step in advance. But when it is made a canopy for national mutilation, and a pretext for castrating the spirit of independence, it is perverted from its original purpose, and debased to cowardly ends. (Loud cheers.) It is a wise and righteous policy between free States ; but it is neither wise nor righteous when invoked to perpetuate tyranny, or shelter the Neros or the Bombas of the earth from contumely and chastisement. (Renewed cheers.) The right of the oppressed to rebel, and the right of free men everywhere to aid them, are elementary rights that no political casuistry can extinguish. (Hear, hear.) They stir the great deeps of the human heart, and ride upon the whirlwind of its passions. They precede all law, and will survive it; for it is an artificial compact, and they are its ultimate principles. A statute of Solon decreed the degradation of whomsoever, in an insurrection, abstained from taking sides. It was a just ordinance—a recognition of the solidarity of humanity. When there is brute force on one side—the rule of the bayonet and halter—and suffering right on the other, neutrality—indifference between good and evil—is moral criminality. England cannot adopt the Monroe rule; neither can she become the "Uriah Heap" of Europe—(hear, hear, and laughter)—or an anchorite among nations. But while I would have England to identify herself with Europe, to sympathise with the adversity and happiness of mankind, and find nothing in human affairs foreign to her, I would not have her run amuck, and tilt at all she meets. (Cheers.) They alone know how to serve their country whose service is consistent with justice. (Hear, hear.) If we have no hostile interest with a nation, it lessens the causes of war; but what forms genuine and durable alliances is the reciprocity of sympathies. Neighbouring Powers will find their best guarantee for tranquillity in combining wise forbearance with mutual respect. Let us hold to every State, whether powerful or weak, friendly but firm language, and observe a courteous, temperate, but unequivocal course of conduct. (Hear, hear.) We gain nothing by trying to conciliate those who wish to intimidate. (Hear, hear, and laughter.) Do not let us mistake cowardice for prudence. The white feather has often been dabbled in blood. If our rights are infringed, our interests imperilled, our honour outraged, address the offenders in the memorable words of Lord Dalhousie:—"I want peace; I have laboured for peace; but if you are bent upon war, war you shall have, and with a vengeance." (Loud cheers.) I have described what the British Empire is, rapidly summarised its extent, character, and population, shown how it was built up, how it is held, and what is the cost of holding it ; I have set set out the obligations it entails, and the benefit it confers, and have educed from them that interest, duty, and honour require us to keep it. (Hear, hear.) I have outlined the policy we have followed with our colonies, and with foreign powers, and indicated where, and in what way, I agree with, and differ from, it. I am for holding our own at all hazards—(hear, hear)—for not meddling in the internal affairs of free States ; for not seeking fresh territory, but for resolutely asserting our rights, and discharging our duties—(cheers)—whatever the cost and sacrifice to oui kindred and our kind. This is the source and sanction of progress. Nothing is sacred but justice, and nothing stable but right. Like the old Crusaders, we should wear on our breasts the symbols of our faith. I believe there lurks beneath the workman's jacket a spark of the sacred fire which burned in British breasts when her heroic sons counted no odds in the fight for liberty. (Loud and prolonged cheering, amid which Mr. Cowen resumed his seat.)

# INDIA, THE SUEZ CANAL, AND AFGHANISTAN.

---

DELIVERED IN BATH LANE HALL, ON THURSDAY EVENING, NOVEMBER 19TH, 1885.

---

CHAIRMAN—COUNCILLOR J. BAXTER ELLIS.

---

Mr. COWEN, who was received with prolonged cheering, the audience rising *en masse*, and continuing the enthusiasm for some time, said : Mr. Chairman, ladies, and gentlemen—the history of that unique political fabric, the British Empire in India, supplies a curious example of the at least apparent influence of small things on great. It was because the Dutch, who had at the time a monopoly of trade with the East, had raised the price of pepper from three shillings to eight shillings per pound—(laughter)—that the East India Company was projected ; it was because the doctor to the English embassy at the Court of Delhi cured the Great Mogul of a bilious attack—(renewed laughter)—that the Grand Charter was conceded ; it was because the cartridges of the Enfield rifles were greased with the fat of a cow, that the Sepoys mutinied, and that the patrimony of the Company was transferred to the Crown. Perhaps, this is mistaking opportunities for causes. That the sequence of events, without the aid of pepper, purgatives, or greased cartridges—(laughter)—would not have led up to the same result, it would be rash to say; but that circumstances, as singular as they were trifling and unforseen, should have carried with them such consequences, is at least curious. In ancient times, India was the principal source of commerce with the Venetians, Carthagenians, and Egyptians. At the end of the fifteenth century, the trade was exclusively in the hands of the Venetians and the Genoese. The merchandise came partly through Egypt, and partly by caravan through the interior of Asia. The position of affairs was revolutionised by the Portuguese reaching India by sea. Half pirates, half merchants, they soon became possessed of the chief ports. They brought the stuffs, the spices, and precious stones of the East to the Tagus, and undersold the Venetians, who had all the cost of land carriage and arbitrary customs to bear. Avarice and love of plunder were the main motives of the Portuguese adventurers. A revolting abuse of power excited the resistance of the natives, who had been armed against each other by the artful policy of the strangers, but who now became united in the presence of a common danger. The Dutch followed the Portuguese, as the Portuguese had followed the Venetians, and wove a commercial net that drew the greater part of the world's wealth within their dykes. Commerce, as her historian says, plucked Holland up half-drowned, and poured gold into her lap. It was from her colonies that she drew the means that enabled her to defeat the designs of Spain, and made her strong enough to defy the combined forces of France and England. When she was supreme in India, she was the first mercantile Power in the world. But England followed, outstripped, and supplanted her. The East India Company, with a capital of £70,000 and 125 shareholders, was formed at a meeting, held in London, under the presidency of the Lord Mayor, in September, 1600 ; and, on the last day of the same year it was incorporated by Royal Charter. The preamble quaintly summarised its objects, which were the honour of the nation, the extension of English discovery and navigation, the advancement of English trade, the increase of the people's riches, and the benefit of the Commonwealth. How this trading company purchased, first, the sites of scattered warehouses; how these expanded to fortified factories, and, ultimately, as if by enchantment, into an empire which rivals in extent that of Alexander or Tamerlane, constitutes one of the most marvellous chapters in the annals of time. (Loud cheers.) The rapidity of the acquisition, the commanding attributes and transforming influence of the dominant race, and the smallness of the means used compared with the vastness of the objects gained, are even more remarkable than the scope of the possessions secured. England is not indebted for her success, as the Tartars were in China, solely to the superiority of armies; nor, as the conquerors of Rome were, to overwhelming masses; nor, as the Arabs were, to religious fanaticism, propagated by the sword; nor, as the Spaniards in America were, to superstition; the natives taking the followers of Pizaro for Centaurs, and the fire from their arms as lightning from heaven. To none of these causes do we owe our ascendency, but to the valour, fortitude, and resource of a handful of Englishmen, capable of any desperate service that has daylight and honour in it. (Loud cheers.) Against the appliances of European civilization, and the magazines of inexhaustible British energy, intelligent but feeble and decrepid Asiatics could make no stand. Our average English politicians systematically ignore India, on the pretext that it is so far, so foreign, and so complex, that they have not leisure to study it. They attach no discredit to the most ludicrous ignorance of the country, its geography, history, and political and social condition. But while thus indifferent to the most costly military investment, and the most arduous political adventure any nation ever embarked in, they can work themselves into convulsions over questions that are both frivolous and far-fetched. (Laughter.) Yet, the slightest reflection would convince them that India disaffected, is a palsy of England's right side—India in rebellion, is a devouring ulcer in her flank. I should like to try to show, as far as my ability and time will permit, how arbitrarily and authoritatively India affects English politics, and how closely its concerns come home to us all in our daily life. (Cheers.) Will you listen? (Cries of "Yes, yes," cheers, and laughter.) Well, then, what is British India? Its length from the Himalayas to Cape Comorin, is 1,900 miles, and its greatest breadth is about the same. This compact domain, along with British Burmah, a strip on the eastern shore of the Bay of Bengal, contains one and a half million square miles, and nearly two hundred and fifty millions of inhabitants. British India, therefore, has an area and a population about equal to the area and population of the whole of Europe, less Russia. It has just ten times the population of England and Wales, and more than double the population that Gibbon estimated was possessed by Imperial Rome. Our Indian dominions include within their boundaries every variety of climate and product; but they are roughly divided into three well-defined regions. The first comprises the Himalayas, which means the dwelling place of snow, the most stupendous range of mountains in the world, and their intermediate valleys and adjacent slopes. The second is the river plains in the north, which were the scene of ancient movements which shaped the civilization and designs of the whole peninsula. The third is the triangular table-land in the south, which has a physical character and race development peculiar to itself. The inhabitants are roughly divided into four great races; but they are subdivided into scores of distinct nations, castes, and tribes. There is great disparity in their physical aspects and forms, in their manners and customs, in their respective advance in civilization of pursuits, and their modes of faith and language. Between the people in the same provinces there is as much difference as there is between the Greeks and Germans, the Italians and Russians, the Spaniards and Swedes. England's task is to devise and direct the administrative machinery, which unites these scattered and discordant races into a pacific and united empire. It is a stupendous undertaking, sufficient to tax the energies of the strongest, and daunt the courage of the bravest. (Cheers.) The passage of the East India Company from a trading to a governing corporation; first its subordination, and then suppression by Parliament, are matters of detail that lie beyond the scope of my argument. It is sufficient, for my purpose, to say that the Secretary of State for India, who is responsible to Parliament, and must be a member of the Cabinet, is now invested with all the powers formerly exercised by the East India Company and the old Board of Control. He is aided by a Council of fifteen members, all of whom must have served or resided ten years in India. The executive in India is vested in a Viceroy, who is assisted by a Cabinet, whose members preside, respectively, over the departments of foreign affairs, interior, finance, and military administration, and by a Council for making laws and regulations. For the purposes of administration, India is apportioned into Presidencies, each with a governor and council of its own. These Presidencies are divided into provinces, and the provinces into districts. There are three Presidencies, fifty-three provinces, and about two hundred and forty districts, with an average population to each district of about 800,000. The administrative system is compact, searching, progressive, and law-worthy. (Hear, hear.) Its defects are exclusiveness and over-centralization. The tendency of all recent reforms, however, has been towards relaxation; and efforts are now made to foster the nascent germs of local life. (Hear, hear.) Formerly, the provincial governors were merely tax-gatherers. Now, they have a certain and growing control over the expenditure. This disposition to decentralization is commendable, and a step towards administrative liberality. It has been accompanied by a concession to the demands of the natives for official recognition and confidence. (Hear, hear.) They are no longer voiceless. Native members have seats on the Viceroy's Council, and on all the councils of the subordinate governors; while native lawyers have reached the highest judicial posts. The old theory was, everything for the people and nothing by them. That is being modified slowly, but still surely and hopefully. (Hear, hear.) Take our Indian administrative system as a whole, it has, in spite of infirmities, mistakes, abuses, and even occasional crimes, well sustained the part of an enlightened ruler, and established a moral claim to a reciprocal allegiance. (Cheers.) Still, it has been, and is, in the main, a despotism—a beneficent despotism, it is true, but a despotism, nevertheless, founded on military power, though modelled and controlled by civil abilities of the highest order. (Hear, hear.) After making every allowance for recent and projected reforms, and for the undoubted disposition of all parties to lighten the burdens and enlarge the liberties of the Indian people, there is no gainsaying the fact that we hold the country by the sword. Our position there, and our position in the other colonies, is very dissimilar. The colonies would not leave us if we wanted them to do so. India would not stay with us unless we compelled her. Are we justified in forcibly retaining the rulership of two hundred and fifty millions of people over four thousand miles away from our shores? It requires great sacrifices at our hands. India has involved us in many a war, and loaded us with many a debt. It has strained our resources, and distracted our energies, by constantly requiring from us a vast expenditure of life and effort to guard it against dangers, and preserve it from attack. Is it worth all this? Especially is it worth it when our self-denial does not secure us the good will of the people we do so much to serve? I think it is, and I will tell you why. (Loud cheers.) First, and chiefly, in the interests of the Indians themselves. I put their case first, for if we cannot show that our rule has benefited them, no advantage that may accrue to us from it would justify its retention. We have been there as rulers just over one hundred years. The primary condition of civilized existence, that which precedes all others, is security for life and property. A century ago, the Indians had not this. Half-a-century ago, they had it only partially. Now, they have it absolutely. (Cheers.) From the earliest times, Central Asian marauders poured periodically over the Indian borders, plundered without restraint, and massacred without mercy. There were six invasions in the hundred years antecedent to Clive's conquest. These invasions were not like those of France by Germany, or Russia by Bonaparte. They consisted of a host of from twenty to one hundred thousand reckless barbarians, who marched through the country, burning and despoiling out of sheer wantonness and cruelty. When they had had a surfeit of slaughter, they usually closed their raid by a final sack and ravage of the capital of the invaded country. The Persian Nadir Shah terminated his invasion, in 1739, by ordering a general massacre in Delhi. One hundred and fifty thousand persons—men, women, and children—were hacked to pieces. The invaders carried off booty amounting to one hundred and twenty-five million pounds, and left the city stripped and desolate. The Afghan butcheries were even more brutal than the Persian, and were attended by incidents that won't bear recital. Such were the invaders from the land-side. But India was open to equally desperate attacks from the sea. Her shores were infested by pirates, who swept down on her ports, sailed up her rivers, harried her villages, and depopulated whole districts, killing or carrying off the inhabitants into slavery. Those were the human devastations. But the peaceful and industrious natives were liable also to incursions of wild beasts, which were quite as disastrous. The fastnesses of the mountains, and the jungles of the plains, furnished covers for ferocious animals. For fifteen hundred miles, along the base of the Himalayas, there stretched a belt of territory from twenty to fifty miles broad, and comprising thirty thousand square miles, which no one dared to cultivate. This desert border-land yielded no food for man, but teemed with fierce beasts of prey, who sallied forth nightly to ravage the herds and hamlets in the open country. Malaria was generated, and deadly fevers bred in this dismal district. They created havoc amongst all who attempted to cross it. But the natives made no attempt to clear it, as it was a partial protection from the savage hillmen on the other side. The helpless and languid Hindoos, who had for ages been trampled on by men of bolder and hardier nature, were thus worried and scourged, robbed and beaten, by beast and man, from sea and land. Lawlessness breeds lawlessness—(hear, hear)—and bands of robbers, the residuum of Afghan or piratical invaders, with here and there a peasant who had been dispossessed of his possessions, ranged themselves into bands, sometimes of fifty thousand strong, who made violence their calling and plunder their means of living. These banditti were associated with professional stranglers, with whom murder was a trade. To add to its miseries, the country was, from periodical drought, and want of means of transit for food and water, liable to famine, in which tens of thousands of people died. Lord Cornwallis reported that, twenty years after the great famine in Bengal, one-third of the territory that was previously populous and prosperous, had been abandoned to wild beasts. The people had perished, and the land had gone back to jungle.

This brief and bald synopsis gives a faint idea of the state of the country when it came under British domination. What is it now? Invasions from Central Asia have ceased. As a consequence, thirteen thousand square miles of frontier jungle have been brought under cultivation. (Hear, hear.) The Director-General of Statistics to the Governor of India, calculates that this reclaimed land will produce eighteen million pounds' worth of food, or more than the average normal cost of the Indian army, and the whole defence of the Indian Empire. (Cheers.) From the fertile valleys of Assam, which were formerly the scenes of periodical devastation, are annually exported, chiefly to this country, three million pounds' sterling worth of tea. And this is but one of the numberless regions which have been similarly transformed. (Cheers.) Piracy has been extirpated, and the Indian seas and rivers are now as safe as the German Ocean or our English waterways. (Renewed cheers.) Robber gangs, and all the special border crimes, have ceased. Crime, indeed, is less in India than in England. For every million of men in Great Britain, there are eight hundred and seventy; and for every million of women there are three hundred and forty criminals always in gaol. In India, there are only six hundred and fourteen male and twenty-eight female prisoners in gaol for each million of population. (Cheers.) In other words, there are more than one-half fewer men, and one-twelfth fewer women prisoners in India than in the United Kingdom. An astounding change! (Hear, hear.) This is the result of civil, not military measures. Dr. Hunter says that the existence of an army is less realized in any rural district in Bengal than in any English county. (Hear, hear.) Of the sixty-three millions in that province, probably forty millions go through life without ever seeing a soldier. The ravages of wild beasts have all but ceased. The ancient Indian lion has disappeared. Wolves are dying out, and the complaint of English sportsmen is that they can seldom get a shot at a tiger. (Loud laughter.) To prevent wild elephants from becoming extinct a close time has been established for them. The only creature that defies the energy of the British Government is the snake. (Renewed laughter.) The deaths from wild beasts and poisonous reptiles, last century, were estimated to be nearly two hundred thousand annually; now, they are near eighteen thousand. Famines have not ceased, but they have been shorn of their intensity. A vast organization of preventive and remedial agencies is constantly kept in readiness to deal with them. Heartrending as was the calamitous dearth in 1877 and 1878, it produced no result analogous to former famines, when it was quite common for half the peasantry of a province to perish, and for the landed classes to be so completely disorganized that one-third of the land relapsed to wilderness. We have given, then, security to property, and confidence to the people. (Cheers.) What have they done with them? Why, the very magnitude of the benefits conferred leads sceptical minds to detract from the achievements, and question their reality. They rest, however, upon too firm a basis to be hurriedly disproved. (Hear, hear.) Here are a few of them. Our rule in India had its origin in commerce, and our efforts have been directed to its development. Former conquerors strove to secure military dominion and religious predominance. The Moguls erected grand palaces; the Hindoos elegant temples; the Mussulmans magnificent mausoleums; and the Mahrattas huge forts. The English have built big cities. (Cheers.) Their designs are industrial and mercantile. The natives are agriculturists. Eighty per cent. of them live on the land; only eight per cent. in this country do so. We have introduced English modes of life to India, and given a stimulus to the population. (Hear, hear.) Formerly, their towns were but camps, around which, as round an old feudal castle, merchants and artificers congregated for protection and traffic. When the courts or the camps were removed, the settlers were scattered, and the settlement reverted to prairie or jungle. Emporiums of trade, such as they now have, they had not. This growth of great towns is characteristic evidence of British ascendency. A century ago, Calcutta consisted of three mud hamlets, barely out of water-mark. It has now a population of 800,000, or nearly double that of any place in the United Kingdom, except London. (Loud cheers.) It is the second city of the Empire. When we took it, its sea-borne trade was not worth £20 a-year. It now amounts to seventy millions—(cheers)—while its home and export trade together is valued at one hundred and ten millions. (Renewed cheers.) Bombay, the second city in India, was, along with Tangiers, part of the dowry of the wife of Charles the Second, and he sold it to the East India Company as a trading station for £10 a-year. (Laughter.) It has now a population of seven hundred and eighty thousand, or nearly double that of Manchester. (Cheers.) We are justifiably proud of the money we have lavished, and the skill we have displayed, in improving the Tyne—(cheers);—but our engineering operations sink into insignificance, when contrasted with the stupendous contest between man and nature that has been successfully waged on the banks of the Hooghly, and amidst the pestiferous swamps of Bengal. (Loud cheers.) There is nothing which reflects the influence of European ideas more than the growth of great commercial centres. It is indicative of the growth of the industrial life of the people. (Hear, hear.) But as great a change has taken place in the methods of Indian manufactures as in the methods of their commerce. India had, along with her agriculture, many skilled handicrafts. It was their goods, as as much as their rich materials, that first attracted European customers. Their fine muslins, their rich silks and brocades, and their harmonious cotton prints, far surpassed our mediæval workmanship. It is customary to credit the Indians with a chronic and unadaptable conservatism. In a sense, this is true; but, in recent years, they have shown a remarkable acuteness in adapting their cultivation to the requirements of commerce. This is shown by the manner in which they have extended their production of jute, cotton, and wheat. When we went to war with Russia, we lost our usual supply of fibres from that country. With remarkable rapidity, the Indian peasants took up the trade, and have ever since kept it. The year before the Baltic was blockaded, the average export of jute from India did not amount to one hundred thousand tons a-year. In twenty-five years, it rose to four and a-half millions—an increase of nearly forty-five fold. (Cheers.) When the American Civil War stopped our supply of cotton, India came to our help. Before the war, the cotton exported from India did not amount, on an average, to more than one and three-quarters millions sterling annually. Now, it amounts to the enormous sum of forty millions. (Cheers.) Thus much for clothing materials. Now as to food. The wheat trade of England formerly oscillated between America and Russia. India is now the third source of supply. Its astounding development will be seen by the following figures:—In 1870, our imports of wheat from Russia were ten million hundredweight; from America twelve million hundredweight; and from India eight thousand hundredweight. That is fifteen years ago. Now, the imports of wheat from Russia are five million hundredweight; from America twenty-two million hundredweight; and from India eleven million hundredweight. (Loud cheers.) Or, to state the facts in another way, our imports from Russia have fallen from ten to five millions; those from America have risen from twelve to twenty-two millions; while those from India have risen from eight thousand to eleven million hundredweight, or nearly thirteen hundred fold. (Great cheering.) We have not yet realized the gigantic probabilities of this new wheat market, nor the magnitude of the stores we may eventually draw from it. If other sources of supply were stopped, we could raise in India all the wheat we require in England. (Cheers.) We take their wheat, and the Indians take our cotton fabrics. We are both benefited by the barter. Contemporaneous with the trade in cotton, jute, and wheat, there has been a development of the coal trade. India has now an annual output of one million tons—about one-fifth that of Belgium, and one-eighth that of America. Cotton mills have followed the opening of the coal-fields. There are now nearly two million spindles employed in that manufacture, and nearly fifty thousand in the manufacture of jute. Twenty-six years ago, there was not a single loom worked by steam-power in India. (Cheers.) In 1830, all the produce that the Indians were able to export amounted to eleven millions sterling. In 1880, they were able to send sixty-six million pounds' worth of Indian produce, or six times as much. (Loud cheers.) Now, the total trade of India—of imports and exports together—amounts to one hundred and twenty-two millions sterling. (Renewed cheering.) These figures imply a stupendous change in the industrial condition of the inhabitants—such a change as has not taken place, in the same period of time, in any country of which we have any record. India now exports, as the products of her soil and workmanship, an annual average of twenty-one million pounds worth of goods more than she imports. With one-third of this sum—or seven millions—she pays interest for the construction of public works. With the second third, she pays for the government that has secured her the opportunity of making so much profit. The last third

—seven millions—goes direct into the pockets of the people, and, to that extent, aids in bettering their condition. (Loud cheers.) Along with increased trade, there has been increased revenue. It has trebled in forty years, and risen twenty-five per cent., even within the last dull decade. (Hear, hear.) The land-tax has, in the same period, increased more than sixty-five per cent., and yet it still only forms one-half its old proportion to the total revenue of India. Land, which was once the most precarious property in India, is now the safest. Money will be lent upon it for one-third the interest got on other investments. This is, perhaps, the strongest proof that can be adduced of the sense of security that English rule has engendered. (Cheers.) We have changed the whole face of the country by covering it with a network of railroads, telegraphs, and canals. They have multiplied and secured its internal resources, while the spacious harbours that have been constructed have brought these resources into the markets of the world. (Hear, hear.) The length of Indian railways now open is twelve thousand miles, and they have cost sixty million pounds. On canal and irrigation works, there have been expended twenty-four million pounds. Sixty-three thousand miles of telegraphs have been laid, while the postal system is nearly as completely developed as in this country. (Cheers.) These are some of the salient, though by no means all the material, results that have come out of British rule. But the efforts to emancipate the Indian people from ignorance, as well as from degrading forms of superstition, are a more splendid memorial of British rule than the material progress that has been made. (Renewed cheers.) We have founded universities, established colleges, built schools, trained teachers, appointed directors of public instruction, and spent large sums of money for educational institutions, old and new. (Cheers.) We have broken in upon the enervating system of caste, and we have now two millions of children receiving instruction in public schools. (Hear, hear.) They are learning that all occupations and professions are open to every native in India as freely as they are to natives in England. (Hear, hear.) The press is free. There are two hundred and fifty papers printed in the vernacular, while an average of five to six thousand books is published every year. Everywhere, we are disinterestedly and skilfully labouring to stimulate and instruct the minds of the people. (Hear, hear.) An enormously increased trade, diminished taxation, immunity from invasion, growing scarcity of famine and dearth, with laws honestly made and justly and purely dispensed, are some of the advantages that have accrued to the people of India from the English Government. (Loud cheers.) This, very incompletely told, is the Indian side of the account. Now for the English. What advantages have we got from India? It is not easy to apportion them with precision, for the relations and advantages are mutual. (Hear, hear.) But let me enumerate some of them. India is not a colony in the sense that Canada and Australia are. It does not offer an outlet for our surplus population as they do. The tropical climate, and the impossibility of transmitting to an Indian posterity the vigour of European constitution, and of promoting general intermarriages between the races, put us at a disadvantage with other conquerors who settled in the country and became part of the population. India is a field of positive duty and prospective usefulness, but it is not an arena for emigration. It is, however, an increasingly valuable market for our goods. At the close of the French war, our total trade with India, imports and exports combined, amounted to eleven millions sterling a-year. It now amounts to little short of eighty millions. India buys from us thirty-two millions' worth of English manufactures, or one-eighth of our exports every year. She takes, annually, five million pounds' worth more goods than America does, and one-third more than Australia does. She is, in fact, our best customer. (Loud cheers.) Our largest trade with her is in soft goods. She consumes about one-third of all we export, taking twenty-five million pounds' worth out of the seventy-six millions worth, which is the amount we send abroad. She buys, annually, about six million pounds' worth of cutlery and hardware, and nearly two millions' worth of machinery and railway plant. (Hear, hear.) A striking fact, and one worth noting, is this:—During the last five years, we have had a languid trade. Our exports have fallen off with all foreign countries materially, and even with some of our colonies. But, with India, the trade has enormously increased during that time. (Cheers.) Our trade in cotton has increased by one-fourth, in woollen goods by one-third, and in railway plant by one-half; while we have sent her three times as much machinery, and nearly twice as many boots and shoes, as we ever did before. (Cheers.) That these large and extending purchases are due to her political connection with England, cannot be doubted, when we compare them with what we send to other countries similarly circumstanced. China is not an unfair parallel to India. India, however, has a smaller and poorer population. Yet, she purchases four times the value of English goods that China does. If we lost the Indian trade —and we certainly should lose it if we lost the country—(hear, hear)—there is not a family in the kingdom but would feel the effect. (Hear, hear.) In some cases, it would be ruin, and in all there would be diminished means of living. (Hear, hear.) I have referred only to the mercantile advantages of our Indian Empire. There are other and greater ones. India makes us a first-class Power in two Continents, and gives us a predominatin influence in Southern Asia. (Hear, hear.) This position commits to us as grand and as beneficent a vocation as any people were ever summoned to fulfil. In accepting it, we incur the double responsibilities of political supremacy and of intellectual pre-eminence. (Cheers.) We hold sovereignity over two hundred and fifty million people—not savages or semi-savages, but bound in the fetters of a most elaborate and antiquated civilization. They are wayward and suspicious children, with some of the irrationality of animals, but with the passions and strength of men. The task of ruling them requires singular delicacy and tact. The task of improving them is one of still more subtle difficulty. A problem requiring such a combination of skill, caution, and courage was never presented to any nation. (Hear, hear.) We have to blend two inherently diverse civilizations, to graft progress on stereotyped forms and canonized stagnation, without risking either social or moral anarchy. We have beneficently to incorporate and imbue Oriental notions with Occidental energy and knowledge. (Hear, hear.) We are not required to furnish the material of the system. That is supplied to our hands. India can support herself. There are millions of acres still to be reclaimed, rivers to dredge, harbours to open, railways to lay, and canals to be made. Its produce may be doubled with energy and science. What we have to do is to supply the head, and, to a limited extent, the hands. We are required to furnish the integrity, the knowledge, the organizing faculty, the indomitable will, and the administrative experience and adaptability. (Cheers.) The natives will supply the rest. The position has been forced upon us. It is our manifest destiny and our manifest duty. (Renewed cheers.) If we neglect or abandon it, all that has been done will be lost. Those who talk of our withdrawing from India have not realized the consequences that would follow from adopting that course. (Hear, hear.) We might abandon Canada, and little if any disturbance would ensue. The Canadians, without disorder or confusion, could either establish themselves as an independent State, or they would enter the American Union. But if we left India, there would be a scramble for the scattered jewels of our crumbling crown. (Great cheering and laughter.) The mutually hostile races would fly at each other's throats. There would be ceaseless war. All progress would be arrested. The public works we have so laboriously erected would be destroyed; the investment we have made would be lost; and civilization would be cast back for generations—possibly centuries. (Cheers.) The native chiefs could not stand alone. They must have some central and binding power to keep them together. The feeling that animates them is not patriotism as we understand it. Such a sentiment is unknown in the East. The cohesive and repelling forces are religious and racial, and not political or national. The struggle is for clan or caste or creed—not for a country. After a succession of internecine feuds, generated by these motives, chaos would come again. (Hear, hear.) There would be a repetition of the scenes that occurred after Nadir Shah sacked Delhi, and the Mogul Empire was overthrown. The cry from Afghan tribesmen and Turcoman freebooters would be the old one—blood and booty. When anarchy had exhausted itself, other, and not such considerate, aliens would step into our vacant place. (Hear, hear.) The people would exchange one foreign ruler for another. They would get a ruler who would oppress and crush them, in the place of one who has committed great wrongs, made many blunders, who has sometimes been unjust and often violent, but who generally meant well in the past, and who always means well now. (Loud cheers.) Is that a result that any patriotic Englisman can contemplate with equanimity and satisfaction? (Cries of "No," and cheers.) It would dash all our dreams of permanent influence and ubiquitous beneficence. It would be fatal to our position as a nation, and irreparably injurious to civilization. (Cheers.) If we must keep India, we must keep the roads to it. (Hear, hear.) There are two—one by the canal and the other by the sea. The former is the shorter, but not at all times the safer. (Laughter and cheers.) The idea of a waterway across the Isthmus of Suez is not new. Fifteen hundred years before Christ, there was one. Herodotus and Strabo both describe the canal in their days. It was then wide and deep—the latter saw it full of ships. It fell into decay, but was restored by the Roman Emperor Trajan. It was again abandoned till about 600 A.D., but was reopened by the Caliph Omar, and kept navigable for 150 years. The old cutting was finally filled up at the instance of a rebellious Moslem leader, with the object of preventing provisions being carried to Mecca. More than one Sultan proposed to remake it. So, too, did Napoleon Bonaparte and Mehemet Ali. No serious beginning, however, was made with the scheme till M. de Lesseps devised, and, with the aid of the late Emperor of the French, and the approval of all the maritime Powers of Europe, except England, completed the present canal. Lord Palmerston held that it was politically undesirable, and Mr. Robert Stephenson maintained that it was physically impossible. Whether the first opinion was right, time will decide; but, that the second one was wrong, the experience of the last twenty years has shown. The canal exactly reversed what took place when the passage round the Cape of Good Hope was discovered. At that time, there were three land routes to India—one by way of Egypt and the Red Sea; another by Bagdad and Antioch; and a third, through Armenia, by Trebizond and Persia. It was over these toilsome tracks that the Oriental merchandise was conveyed to ports in Egypt and Asia Minor, whence it was passed on to the West by the vessels of the Venetians and

Genoese. When Vasco di Gama got to Goa, direct by the sea, the longer but cheaper way was resorted to, and used exclusively until Lieutenant Wagner initiated the overland mail route in 1845 ; and M. de Lesseps inaugurated his canal in 1869. The canal has revolutionised the carrying trade, and largely helped to displace sailing ships. Special interests have, without question, been injured by it. Indian produce, which formerly came to England, and was subsequently redistributed over Europe, now goes direct to its destination without paying toll to our Customs, or finding freights for our ships. We are sectional sufferers to that extent. On the other hand, the community at large has been immensely benefited by the impetus which the short route has imparted to commerce. (Hear, hear.) Fully 85 per cent. of the goods we send to India go by way of the canal, and fully 50 per cent. of the goods we get from India come by the canal. Last year, 2,537 British ships, with a tonnage of 6,200,000, went through the canal. In the same time, all the rest of the world sent only 760 ships, with a total tonnage of 1,900,000. (Hear, hear.) We have, therefore, 80 per cent. of the traffic, pay more than 80 per cent. of the dues, and hold one-half of the canal. (Cheers.) These figures demonstrate at once the preponderance of our Eastern trade, and our stake in the canal. Both for mercantile and strategic purposes, it is of first importance to the British Empire. Is it politic to have the vast imperial and commercial interests of the nation dependent on a ditch, cut through a foreign, and possibly hostile country, and managed by a company having rival if not antagonistic purposes ? (Cries of "No," and cheers.) One of the effects of the application of science to military operations has been to render the breaking out of hostilities more sudden than formerly. If we should unexpectedly be involved in war in India, it would be easy to cut us off from ready access to the East by the use of a few pounds of dynamite, by the sinking of a few barges, or by the sacrifice of an ironclad. (Hear, hear.) The canal is the weakest link in our imperial chain. Our position with respect to it is altogether anomalous, and is neither dignified nor safe. (Cheers.) We opposed its construction, and now we are its principal customers. We recognize it to be the gate to India, and we leave the key in other hands. We pay its expenses, while others make the laws under which we are permitted to use it. The late Government proposed to neutralize it; but that would not serve us. At the very time we needed it most we might be deprived of its use. (Hear, hear.) Neutralization would benefit all other maritime Powers more than it would us. Our power on the sea is supreme; and to neutralize any portion of it would be to remove it from our control. Our interest is to extend as widely as possible the activity of our fleet in times of war; and to declare any waters neutral is to limit that activity. (Cheers.) If the canal is neutralized, we must guard its extremities; but, if we cannot traverse it, we derive no advantage from its existence. The accidental block might be timed to occur coincident with the arrival of the British transports at the entrance. (Hear, hear.) The entire length of the Mediterranean would then lie between the fleet and the alternative Cape route, if it should be decided to resort to it in preference to waiting an indefinite time for the restoration of the channel. If fighting were excluded from the neutral waters, it would rage outside. Our ships would be exposed to attack before entering, and after leaving the portion of the way protected by international police. What is wanted is the undivided command of a road to our possessions, as short as the canal, and as safe as the ocean. (Loud and prolonged cheers.) Existing arrangements give us neither security in time of war, nor adequate accommodation in times of peace. (Hear,

hear.) Neutralization will leave our risks unguarded, and weaken our power of defence. What has been may be. (Hear, hear.) As Mahomet-ben-Abdoullah-ben-Hassan-ben-el-Horem-ben-Ali-ben-Abou-Thaleb—(roars of laughter)—a vassal of the Caliph Irac—closed the canal in the hope that it would cripple his chief, so some modern rebel leader, with not so long a name—(renewed laughter)—but with an equally long head, may try to cripple us by doing the same thing. (Hear, hear.) It was Napoleon's intention to seize Egypt, construct a canal, and use both as a base for his contemplated operations against our possessions in India. May not recent geographical re-arrangements prompt the revival of this programme by some future Napoleon? It is a contingency not to be overlooked or under-estimated. (Hear, hear.) The disparity between our military interests in the canal, and those of all nations put together, is even greater than that between our shipping and theirs. They have isolated colonies, calling for little beyond formal protection and efficient police. We have a vast Empire to govern and defend. Whether the additional way of reaching it is to be got by another canal through the Isthmus of Suez, by one through the Valley of the Jordan, or by a railway through the Valley of the Euphrates, is a question that cannot appropriately be dealt with now. It is a politico-engineering inquiry. But that additional and independent facilities for getting to India will have to be found, is admitted alike by military, naval, and mercantile experts. (Loud cheers.) The trade has outgrown the capacity of the present canal. It was constructed for a traffic of 6,000,000 tons. It now carries over 10,000,000, and the dividends range from 16 to 21 per cent. While our influence is dominant in Egypt, we have some security, but not a sufficient one, that our road to the East will not be wilfully destroyed. (Hear, hear.) We shall never be safe, however, until we can command a route whose direction shall be free from the disputes of competing traders, and the intrigues of rival nations. (Cheers.) In 1872, a Select Committee of the House of Commons made an exhaustive inquiry into the feasibility of constructing a railway between the Levant and the Persian Gulf, by way of Aleppo and the Euphrates Valley. They reported that the project was practicable. There were differences of opinion as to whether a railway or a canal would be better, and as to which route the railway should take. But both the witnesses and committee-men concurred in the necessity for a new and alternative route. The harbour of Alexandretta, the proposed terminus, is sufficiently capacious to contain the whole British navy. By a route from there to the Persian Gulf, the journey to India would be shortened by one-half. Bombay would be reached in ten days. (Hear, hear.) With a railway there is the disadvantage of transhipment, but there is the advantage of speed. A line through Asia Minor would not only bring the vast population of India into closer contact with Europe, but it would lead to the colonization of rich and historic lands ; the resuscitation of Babylon and Nineveh ; the re-awakening of Ctesiphon and Bagdad ; and the resumption of their places amongst the civilized nations, of regions that were once thought the fairest and most prosperous on earth. (Loud cheers.) We must not only guard the road to India, but we must guard her frontiers. (Cheers.) These are safe on three sides ; unsafe on the fourth. We are master on the water, and can easily protect her sea-board. (Hear, hear.) We may have trouble with, but no danger from, the Asiatic empires and tribes on the east and north ; but on the north-west our Empire is assailable. It is through the passes of the Suliemans that the martial hosts of Alexander—the unorganized hordes of Genghis Khan, Tamerlane, and Nadir Shah—the robber bands of Turcomans and Afghans—have swarmed, laying waste the country, and inflicting on unoffending nations the most appalling cruelties. It is through these same mountain gateways that the Muscovite generals hope some day to pour their whiskered pandours and fierce hussars. (Hear, hear.) Are we prepared to stop them? Our immediate neighbours to the west are the Beloochistanis. Their country is destitute of regular government; and, if the Khans desired to attack us, they would have to depend for military service on legions of freebooters—not a formidable force. Beyond Beloochistan is Persia—a country of more importance, but equally unequipped for aggressive purposes. Russia might strike her spurs into Persia's flanks, and try to drive her to discomfiture; but it is not likely. Should the spectre of a Persian army appear on our borders, it would not be difficult to cut its communications. (Cheers.) The Persians, even with external aid, could not sustain an army with nearly 500 miles of desert and mountains between it and its base of operations. It is, however, unnecessary to discuss the chances of trouble from these quarters. (Hear, hear.) Beloochistan is virtually ours. We have subsidised all its chiefs. They are harmless, if not friendly; and Persia has neither the means nor the desire for aggression. All she wants is to be left alone. The only chink in our armour is to be found through Afghanistan. There we can be struck in a vital part. (Hear, hear.) The circumstances have changed, and the changed conditions necessitate strengthened barriers. If you live amongst an honest and thinly-scattered population, your dwelling requires little further fastening than will keep out the weather; but if you dwell in the neighhourhood of thieves, you require to take precautions against experts in the use of housebreaking instruments as well as against wind and rain. (Laughter and cheers.) The Afghans are restless, and, at times, troublesome, but they are not dangerous neighbours. Behind these Oriental highlanders, however—(laughter)—like a dark mountain slowly emerging from the rising mist, we can now distinguish the broad outlines of a hostile and threatening Power. It is not the Asiatic Roderick Dhus that trouble us—(laughter)—but a more powerful potentate in the background. (Hear, hear.) A cordon that was protection enough against the one is not sufficient against the other, skilled as he is in the arts and implements of political burglary. (Cheers and laughter.) That better security is wanted against the trained forces of the Czar than against the loosely-organized militia of any Afghan Ameer, does not admit of controversy. (Hear, hear.) We are often invited not to distrust Russia, and we are assured, in the blandest terms, that our fears of her are exaggerated. My reply to such remonstrances is brief and complete. Nations have often fallen from excess of confidence, never from excess of caution. (Cheers.) All the smooth phrases in the vocabulary of diplomacy cannot gainsay the fact of Russia's unflagging and persistent absorption of adjacent States. She stands on the confines of two continents, with one sword pointed at Constantinople, another to the Persian Gulf, and a third to India. (Cheers.) Her ambition expands as her frontier advances. At one time it is the Crimea; at another the Pruth; then the Danube; and now, in fact although not nominally, the Balkans. In another direction, her outposts were, in the lifetime of many now living, on the Don, then on the Caucasus, now at Batoum and Kars. Her dominion was, a generation ago, bounded by the Caspians, then it was pushed to the Oxus, and now it reaches to Afghanistan and China. (Hear, hear.) She aspires to be the chief gendarme of Asia, and would plant in every corner of that continent a musket or a spy. (Hear, hear.) It is this Power, the friend of all re-action and the foe of all freedom—(cheers)—the very existence of which is an absolute negation of the principle of nationalities, that is hovering on our Indian frontiers. (Hear, hear.) Her Cossacks are on the Heri-Rud, and her engineers beyond Kizil Arvat. She says she has no designs on Afghanistan—(laughter)—but she said the same thing about Khiva, Merv, and a score of other places. (Hear, hear.) We believed her, we were deceived, and we know what has happened. (Hear, hear.) When her railway is complete, and her troops are ready, she will resume her stereotyped tactics—pick a quarrel with the Afghans, and use that quarrel as a justification for an attack on Herat. (Cheers.) When she does this, we will be bound to protect it. Every conqueror of India has secured, first, Merv, and the oasis on the lower course of the Murghab, and then Herat. The Ameer is our feudatory. We pay him £120,000 a-year, and provide him with arms and ammunition. He permits us to control his foreign policy, and we have engaged to sustain his authority. We do not want Afghan territory; but we *do* want to keep the Russians out of it. (Cheers.) And for this all-sufficient reason. If the Russian and British dominions become conterminous, it will require a capital expenditure of from twenty to thirty millions to put the frontier in a state of defence; and it will require an addition to our military expenditure of from two to five millions a-year to maintain and garrison it. (Hear, hear.) In our wide dominions, we have now no great aggressive State for a neighbour; but Russia, in Afghanistan, would be one. Her presence there would necessitate us doing what France has to do with her German, and Germany with her Russian, border—uphold a long line of entrenched strongholds bristling with cannon and crowded with soldiers. Whether Russia seeks to threaten us in Asia, to cripple us in Europe, or whether she seeks to sack India, preparatory to conquering the East, as her military men say she does, is immaterial. Her presence on the confines of our dominions would be a permanent addition to our expenditure, a perpetual source of disquiet to our peoples, and a standing menace to our Empire. (Cheers.) Dost Mahomet, when talking to Sir Alexander Burnes, said the danger he apprehended from Russia was the same as when you saw a stranger looking over your garden-wall. He might be on his own side of the fence, and he might make no seeming attempt to come over; but as you know he is there for no good, you do your best to dislodge him, and do not rest until you have done so. (Laughter and cheers.) This is a subject on which English statesmen are unanimous. (Hear, hear.) Some were credulous enough to trust Russian professions. Others, who were not doubtful as to her designs, were doubtful as to her means. But those who thought she did not mean to advance, and those who thought she could not, were wrong. (Hear, hear.) It is of small importance what balance of blame or praise, of wisdom or folly, is due to either partizans. (Hear, hear.) The dead past can bury its controversy. We have to do with the living present and the coming future. (Cheers.) We are confronted with a slowly-gathering, and long-threatened, peril. A cloud, big with storms, is overhead. It would be calamitous if a question of such vital national importance were discussed with bitterness and recrimination, or if the real points at issue were either overlooked, forgotten, or defaced, by the struggle of some to secure a party victory, and of others to register a party defeat. (Loud cheers.) If there be one lesson that history proclaims more clearly and forcibly than another, it is that the fate of a nation is doomed when party passions and personal rivalries are allowed to over-ride or outweigh national interests. (Renewed cheers.) It may be months, or it may be years, but it is as certain as anything contingent can be certain, that we will have to fight with Russia for India. (Hear, hear.) As General Kaufmann says, "Russia means that the cost of absorbing the Khanates shall be recouped from the spoil of Delhi and Lahore." Whether the inevitable battle has to be begun before Herat or before Candahar, on the Heri-Rud or on the Helmun, is a question that experts and circumstances will determine. When it does begin, I hope we shall beware of the wounded wolf. If not killed, he will kill us. (Hear, hear.) There are two theories about Afghanistan—that of a buffer State, and that of a scientific frontier. By the former, we have bound ourselves to encounter the Russians immediately they enter upon Afghan soil, and the Ameer asks our aid. That is our treaty with Abdur-Rahman—(hear, hear);—and if we don't keep it, the Afghans, who are an aggregate of tribes and not a nation, and are mercenary and perfidious to a proverb, will speedily transfer their alliance to our enemies. (Hear, hear.) Lord Lytton's plan, on the other hand, did not pledge us to defend Afghanistan. He bound us to subsidise them, and we got, in repayment, the direction of their foreign relations and a new frontier. By his bargain, it was open to us to resist the Russians on the borders of Turkestan, though we were not bound to do so. We secured command of the crests of the mountains and the passes. In military language, we got the issues of the frontier. (Hear, hear.) The marauding hillmen were to be organized as patrols. A line of fortresses was to be built; a railway was to be laid to Quetta; and Candahar was to be put under a friendly Vali. This was the scientific frontier theory which was assented to by Yakoob Khan, and embodied in the treaty of Gandamak. The idea was to sustain Afghanistan on the basis of the arrangement made by Lord Dalhousie with Dost Mahomet in 1855, but not to bind us to maintain the ruling or any succeeding Ameer. We were to aid the Afghans, but not to put ourselves in their power. We could defend the new frontier, if need be, against the Russians and Afghans combined, and we were under no obligation to fight for any Afghan fortress or territory. The late Government reversed this policy, abandoned the new frontier, pulled up the railway—(laughter)—and other defensive preparations, gave Abdur-Rahman a more liberal allowance, and entered into more binding engagements for the support of his authority. If the Russians had kept their bargain, this treaty might have worked satisfactorily enough; but they did not, and the Liberal Ministry realized, when too late, the onerous character of the obligations they had contracted with the Afghans, and the untrustworthiness of the Russian professions. The abandoned railway works were resumed; another line through the Bolan Pass was projected; a chain of fortresses designed, and troops and war material hurried to Quetta—all very commendable work. The only regret is that it was not done before, and that the defences initiated by Lord Lytton were discontinued. (Cheers.) The present Government are energetically carrying out the intentions of their predecessors, and amplifying them. It is a race whether our railway shall reach Candahar, or the Russians shall reach Herat first. Our Afghan policy, therefore, is now a national one. (Cheers.) Afghanistan is the only entrance to India that is open. If it is forced, that marvellous monument of English skill and courage, of enterprise and endurance—British India—will fall. Alexander's empire passed away in a blast of mutiny; the Mogul went out in a convict ship; the Portuguese crept stealthily away; and the Dutch perished for very greed. If the English goes down, it should be with torn sheets and battered sides, but with colours flying, and every man at his post. (Loud and prolonged cheers.) I must apologise for having troubled you with such a mass of figures—(cries of "No, no," and "Go on," and renewed cheers);—but they were essential to my argument, which is that, whatever may be our opinion as to the way India was won, there can be no disagreement as to the wisdom and necessity of our holding it now that we have it. (Cheers.) We must do this for the sake of the natives, of ourselves, and of civilization. (Hear, hear.) To do so, we must guard its frontiers and its approaches. The only vulnerable point is the north-west frontier, and that is menaced by Russia. We must defend it, if need be, with all the strength of the Empire. (Great cheering, in the course of which Mr. Cowen resumed his seat.)

# FIRST "HECKLING" MEETING.

HELD IN THE LECTURE ROOM, NOVEMBER 21ST, 1885.

CHAIRMAN—CAPTAIN NEWSTEAD.

Mr. COWEN, who was received with loud and enthusiastic cheers, on rising, said : Mr. Chairman, ladies, and gentlemen,—I have called this meeting, primarily, for the purpose of getting and giving information, and, secondarily, for affording everyone an opportunity of interrogating me on anything that may appear doubtful in my conduct in the past, or obscure in my professions for the future. (Hear, hear.) Formerly, candidates, unable or unwilling to do so personally, could pay persons to canvass each elector. That practice is now prohibited. It had many drawbacks, but it had some advantages. The vast majority of electors do not attend election meetings, or read what is said at them; but when a candidate or his deputy visited them they could cross-question them. That cannot now be done—at least by me. (Hear, hear, and cheers.) If I were willing, I could not call on thirty thousand electors between now and the election day. I cannot pay anyone to do so for me. It would be illegal. (Hear, hear.) And I have not, like my competitors, an organization whose members undertake the work gratuitously. Indeed, I would not consent to my friends undertaking so laborious and troublesome a task on my behalf. (Cheers.) Unable, therefore, to meet you singly, either myself or by representative, I have asked you to meet me in a body, when the inquisitive can interrogate and the captious and the crotchety can "heckle" to their hearts' content. Facilities for doing this are afforded at the close of every meeting, but they are scarcely sufficient. After a man has been speaking for over an hour, he is not always able to give, or the audience is not always willing to listen to, replies sufficiently copious to make his meaning plain. Both the person who asks and the person who answers are thus placed at a disadvantage. But when a whole night is set apart for the purpose, time is afforded to the inquirer to frame his questions and the speaker to reply to them. (Hear, hear.) We will proceed on the Socratic method. (Cheers.) For the nonce, we will all discard speechifying, and betake ourself to the dialectical style of discourse. Socrates was the special opponent of rhetoric. He said it was not an art, but an adulation. Plato described it as a kind of skill, like cookery, which he regarded as a branch of the same pursuit. (Laughter.) Orators and despots belonged, in his opinion, to the same genus. (Renewed laughter.) Hobbes condemned an orator as a base and pernicious despot, whose chief requisite was impudence. (Laughter and cheers.) Orators have often been accused of being the ruin of every State in which they obtained predominance. All this is very hard on the orators. (Laughter.) Fortunately, it is not true. (Cheers.) If orators have ruined some States, they have saved others. (Hear, hear.) There was a time when there were only two forces in Greece—Alexander the Emperor and Demosthenes the orator. The power to detach, and to magnify by detaching, to fix momentary eminence on any subject, to unite the logical arguments that satisfy the reason with the language that delights the imagination, is the essence of rhetoric; and that power has oftener been wielded by patriots for their country's benefit than by demagogues for its injury or for their own gain. (Loud cheers.) We are governed by public meeting; and every citizen will be better able to fulfil his duties if he can expound his principles and opinions with freedom, perspicuity, and directness. Without, therefore, accepting Socrates's views anent rhetoric, let us try to adopt his system of exposition and discussion, and strive after, at least, an approach to his colloquial magic. I am ready now to reply to all relevant questions that you care to ask me. If I have deceived any man, let him point out where and when. (A Voice: "Never," and cheers.) If I have violated any pledge, let him who thinks so specify it. (Renewed cheers.) If I have neglected my duty, tell me the occasion. If I am incompetent or unfit to be one of your members, tell me why and how. (Cries of "No, no," and cheers.) If there is any man who has a grievance against me, let him state it. I court the most searching inquiry, and promise the fullest, frankest answer, explanation, or defence. (Hear, hear, and cheers.) This room recalls stirring associations. It was the Newcastle Forum. It has been the scene of many a memorable gathering. Within these walls, Mr. Larkin, Mr. Doubleday, Sir John Fife, Mr. Attwood, Dr. Newton, and a crowd of famous Tynesiders have done yeoman service for Radicalism. (Loud cheers.) I was the youthful ally of the fathers of our faith. I have spoken here on political questions as often perhaps as any man in Newcastle. (Renewed cheers.) I gather fresh impulse from this spot and its associations. (Great cheering.) The Highland chieftain, when he returned to his mountains and felt himself free from the restraint of city life, proudly proclaimed, "My foot is on my native heath, and my name is Macgregor." Returning from the enervating atmosphere of the Metropolis, I may be allowed to paraphrase the exclamation. My foot is not upon any heath, and my name is not Macgregor, but it is upon my native platform—(cheers);—and I am here to plead for the old cause with undiminished earnestness and matured convictions. (Loud and prolonged cheering, the audience rising and waving their hats.) To render discussion effective, it is requisite to make arrangements, and follow them. I have received a number of questions at the different meetings I have addressed. I propose to answer them first, as they have been sent first. (Hear, hear.) I will next answer the questions which have been addressed to me by public bodies. I have received a number of inquires about Ireland, but as I mean to speak on Irish matters on Tuesday night, the gentlemen who have written me will find all the information they ask for given in the remarks I make that night. (Hear, hear.) I have found it a very difficult task to summarise and arrange all the questions that have been forwarded to me. I counted upwards of three hundred; and when I got to that number I abandoned further enumeration. (Laughter, cries of "shame," and cheers.) Many of them are repetitions. Some gentlemen have gone so far as to send me as many as twenty inquiries on one sheet of paper. I don't suppose any Parliamentary candidate ever had such a number and such a variety of questions addressed to him. (Laughter.) They cover all subjects. They are personal, political, philosophical, literary, local, and antiquarian. (Renewed laughter.) I could not answer them all if I had five nights, instead of two; but I hope to be able to reply to the most important, to-night, and on Wednesday, when I hold a similar meeting to this at St. Peter's. (Hear, hear.) I have grouped the topics as far as I have had time, and their variety would permit, under heads. Many of the personal questions are simply vulgarities—(cries of "shame" and hisses)—meant, I suppose, to be annoying. The authors exhibit their ill-will by sending me, by means of anonymous questions, an unfriendly expression of opinion. ("Shame," and loud cheers.) I have been amused, not disturbed by them. I remember a story told of an American politician. He went home to his dinner one day; and before he sat down to the table, he asked his wife, with great vivacity and volubility, if she or any of her relatives had ever committed a great crime; if they had ever been guilty of manslaughter, robbery, burglary, forgery, or murder; if any of them had ever run away with another man's wife—(laughter)—or committed an unmentionable offence? The good lady was startled at the earnestness of her husband's inquiries. She conceived that some terrible calamity had happened, and besought him to inform her what had occurred. He said a calamity had happened, because he had consented to become a candidate for one of the divisions of New York—(laughter);—and he knew, before the election was over, every one of the crimes he had mentioned would be laid at the door of himself, or some of his relatives or their connections; and he was anxious before the battle began to be put in possession of the facts. (Renewed laughter and loud cheering.) Some of my interrogators—only an insignificant number, I suspect—have verified the forecast of the American candidate by making to me mean and despicable insinuations under the guise of questions. (Cries of "Shame," and hisses.) I have put them into the fire—(hear, hear, laughter, and cheers)—and I don't mean to further allude to them. (A voice: "Quite right," and renewed cheers.) One of the first relevant subjects that I have been interrogated upon is about further changes in our representative system, the comparative position of English and foreign members of Parliament, the labours that they respectively undertake, and the remuneration they receive. To begin—

"Are you in favour of putting the legal cost of taking Parliamentary elections on the rates?"

Of course I am. (Cheers.) I have said so scores of times, in and out of Parliament. It is a gross injustice to compel the men who give their services gratuitously to the State to bear the cost of the booths, ballot-boxes, and other electoral paraphernalia. There is not another country in the world where such a practice exists. It imposes a monetary qualification on members. (Hear, hear.) It is indefensible under any circumstances, and it is entirely inconsistent with an extended suffrage. One of the first works of the new Parliament will be to pass an Act requiring every constituency to provide the machinery for elections and the men for managing it. (Cheers.)

"Are you in favour of the payment of members?"

Yes. (Hear, hear.) There are advantages and disadvantages in the present system. Whether the one or the other overbalance, this is certain—the change cannot long be delayed. (Cheers.) I confess I don't like professional politicians. They are usually men of easy consciences. (Laughter.) They will do anything to oblige the voters or their leaders—change their principles as readily as they change their coats. (Renewed laughter and cheers.) But there are exceptions—let us hope they will be numerous. We should take as a model our own Andrew Marvel, or Baudin, the French Republican Deputy, who fell on the barricades on December 2nd, 1851. When urging his countrymen to rise against Louis Napoleon and defend the Assembly, the Parisian workmen shouted, "We will not sacrifice ourselves for the salaried servants of universal suffrage, who play the patriot for twenty-five francs a-day." "You shall see," replied Baudin, "how a man dies for twenty-five francs a day"—(cheers)—as he shouldered his musket and marched to death and immortality. (Great cheering.) I trust our professional politicians may emulate the spirit of this French Republican, and not that of the caucus-made machine-men of New York. (Hear, hear.)

"At what hours do other Parliaments assemble, and how long do they sit?"

In Austria, the Reichstag sits in autumn, and the session lasts from three to four months; business begins at eleven a.m., and ends between four and five p.m. In Hungary, the session is convened in October, and sits four months; the Assembly meets at ten, and separates at two o'clock. In Belgium, the session begins in November, and lasts eight or nine months; the House, however, sits only four days a-week, and has various holidays; it meets at one o'clock, and separates at half-past four. In Denmark, the average number of days in a session is 196. The average number of working days is 145; and the House meets at one, and sits till about five o'clock. In France, the session lasts five months; the House meets at two, and closes at six. In Germany, the Reichstag sits four to five months; meets at eleven, and closes at four. In Italy, the session lasts six months; the House meeting at two, and closing between six and seven. In Holland, the session lasts from four to five months; the House meets at eleven, and sits four and a-half hours. In Portugal, the session lasts three months; the House meets at two, and sits till five. In Spain, the session lasts four months; the House meets at two, and sits four hours. In Sweden, the session lasts four months; the House meets at ten, and sits four hours. In Norway, the session lasts three months; the House meets at ten, and sits four hours. In Switzerland, the session lasts three months; the House meets between eight and nine, and sits till two. In the United States, the session lasts four or five months; the House meets at noon, and sits till half-past four. There are holidays in each country, of greater or less length, when the various assemblies do not sit. Out of thirteen Parliaments, eight meet at noon or before it; two meet at one; and four meet at two o'clock. None meets later. The average sittings are little over four hours' duration, and none more than five hours. The average length of the session is eighteen weeks, not counting holidays. The sessions of the English Parliament can be seen from the following table:—

| Session. | Sat Weeks. | Days it Met. | Average Length of Sitting. | | Hours After Midnight. | | Number of Hours Sat. | |
|---|---|---|---|---|---|---|---|---|
| | | | H. | M. | H. | M. | H. | M. |
| 1880 | 27 | 121 | 8 | 36 | 163 | 30 | 1,040 | 5 |
| 1881 | 31 | 154 | 9 | 5 | 238 | 35 | 1,400 | 5 |
| 1882 | 26 | 162 | 8 | 51 | 231 | 45 | 1,434 | 27 |
| 1883 | 26 | 129 | 9 | 1 | 179 | 10 | 1,163 | 30 |
| 1884 | 25 | 126 | 8 | 49 | 166 | 50 | 1,102 | 50 |

The number of hours after midnight has decreased triflingly the last two or three years, because of the number of morning sittings; but these figures show that the sessions of the English Parliament are much longer, that the hours the House sits are longer, and the hour at which the House meets is much later than it is in any foreign Parliament. (Hear, hear.) I have taken some trouble to collect this information. It is to be got only from a number of scattered publications. My object in doing so is to emphasise the opinion that, of all practical reforms in Parliamentary procedure, there is none so pressing as one in the time when the session meets and the House sits. (Hear, hear.) Three-fourths of our huge taxation are voted in the presence of a score or two of sleepy legislators, most of them officials, in the early hours of the morning. Nearly all the mischief done by Parliament is done after midnight. (Hear, hear.) The new electorate should insist on the work of the nation being done in daylight, and in natural and reasonable hours. (Cheers.) You may depend on it the subject is more important than to outsiders it may seem to be.

"Do not all other countries pay their representatives salaries; and what is the average amount?"

I don't know whether all do so, but certainly most of

them do. In Belgium, each member of the Chamber of Representatives receives 200 florins, or £16 15s. a-month while the House is in session. In Denmark, the members of the Landsthing and the Folkething are paid the same salary—about 15s. per day. In Portugal, Peers and Deputies receive an annual stipend of £67. In France, Senators and Deputies each get 19,000 francs, or £356 a-year; the colonial representatives getting, in addition, their travelling expenses. In Sweden, members of the Diet receive 1,200 rix-dollars—equal to £66 14s.—for a session of four months, and their travelling expenses. Members of both Chambers are fined 10 rix-dollars, or 11s. a-day, if they do not attend. (Laughter.) In Switzerland, members of the National Council receive 10s. a-day, which is paid out of the Federal treasury. Members of the States-Council are paid by the Cantons, and their salaries vary from 6s. to 10s a-day. In the United States, representatives and delegates each receive £1,041 a-year, and their travelling expenses, at the rate of 20 cents per mile. In Norway, the members of the Storthing receive 13s. 4d. a-day while it is sitting, which is usually about twelve weeks. In Italy, neither Senators nor Deputies are paid, but they get free passes over all the railways in the kingdom, and some other concessions as to taxes and patronage—a most objectionable mode of payment. (Hear, hear, and cheers.) In Spain, the members are not paid. In Greece, Senators get £20 a-month, and members of the Representative Chamber £10. In all the local Legislatures in Germany, the members, with one or two exceptions, are paid; the salaries ranging between 9s. a-day in Prussia, and 20s. in Austria. In Canada, New Zealand, Victoria—indeed in all our colonies—members of the Legislature are paid, usually at from £250 to £400 a-year. Members of the English Parliament receive no pay, have no patronage, and are required to pay all election expenses.

I have had a series of questions forwarded to me about India and Afghanistan. I propose to take them *seriatim*. The first is—

"Do the English still hold the scientific frontier secured after the last war by the Treaty of Gandamak?"

Partly so. The Treaty of Gandamak was concluded with Yakoob Khan, the son and successor of Shere Ali, in May, 1879. The principal articles gave to the English control of the Khyber Pass and the valleys of Kurum and Pishin. It also provided that England should direct the foreign policy of the Ameer; that there should be a British Resident received at Cabul; and that British agents should be stationed in three or four of the large towns. In consideration of these concessions, the English Government agreed to pay the Ameer £60,000 a-year, to assist him with arms and ammunition, and to protect his country from aggression. Sir Louis Cavignari, our agent, went to Cabul in 1879, and shortly afterwards was killed. Yakoob Khan then abdicated; and some of the provisions of the Treaty were allowed to lapse, although England has kept possession of a portion of the territory that was comprised within the scientific frontier. (Hear, hear.)

"Have we a Treaty with the present Ameer of Afghanistan to defend him, and is there any record of the money we have paid him, and the arms and ammunition we have supplied him and his predecessors with?"

The engagement with the Ameer was made in a letter written by Sir Lepel Griffin on the 7th of August, 1880, and was renewed in the same terms in two letters from the Viceroy to the Ameer on February 22nd and June 16th, 1883. The letter from Sir Lepel Griffin, which constitutes the Treaty, is as follows:—

"Your Highness has requested that the views and intentions of the British Government with regard to the position of the ruler at Cabul in relation to foreign Powers should be placed on record for your Highness's information. The Viceroy and Governor-General in Council authorises me to declare to you that since the British Government admit no right of interference by foreign Powers within Afghanistan, and since both Russia and Persia are pledged to abstain from all interference with the affairs of Afghanistan, it is plain that your Highness can have no political relations except with the British Government. If any foreign Power should attempt to interfere in Afghanistan, and if such interference should lead to unprovoked aggression on the dominions of your Highness, in that event the British Government would be prepared to aid you to such extent, and in such manner, as may appear to the British Government necessary in repelling it, provided that your Highness follows, unreservedly, the advice of the British Government in regard to your external relations."

Various documents have been submitted to Parliament from time to time, showing the amount of money that was paid to Dost Mahomet and to Shere Ali, and the arms and ammunition that were supplied them. I have not the data, but it has run up to a considerable sum. The amount that we pay to the present Ameer is £120,000 a-year. (Hear, hear, and cheers.)

"Is it true that the late Government stopped the railway to Quetta, pulled up the rails, and dispersed the plant ?"

After the last war, and for the double purpose of improving the means of trade with Afghanistan, and strengthening our frontier defences, the line was projected and surveyed under orders from Lord Lytton. It was intended to lay it from Sibi to Candahar, through Quetta. By such a line, Southern Afghanistan would be brought into direct railway communication with India. The work was begun in 1879, and partly constructed before Lord Beaconsfield's Government went out of office. (Hear, hear.) In 1880, the late Government stopped and dismantled the works, and scattered the plant ; but in 1883, when the Russians took Merv, and affairs in Central Asia looked threatening, they recommenced it. While admitting that they stopped the line, the late Ministry deny that they ordered its destruction. They allege that the cost of construction, and not a desire to reverse Lord Beaconsfield's policy, was the cause of its abandonment. Perhaps, their objects were mixed. (Hear, hear.) They did not then believe in a Russian advance, and they wished to show the Afghans that they disapproved of the policy of their predecessors. They wanted also to curtail the expenditure, so as to enable them to abolish the Customs duties on Lancashire goods entering India. But be this as it may, the stoppage of the railway was a great blunder, and has certainly not been a saving. (Hear, hear, and cheers.) The statement that little work had been done, when orders were issued to suspend it, is not correct. At that time, engines were running between Sibi and Nari Gorge; and from the latter place onwards twelve and a-half miles of bank had been made, and plate-laying had commenced. At eleven stations, the necessary buildings were either completed, or in course of construction. At all of them, defensible store-yards had been erected. A surface road had been made nearly to Kach, and one was staked out to Quetta. A quantity of permanent material had been carried forward, six miles of line were laid north of Nari, and several detached miles were laid in the hill country beyond. (Hear, hear.) The total sum expended, according to the Budget, was £560,000; and if the work had been persevered in, it would have been completed to Candahar in 1882. According to the report of an eye-witness, whose testimony has been cited in Parliament, and never impugned, the loose plant and the sleepers were left on the ground, and no attempt was made to collect them, and take them back to the depôt on the Indus. Some of the rails in the immediate vicinity of Sibi were utilised, but all the other property, including the accumulated stores, was abandoned to the plunder of the tribes. A gentleman engaged in the work says that the orders sent to the engineers were to destroy the earthworks, and that they were accordingly shovelled down to the level of the ground, with the result that in some districts no trace of the line remained. This entailed not only a serious loss of money, but a greater and more serious loss of time, the disastrous consequences of which we should have experienced if we had gone to war with Russia. (Hear, hear, and loud cheers.) Sir Henry Rawlinson, the Vice-President of the Council of India, gave his opinion on the importance of the railway in 1880, and it was very decisively in favour of its immediate construction. Sir Rivers Wilson, another member of the Viceroy's Council, condemned the abandonment of the line in much more energetic language than even Sir Henry Rawlinson used. I can read these minutes if you think it necessary, and also private letters I have from General Roberts — (loud cheers) — confirmatory of the opinions there expressed. The late Government ultimately repented of their action, and in 1883 they recommenced the line. It is now being pressed forward vigorously; and it is expected that it will be open for traffic in 1887, or the beginning of 1888. (Hear, hear.) It is calculated that the whole of the line and its approaches will cost between three and four million pounds. While condemning the late Government for their conduct about this railway, I am glad to commend them about another. When their fears about Russia were really aroused, and they realized the danger of her advance, they not only resumed the construction of the old Candahar line, but they began a more direct line to Quetta through the Bolan Pass. (Cheers.) The Pass was levelled during the last war; and the construction of the new line is, therefore, both easy and cheap. It is expected to be completed by the beginning of next year. In addition to these two lines—the one through Sibi and Nari to Quetta, and the other through the Bolan Pass, the late Government ordered the construction of a series of frontier railways, roads, and bridges, which will entail an immediate expenditure of over five millions. These works are to be supplemented by a series of fortresses. When they are built, they will save India from periodical scares, which are both dangerous and costly. (Hear, hear, and cheers.) When the people feel their frontiers to be safe, they pursue their career in peace, and develop, unmolested, the vast resources of the country. (Loud cheers.)

"Are not the famines in India the cause of discontent and evidence of bad government?"

Famine-stricken people are not rebellious. They suffer too severely. There have as many as three millions died in some Indian famines. Famines are generally caused by want of rain, but sometimes by storms and floods, by swarms of rats and locusts which eat up the crops, and by a combination of these causes. The construction of canals and the development of a system of irrigation act as preventives of famines; and railways afford the means of distributing food when famine arises. (Hear.) The famine in Bengal in 1874 cost, in providing remedial measures, nearly seven million pounds; and that in Madras in 1877 cost over ten millions. They both arose from drought. This money would have been better spent in promoting irrigation, and thus providing against famine, than in feeding the people when famine came. It was proposed by Sir John Strachey to set aside two million a-year as an insurance against future famines. Whether that has been done or not, I don't know.

An inquiry is made as to the meaning of the word "ben," that appears so often in the long name of the Moslem rebel, who filled up the Suez Canal. (Laughter.) "Ben" is an Eastern prefix to a name, equivalent to the Scotch "Mac," or the Irish "O." They all mean son, as Macdonald, son of Donald; O'Donoghue, son of Donoghue; and Benjamin, son of the right hand—Jamin. (Hear, hear.) "Ben" in Scotland means a high hill, as Ben Nevis, and Ben Lomond. It means also the inner part of a cottage, as "but" means the outer.* (Laughter.)

"What is the tenure on which we hold the island of Cyprus, and is it a loss to this country?"

The Queen is the lessee of Cyprus rather than the sovereign. By the convention we concluded with Turkey in 1878, England entered into a defensive alliance with the Sultan. Asiatic Turkey was placed under British protection, and we engaged to defend it against any invader by force of arms. In order to make the necessary preparations, the Sultan assigned Cyprus to be occupied and administered by this country. There are 187,000 inhabitants in the island. The regular revenue and expenditure, including a tribute to Turkey of £90,000 a-year, nearly balance. But there are improvements going forward in the island—roads are being made, harbours cleared out, and the locusts are being destroyed. Thus an extra expenditure has been incurred, and £15,000, annually, has been paid in aid of these improvements for some years. The inhabitants of the island have greatly benefited by British administration, and the island now is fairly prosperous. I have the last report respecting the island here, and the gentleman who asks the question can have it, if he likes. (Hear, hear.)

"Do you approve of the late Government allowing France to make rice a contraband of war?"

I am not aware that the late Government consented to France's contention; but if France *did* declare rice to be con-

* Dr. Jamieson, in his "Etymological Dictionary of the Scottish Language," states that the terms *but* and *ben* seem to have been primarily applied to a house, consisting of two apartments, the one of which enters from the other. The word *ben*, according to the same authority, is used as an adverb, signifying towards the inner apartment of a house corresponding to *but*.

traband, she would be just following the example set by England, when in 1784 we prohibited all trade with France in all articles of food, and ordered our cruisers to stop all ships bound for France with grain. (Cheers.) The neutral Powers protested, but we were then masters of the sea, and disregarded their protests. It is a question of international law, and I am not a lawyer; but when two nations are at war, it is the whole people that are engaged in the conflict. (Hear, hear.) The soldiers are merely the militant section. It is possible that the losses inflicted on the non-combatants will do more to bring about peace than losses inflicted on the army; and if so, I think it is likely jurists will hold that a nation in arms may, if it choose, treat food as contraband. (Hear, hear, and cheers.)

"Will you vote for the abrogation of the Declaration of Paris?"

Six other Powers as well as England joined in the Declaration of Paris, and the British Government have neither the right nor the power to abrogate it. (Hear, hear,) But I would vote —and have already done so—in favour of England withdrawing from it. (Loud cheers.) The English people have never seen the injury this Declaration may do them. (Hear, hear.) Its history is suggestive. Before entering into the Crimean war, England renounced the right of seizing its enemy's property, except articles contraband of war, when embarked in neutral vessels. This was the price paid for the alliance of Louis Napoleon. He required it of us, and we consented to his dictum provisionally. At the conclusion of the war, the agreement was confirmed and extended. France, England, Russia, Prussia, Austria, Sardinia, and Turkey declared, in concert, first, that privateering should be abolished, that free ships made free goods, except articles contraband of war; second, that neutral merchandise, with the exception of articles contraband of war, should not be subject to seizure on an enemy's ship; and further, that blockades, to be binding, must be effective. This is the maritime code of the Powers who are parties to the Declaration. Consider how it will cripple us when we go to war with a great power. Our ships are our protection, but of what avail will they be, if our enemy is to be allowed to carry on his commerce under a neutral flag? What use are all our cruisers, if our enemy is to save himself by carrying on his trade in the vessels of other countries? We cannot attack him by land; we have no army capable of doing so; and if we cannot assail his trade, we will be powerless. I would rather coerce an enemy than kill him. (Hear, hear.) I prefer to take his goods rather than his life. (Cheers.) To do this, we must exercise the right to search and capture—(hear, hear)—burn or destroy his goods, whether found in his own ships or in those of another. (Loud cheers.) If we cannot do so, our navy is a gigantic, costly, and useless toy. The sea is our safety when we are all-powerful, but will be our danger when we are not so. It is impossible to have all the advantages of commerce and peace amidst the ravages of war. (Hear, hear.) The soonest way to get peace is to disable your enemy. (Cheers.) I am, therefore, in favour of withdrawing from the Declaration of Paris, and for our re-asserting the right of search, and liberty to issue letters of marque. (Hear, hear, and cheers.) Neither Spain nor America agreed to the Declaration of Paris.

"Is there any precedent by which Sir Stafford Northcote was made First Lord of the Treasury, with a salary and no duties?"

The office is anything but a sinecure. It has responsible duties attached to it. The arrangement is not a new one. It was resorted to by Lord Chatham at least on two occasions. Although Chatham was at one time the head of the Government, he only held the office of Privy Seal, and the Duke of Grafton was Prime Minister. At another time, Chatham was Secretary for the Northern Department, and the Duke of Newcastle was First Lord of the Treasury. All students of "Junius" will remember this case; and there are others, I believe, which I don't recollect, but which constitute adequate precedents for the course taken in separating the Premiership from the office of the First Lord of the Treasury. (Hear, hear.)

"We are often told how much money great soldiers and lawyers have got from the State. Can you tell us how much great statesmen, say, Mr. Gladstone and Lord Granville, have got from the State for their services?"

I cannot off-hand; but the curious on the point can easily get the information by referring to Debrett, counting the number of years the two statesmen have been in office, and adding up their salaries. Mr. Gladstone has been over fifty years in Parliament, and in office about half that time. Lord Granville has been in the two Houses of Parliament nearly fifty years, and in office more than half that time. At a guess, I should say Mr. Gladstone may have received, in salaries from the State, from £100,000 to £120,000, and Lord Granville from £90,000 to £100,000. I don't know the exact figures, and merely give these as an approximate amount. But why ask the question? (Loud cheers.) Surely "the labourer is worthy of his hire," whether he is a soldier, lawyer, or statesman; and it is shabby to reckon up the receipts in any case. (Hear, hear, and renewed cheers.) The assumption is that the country gets value for its money.

"What sum is annually paid for secret-service?"

The amount has been doubled under Mr. Gladstone's Government. It used to be about £25,000 a-year, but last year £50,000 was voted for secret-service in the estimates, and

£10,000 was paid out of the Consolidated Fund. In all, the country paid £60,000, for which no account was rendered. No one knows exactly how the money is spent. (Hear, hear, and laughter.) It transpired accidentally, however, a few years ago, that a portion of the money was paid away in the shape of increased salaries to officials in the Foreign Office. Some of it probably goes to pay the cost of such special missions as that of Mr. Errington at Rome; and other portions to pay for secret police in Ireland and secret agents abroad. (Hear, hear.)

"Will you aid the Salvation Army—(laughter)—in having justice done to it, and not having its meetings forcibly broken up?"

Parliament has no authority in this matter. The law is strong enough to restrain, and, if need be, to punish rioters. All it wants is to be applied. The Salvation Army has as much right to protection as any other public body—(hear, hear);—while the zeal and earnestness with which its members prosecute their self-imposed labours entitle them to the sympathy of all advocates of social improvement.

I have received from two or three persons copies of a series of questions issued by the Shipowners' Society. I sent an answer immediately I received the first copy to my friend, Mr. Welford, the secretary. I believe that my views on all the points are substantially in accord with those of the shipowners. (Cheers.)

I have got from sundry members of the Amalgamated Society of Railway Servants a series of questions. I have answered one or two of them already in the meetings I have attended; but I desire now to repeat that I am in favour of all the five points that the railway servants ask to have settled. (Loud cheers.) If I should be a member of Parliament again, I shall certainly vote in favour of legislation to give them effect.

I have had four questions sent me respecting the police. I am in favour of all the demands of the police. (Cheers.) I was one of the members who introduced the Bill to give the policemen votes at elections, and I have been in constant communication and co-operation with General Alexander during his efforts to secure the passage of the Police Superannuation Bill. I think the police have very grave grounds for complaint at the manner in which they have been treated by Parliament and by recent Governments. (Hear, hear, and cheers.)

I have got several communications about the carriage-tax, but it is scarcely necessary for me to say that I am in favour of its immediate and total abolition. (Hear, hear.) I seconded the motion which Lord Algernon Percy moved on this subject last year, and I am in entire sympathy with the coach-makers. I think it is a most objectionable tax. It is really a tax upon industry, and not, as its supporters say, a tax on luxury. (Hear, hear.) The Newcastle coach-builders are to be commended for the energy and earnestness with which they have urged the agitation for its abolition. (Hear, hear.)

Five or six persons have asked me if I am in favour of subjecting to the income-tax persons who may be in receipt of less than £150 a-year. I certainly am not. (Cheers.) I think the exemption rightfully goes up to that sum ; and I shall oppose any attempt to alter it—certainly in the way of reducing the amount upon which the tax should be levied. (Renewed cheers.)

"Are you in favour of voting by ballot in the House of Commons, and if re-elected will you bring forward and support a motion to that effect ?" (Laughter.)

There have been occasions when it has been desirable for members of the British Parliament to vote in secret—(hear, hear);—but that was when they were afraid of being imprisoned and fined in consequence of acting in hostility to the Court or the King. But that day has long since passed—(cheers);—and it is clearly the right of the constituencies to know how their representatives vote. (Hear, hear.) A member of Parliament is a trustee, and the people who commit to him the trust ought to know how he discharges it; and this they could not do if he voted by ballot. (Cheers.) The position of a member of Parliament and an elector is different. Instead of decreasing the responsibility of members, I would be inclined to increase it. (Hear, hear.) I quite see the drift of the inquiry. (Loud laughter.) The gentleman who sends it evidently thinks that if members could vote by ballot, they would vote differently from what they sometimes do. (Renewed laughter.) That would very likely be the case. (Hear, hear.) Members are very often driven to vote contrary to their convictions, or their sense of right and wrong; but still the disadvantages of allowing them to vote by ballot would be greater than the disadvantages of the present system. (Cheers.)

I have here several questions about the Liberal Association. (Laughter, and cries of "Don't answer them" and "Tear them up.") I do not wish to be drawn into further controversy with that body. I have said all I care to say. (Hear, hear.) The leaders of the association have been systematically abusing and attributing all manner of unworthy motives to me for years past. I took no notice of them. (Cheers.) But when the election came, it was necessary for me to reply to their charges. I have done so; and so far as I am concerned the dispute may rest there. (Cheers.) The public know—or at least that section of them who interest themselves in the controversy—what I am accused of, and they know my answer, and can judge between us. (Cheers.) I do not mean to fight over the business further. Newcastle is big enough for both me and the caucus. They can go their way—I will go mine. (Loud cheers.)

Recriminations will not mend matters, and reconciliation with some of these gentlemen I know to be impossible. They are opponents for personal reasons, and it is useless saying anything further to them. But to others who have no personal feeling, I will, in a sentence or two, summarise again my grounds of difference. I put first Liberal principles. (Cheers.) They put first the Liberal party. I care most for measures. They care most for men. (Laughter and cheers.) In this lies all the quarrel. There were many Liberals who thought the suspension of trial by jury in Ireland and the imprisonment of men there without trial a great offence. (Hear, hear.) It shocked their sense of justice; and if the Tories had done it they would have opposed it strongly. (Loud laughter.) But it was done by the Liberals, and they gave it their approval. They thought again that the restriction of the right of free speech in Parliament was a violation of principle; and if the Tories had proposed it they would have had endless meetings and memorialised against it. (Laughter.) But being done by their own party, they supported it. They were against the war in Egypt, and would have roused the country on the question if the other side had embarked in it. But as it was done by Mr. Gladstone, they pocketed their principles and supported it. That is their position. Mine is the very opposite. (Great and prolonged cheering.) A thing is right or wrong whoever does it—(cheers);—and I don't care the cast of a copper who the men are, whether they call themselves Liberals or they call themselves Tories, if they do what I believe to be wrong, I shall oppose them; while if they do what I believe to be right, I shall support them. (Cheers.) Party is merely a means to an end. It is not *the* end. (Hear, hear.) Leaders are all very well in their place, but none of them is infallible, and I will surrender my judgment in matters of principle to no man, however powerful, and to no body of men, however numerous. (Loud cheers.) With this, I dispose of a whole batch of questions referring to the same subject. No. I will tell you a story bearing on the subject—(laughter)—and with that I will close all reference to the Liberal Association. Samuel Butler, a man who, it was said, was a whole species of poets rolled into one, wrote a polemical and satirical poem entitled "The Elephant and the Moon"—(laughter)—which is only less famous than Hudibras. Butler describes a society of learned men who, amongst other treasures, possessed a telescope. One of the members saw through it a startling sight—nothing less than a battle in the moon. (Laughter.) Battalions of lunar warriors manœuvred about and then disappeared, sometimes into dark caverns and into places behind precipices. Their movements were ever and anon disturbed by a prodigious monster, a cross between an elephant and a hippopotamus, whose presence shut out all sight of the sidereal luminaries. It was marvellous. (Laughter.) The discoverer speedily summoned his colleagues to witness it, and they came in hot haste—a veritable caucus. (Laughter.) They listened wondrously and credulously to his expatiation, but there were some doubters, believers, no doubt, in Occam's theory, that no occurrence that can be explained by ordinary, should be attributed to supernatural, causes. These scientific Peters—(laughter)—did not exactly know how, but they suspected it was only an optical illusion. But they were overridden, and the members retired to record their discovery in a resolution. (Loud laughter.) While they were busy, some inquisitive schoolboys wanting a peep, pulled the telescope out of its position, when, lo and behold! an accumulation of dirt and flies and a whole army of midges slid down the shaft. (Laughter.) The instrument had been strung up so long a time at the same angle that it had got foul. The elephant turned out to be a mouse, which had crept in between the lenses. (Laughter.) When the philosophers' sederunt broke up, they saw and were astonished at what had occurred. They were loth to admit their error, they shook their heads, muttered their misgivings, and separated sulkily. (Laughter.) They did not want their illusion dissipated, but the sceptics smiled, and were satisfied. (Laughter and cheers.) When Butler wrote this poem, he must have had some premonition of our Newcastle Caucusians. (Renewed laughter.) Their political lenses have been twisted and distorted, coated with rusty prejudice and the canker of suspicion. (Hear, hear, and cheers.) They magnify mice into elephants and flies into soldiers. (Laughter.) I am trying to play the part of Butler's scholars—to readjust their glasses, or lixiviate or swab their political telescope. (Loud laughter and cheers.)

Some questions are addressed to me that would be more appropriately addressed to *Notes and Queries*. Amongst them is one from a gentleman, who asks if I could tell him the author of the lines which he says I quoted in a recent address I made—

> "I do not like thee, Dr. Fell,
> The reason why I cannot tell," &c.

I only got the note this morning, and have not had time to refer, but I believe the lines are to be found in the poems of Tom Brown, a poet who lived about the Revolutionary period of 1688.*

I have really received such a flood of questions that they have got mixed. (Laughter.) It is not easy to keep one from overlapping the other. This reminds me of a tale that was told of Lamartine. M. Senior relates it, and I think I was told the same story by M. Ledru Rollin or M. Louis Blanc. It was this.

*As to the use of the familiar rhyme by Tom Brown, Mr. Cowen is doubtless correct; but, it may be interesting to state that the lines are a very literal translation of the following epigram by the Latin poet, Martial:—

> Non amo te, Samidi, nec possum dicere quare;
> Hoc tantum possum dicere, non amo te.

Lamartine was President of the French Provisional Government in 1848. When sitting in council with his colleagues, he used to jot down indiscriminately hints for the Administration. In a paper, containing amongst other things a list of Prefects, was found the word David. (Laughter.) M. David appeared, therefore, next day in the *Moniteur* as Prefect. No one knew M. David, and when Lamartine was asked to give his address he could not remember. (Laughter.) The name was certainly there, but he could not tell why. At last, he recollected he had put it down as a memorandum of some allusion to King David to be introduced into a poem. (Loud laughter.) So a notice had to appear in the *Moniteur* nominating A. B. Prefect in place of M. David sent to other functions. (Laughter.) It will not be difficult for me to mix up one question with another, or to confound, as a certain historic personage is supposed to have done, the hundredth Psalm with "God save the King." (Laughter.)

Here is a gentleman who tells me that I will not be elected. (Laughter, and a voice: "Ah, but you will," and cheers. Mr. Cowen tore up the question. A voice: "That's right; tear it up," and cheers.) Well, I don't know that. No one will know it till next Saturday night. But if I am not elected—(cries of "Top of the poll," and cheers)—all the difference will be this: I will live at Blaydon instead of at London, which will be a little more agreeable. (A voice: "And make more bricks.") Yes, and make more bricks. (Laughter.) The gentleman may be right, and I may not be re-elected. But I mean to give the people of Newcastle an opportunity of pronouncing an opinion upon my Parliamentary conduct and the principles and policy I have upheld. (Loud cheers.) I am desirous for their decision on public grounds, but personally I will be content with any result. I often wonder at the anxiety which some persons exhibit to embark in a Parliamentary career. It is an honourable position, no doubt—one of the most honourable within the reach of an average English citizen. It affords great possibilities. It is a platform from which a man may preach to the world. But, like everything else, it has its drawbacks. It is not all glory, and fewer results are realized for the labour expended than are to be obtained in any other department of public effort. (Hear, hear.) Looking back at the last ten years, it makes me melancholy to reflect upon the time I have given for no useful purpose. A considerable span of my life, by a contradiction of fate, has been spent for little good to any one. ("No, no.") Routine, petty business details, and formal correspondence have occupied half my days; and the other half has been spent in listening listlessly to dull debates, or fretfully watching for an important division. I receive as many letters during a session as a considerable mercantile firm receives. (Laughter.) They are of little intrinsic importance, and, in a counting-house, could be disposed of by a clerk for 30s. or 40s. a-week. But a member cannot delegate his duties—(cheers)—and he is thus occupied on trivial, often irksome, but urgent affairs. If M.P.-dom has its honours and its usefulness, it has also its drawbacks. (Hear, hear.)

Mr Cowen, having examined into a batch of questions before him, said: Here is a gentleman who says I have badly repaid the Liberal party for their services to me. Repaid the Liberal party for their services! (Laughter.) What services did they ever render to me? (A voice: "Never any," and cheers.) I owe them nothing. (Cheers.) I never cadged for a constituency. (Renewed cheers.) The Liberal managers sought me. I never sought them. (Hear, hear.) I fought their battle regardless of either health or cash. (Cheers.) I claim no credit for what I did. It was only my duty; but when I am chided with ingratitude, and reminded of payment of services, I will speak the truth right out. (Loud cheers.) I have been engaged in political work for thirty-seven years now. I have travelled hundreds of miles, laboured long and hard by night and day; and I never, either directly or indirectly, took a farthing even for travelling expenses, much less for services. (Cheering.) I would not have taken, if they had offered, the most insignificant of the recognitions that party politicians seek for and usually secure. As showing their disposition, I might cite one fact. I could, if necessary, cite others. My name was sent, without my knowledge, desire, or approval, three times to Liberal Lords-Chancellor to be put on the Commission of the Peace for Newcastle. It was three times rejected. I would not have accepted the position, but I notice the circumstance—(loud cheers)—to show the disposition of the persons who reproach me with ingratitude. (Hear, hear.) Recently, my name was proposed by the present Lord-Chancellor to be a Justice, but I have refused to take the office. (Cheers.) All the time I have been in political life, I have had to encounter the persistent opposition of the heads of the Liberal party. Until 1874, I was always either outside or in advance of them—very often ostracised by them. All the democratic efforts I was engaged in were in opposition to the orthodox leaders. Not one of the men who now sit as my censors either gave a shilling of money or an hour of time to further these movements, in their early stages, that they now profess so keen an interest in and claim so much credit for. (Laughter and cheers, and a voice: "Hit them hard, Joe," and "Gie them it hot.") I could a tale unfold about some of these new-fangled Liberals' labours—(loud laughter and cheers)—for Liberal principles that would rather surprise the younger section of the community, if it were worth while telling. I am not complaining. I never sought, I never wanted, I would never take, either their pay or their honours. (Cheers.) I only did my duty To have done less, I should have been recreant to my trust. I am only driven to say this much in refutation of the insinuations which are as cowardly as they are false. (Loud and prolonged applause.) When men charge me with being ungrateful to the Liberal party and not repaying them for their services, I throw the accusation back again, and repudiate the charge. (The audience here rose and cheered enthusiastically.) I have no desire to refer to these matters. It is repugnant to me to do so. I think you will do me the justice to admit that. I never refer to them but when driven to it. (Cheers, a voice: "Give them another blow," and laughter.)

Here is a question. I take it at random out of the lot before me. I daresay the man who sent it—there are three or four of the same kind—did so in good faith.

"It was stated the other day that you voted in Governmental divisions in 1881-2 as follows:—For the Government in one year, 26; and in another, 12. Against it in one year, 104; against it the next year, 131."

(A voice: "Now for it," and laughter.) Now listen. This is a specimen of the criticism that a handful of bilious and imperfectly-informed individuals indulge in. In 1881, as you know, the Coercion Bill was before Parliament. It occupied nearly two-thirds of the session. There were divisions on almost every line—certainly on every clause. We fought the bill on its principle, in committee, on report, and on the third reading. Every man who knows anything of current politics knows this. I proclaimed, in all conceivable ways, that I was opposed to the bill—that I would resist it on all and every occasion. (Hear, hear.) I kept my word. I did so. (Cheers.) These votes they talk of as being against the Government were against the Coercion Bill. (Cheers.) Yet, my dishonest censors wish to convey to the public the idea that I voted 104 times against the

Government on 104 different questions, when the votes were all, or nearly all, on one measure. ("Shame.") The same remark applies to the Cloture divisions in the year following. Every proposition that tended cloture-wise I voted against. But the votes, although separate, were really one, as they referred to one question. (Hear, hear.) Let my opponents be fair and state the other side. (Hear, hear.) I supported the Land Bills, Irish and English, of the Government as cordially as I opposed the Cloture and Coercion. (Cheers.) On the Representation of the People Bill, I did what no other man in the country did. (Loud cheers, and a voice: "And never said a word about it.") I voted on every division, and, except on the question of women's suffrage, on every occasion with the Government. (Cheers.) I ask you whether such criticism as these questions cover is fair? (Cries of "No.") Is it an honest way of conducting political discussion? ("No," and "Unmanly.") The Coercion Bill confiscated the most cherished rights of our British Constitution, and I resisted it both on principle and in detail. (Cheers.) It stirred the very fibres of my soul. (Cheers.) I have, times out of number in this room, denounced the coercion of the old Radicals by Sidmouth and Castlereagh, and of the Chartists by later Administrations. And was I, an English Democrat, sitting there in Parliament to represent a Radical constituency, to sacrifice the principles of my life to serve a party? Never! ("No," "Certainly not," and the audience again rose and cheered the candidate.)

I will take the questions *seriatim*, if you like, but it is impossible to answer them all to-night. I pick up this one:—

"Did you ever refuse to present a petition in favour of Sir Roger Tichborne?"

I certainly didn't. I not only did not refuse, but I was the only member of Parliament, along with my friend, Mr.

Whitworth, who signed a petition in favour of limiting his sentence. (Hear, hear.) Why, I presented a petition to Parliament for the impeachment of Lord Beaconsfield—(laughter)—and another for the impeachment of Mr. Gladstone. (Laughter.) I will present any petition to Parliament that any number of citizens sign and send me, provided it is respectful and in legal form. (Hear, hear.) I showed the Speaker the impeachment petitions, and he said they were in order. I am disposed to think that the old plan of impeaching Ministers was better than the new one of moving votes of censure. (Laughter.)

There are three or four questions about the Criminal Law Amendment Bill. The opinion the questioners evidently hold is that that Bill was carried in consequence of the agitation got up about it. (Hear, hear.) That is an entire delusion. I know all that took place with respect to that Bill. It was the outcome of the action of a committee of the House of Lords, promoted chiefly by the late Archbishop of Canterbury, and the venerated but now deceased Lord Shaftesbury. (Hear, hear.) The committee reported in favour of an alteration of the law, and a Bill based on the report passed the House of Lords twice—last year and this. Mr Gladstone, long before the session closed, said that it was one of the Bills the Government were pledged to carry. Lord Iddesleigh, speaking on behalf of the Opposition, intimated his approval of the late Premier's resolve. When the present Government took office, the Bill was taken charge of by Sir Richard Cross. I have heard Sir Richard Cross and Sir William Harcourt say repeatedly in public, and more than once in private, that they both meant to do their utmost to carry the Bill, and I believed them. I am sure they meant what they said; and I am equally sure the House of Commons would have passed the Bill if not a single meeting had been held. (Hear, hear.) This question and others have been put apparently to induce an expression of my opinion on a distasteful subject. I make this answer. There are some things in life we had better say as little about as possible. (Hear, hear.) I have no sympathy with either men or women who take a pleasure in discussing prurient topics—(cheers)—either on the platform or in the press. There are some dirty pools that had better not be stirred. I heard of things done and said in London last autumn that I was ashamed at. They could not be repeated. I will tell you a circumstance which these questions bring to my recollection. It shows one way, and, in my judgment, a better way, of dealing with the nasty business referred to by my interrogators. There was in London, some years ago, a circle of young men, very foolish and somewhat depraved, who indulged in unmanly and discreditable practices. Information respecting them was brought to Lord Beaconsfield, who summoned the authorities responsible in such matters, and informed them what he had learnt was going on. He said: "I ask for no details. I stipulate no conditions, but you must find admission to the room where these misguided young men assemble, and get the names of every one of them." This was done. Entrance to the room was got, the doors closed, and the names of every person there, to the number of some thirty or forty, many of them dressed in women's clothes and indulging in improper antics, were obtained. They were not arrested, but communications were made to the parents of all of them. Those who were young enough were chastised or reproved by their guardians, and the older ones were severely taken to task by others in authority, censured, and warned. The consequences of their conduct were brought vividly before them. The young men's careers were not blasted by exposure, and the world was not scandalized by a demoralizing investigation. (Hear, hear.) That was, in my opinion, a better method of dealing with a degrading evil than seeking to check it by deluging our streets with filth. (Cheers.)

"Will Mr. Cowen vote for an increased capitation grant to volunteers?"

Unquestionably. (Cheers.) I know of no body of citizens who are more deserving of encouragement. (Cheers.)

"Mr. Cowen, Sir,—Will you kindly let us know whether private members are paid for sitting on commissions, like the Shipping Commission, and committees? The reason for asking this is that it is always cropping up at meal hours."

I have answered this question before. I think I did so at Elswick the other night, but I will do so again. Members get no pay of any kind, either for serving on commissions or on committees. There is a commission sitting on shipping just now, and not one of its members will get a farthing. They receive travelling expenses if they leave London, but nothing beyond that.

I am asked respecting the relative transactions of tradesmen and co-operative stores. I thought I had replied to this inquiry early in the evening. I think the stores and the tradesmen should stand absolutely on an equality. (Hear, hear.) I know that wealthy men—members of the aristocracy—deal with the stores in London. You can see, any Saturday, miles of carriages standing at the doors of the palatial establishments in Victoria Street or Haymarket. These aristocratic co-operators are tradesmen; and I cannot see the justice of exempting them from any legitimate taxation that struggling tradesmen have to pay. (Cheers.) (A voice: "They do pay income-tax.") Well, I am speaking on the assumption that they don't.

"As an electer, and one deeply interested in the religious

and political welfare of the nation, I presume, Mr. Cowen, you wi. not consider the question 'What is your religious belief' an irrelevant one, and don't forget to give a clear answer to it?"

(Hisses, and cries of "Tear it up" and "Don't answer it.") No, I won't answer it. (Cheers.) I will answer any question as to citizenship; I will answer any inquiry as to my duties as a representative; but I will not reply to any question as to my religion. (Cheers.) I have no doubt my interrogator is a sincere and worthy person, but if he has ever read what I have said, he must have little difficulty in evolving a clear enough conception as to my religious views. (Cheers.) But, to make a man's creed a qualification for, or a disqualification from, discharging the duties of any civil office, would be to set up a theological test. (Loud cheers.)

There are several questions asked me with respect to my competitors in this contest. (Laughter.) I think it undesirable to refer to them. (Hear, hear.) I am appealing to you—no, I am not appealing. (Cheers.) The electors of Newcastle want two members. I have been one of them for eleven years. I am willing to serve them again, if they want me. I ask no man for a vote, and no man is empowered to ask for a vote for me. If you choose to elect me, well. If you don't, again well. I will go about other business. (Laughter and cheers.) I don't care to say a single word calculated to irritate opponents, or to engender any ill-feeling during this contest. It will soon be over. I hope, when it is, no one's friendship will have been disturbed, and that no sediment will be left.

"How long must a householder be in a borough before he is entitled to vote?"

Twelve months, I think.

"What does the Church derive from the taxes?"

Nothing. The Church—no church—gets no money from the Estimates. The Protestant Dissenters in Ireland used to get an annual grant known as the Regium-Donum, but that ceased with the disestablishment of the Church in that country. (Cheers, and a voice: "Answer no more," and "You have answered plenty.")

"Will Mr. Cowen tell us what are his party colours?"

This comes from a lady-admirer. (Cheers.) The Radical colours used to be white and green. Those were the colours that were worn by Mr. Attwood, Mr. Aytoun, Mr. Beaumont, and the Radicals generally in the olden times. I suppose the same colours now will do. (Loud cheers.) I hope the white does not mean any indication of want of courage. (Laughter.) I believe the use of colours is very stringently restricted by the Corrupt Practices Act; and I trust no one interested in my election will involve himself in any liability on the score of expense in providing colours. No candidate can pay a farthing for such a purpose. (Cheers, and "That will do," and "You have answered enough.") I am quite willing to go on. (Loud cries of "No, no," and "Sit down now.")

Mr. Cowen then resumed his seat, the audience rising and cheering him with great enthusiasm.

# EGYPT AND THE WEST AND SOUTH AFRICAN COLONIES.

---

DELIVERED IN THE BYKER BOARD SCHOOL, ON MONDAY, NOVEMBER 23RD, 1885.

---

CHAIRMAN—COUNCILLOR BIRKETT.

---

Mr. COWEN, who was received with prolonged cheering, said: Mr. Chairman, ladies, and gentlemen,—have you ever inquired how the politicians who attained power as the opponents of territorial aggression, and the friends of peace, should have involved the country in one of the most unprovoked, sanguinary, and costly military adventures of modern times? Their professions, and their practices, can only be reconciled on the hypothesis that deeds are good or evil according to the persons who commit them. (Laughter.) Evidently war, in the judgment of the late Ministers, is odious and sinful when originated by one set of men, but honourable and virtuous when originated by another. (Renewed laughter.) This may be so, but, if it is, I have a very incorrect conception of Christian morality. (Hear, hear, and cheers.) The attitude of the public, during the course of the deplorable events in Egypt, may be explained by the systematic indifference with which they regard all foreign complications until we are involved in them. It usually happens that, by the time the constituencies have mastered the matters in dispute, the Ministry of the day have committed the country to a definite course. The question is then fought out on strictly party lines. Remonstrance is unavailing, and reason is denied a hearing. If the people had heeded the warning, and acted on the counsel plentifully tendered when the trouble in Egypt was brewing, they would have been saved the sad and mournful story of the past five years. (Hear, hear.) But they would *not* listen, and they have had to pay for their temerity. (A voice: "Served them right," and hear, hear.) When the Cabinet had our fleet roving the eastern waters, ostentatiously brandishing their arms before Dulcigno, as they afterwards did with such direful effect before Alexandria, they were told that this naval roystering might go a step too far, and that Mussulman fanaticism might be roused to reprisals. But all such sober caution was set down to partizan malice or spite against the late Prime Minister. If there are any here who can carry their minds back to the naval promenade in the Adriatic five years ago, recall what I, along with others, said about it—(cheers)—and compare the predictions then made with what has since occurred, they will allow that the protest was prompted by something else than partizan malevolence. (Hear, hear.) A course calculated to produce like embroilments has been pursued, unnoticed, in Afghanistan. The Liberals objected to the action of Lord Beaconsfield in that country, and reversed it. In doing so, however, they have committed us to engagements much more onerous, as they will find when we are called upon, as we can be with our Treaty with Abdur-Rahman, to defend, not the Passes of the Suliemans, but the whole of wild Afghanistan. (Hear, hear.) But it was a party bargain, and scarce a voice has been raised against it. I know all protestations would have been unavailing. The part of Cassandra is an unpleasant one for a man to play. It makes others uncomfortable, and himself unpopular. People detest, and usually resent, being told of impending peril. It is, too, impossible to induce a busy community, swayed by a thousand different and conflicting interests, to give continuous attention to the multitudinous and complicated questions that our relations with other States are constantly raising. They don't know what has been devised in the diplomatic laboratories, and, in despair, they surrender themselves to the guidance of professional leaders. Professional politicians, like professional cricketers, have only one object—to win their game. (Laughter.) They do not commit themselves until they see, or think they see, which course is best for the party to take; and then they will do anything with the game but lose it. (Laughter.) National interests are made subservient to sectional and irrelevant considerations. Thus, between the indifference of the public and the schemes of party chiefs, the country staggers into war, or engagements that lead to war, much as a drunken man staggers into a ditch without knowing it. (Laughter.) If the people had dispassionately investigated the initial stages of the Egyptian dispute, the Ministry would never have been permitted to oscillate into the embroglio in which they have landed themselves and England. (Cheers.) We cannot recall the past, but we may extract from it guidance for the future. (Cheers.) The disturbing influences which have caused so much misery, bloodshed, and perplexity, have disappeared. Arabi and the Nationalist leaders are in exile. The Mahdi and his able lieutenant are dead. So, too, is the heroic Gordon, as well as the Government that despatched him on his chivalrous but bootless mission. ("Shame.") Egypt is bankrupt; and our army has returned vanquished, but not dishonoured. (Hear, hear.) The followers of the Egyptian patriot, and of the Soudanese prophet, are bewailing their fate in dismantled homes and decimated families. The most vivid imagination cannot depict the sickening reality of our desert butcheries. The patient work of generations—agriculture, commerce, progress—has been sacrificed to fanatical credulity and political vacillation and indecision. (Hear, hear.) Egypt ruined, the Soudan abandoned to slavery and savagedom, England discredited—these are the trophies of British intervention. (Hear, hear.) Now, when the centres of the opposing forces have played their parts, and have vanished, we may inquire what object we had in going to Egypt. The caucus Liberal, who buys his opinions as he buys his dinner, ready cooked—(laughter)—will tell you that the root of the evil lay in the Dual Control, which Lord Salisbury and M. Waddington concocted, and bound their respective countries to uphold. The statement is not correct. If the Dual Control was obligatory on us, it was also so on the French. They did not sustain it by force of arms, and we need not have done so unless we liked. (Cheers.) But let that pass. Admit that the Anglo-French bargain carried all the obligations it is credited with, why did we enter into it? If the Control caused the war, what caused the Control? That is the question. There is a reason for most things, and there will be for this amongst others. What was it? British interests—not a sentimental, but a substantial reason. (Hear, hear, and laughter.) We are interested in Egypt, because a large number of our countrymen have heavy investments, and do a large business there. (Hear, hear.) Lord Beaconsfield defined foreign affairs to be the affairs of Englishmen living in foreign countries. The affairs of Englishmen living in, or connected with, Egypt, led our Government, as the affairs of Frenchmen led the French Government, to organize the Dual Control. Whether it was a wise or unwise arrangement, I am not now discussing. I am only explaining its origin. Egypt has been the brightest jewel in the crown of many a conqueror —the objective point which, in the internecine struggles of the East, all have striven to gain. Xerxes, Alexander, Ptolemy, Augustus, Saladin, and Napoleon, each, in turn, devoted his bravest legions and untiring energy to its conquest. (Cheers.) Bonaparte told the French Directory that, by seizing and holding Egypt, he could command the destinies of the civilized world. Its geographical position has destined it to be a great commercial emporium. Historians and political philosophers have discoursed eloquently on its natural resources, and on the power its possession confers. One of its eulogists points out how, being placed in the centre between Europe and Asia, on the confines of Eastern and Western civilization, at the extremity of the African Continent, and on the shores of the Mediterranean, it is fitted to become the central point of communication for the varied productions of these different regions of the globe. The waters of the Mediterranean bring it all the fabrics of Europe; the Red Sea wafts to its shores the riches of India and China; while the Nile floats down to its bosom the produce of the vast unknown regions of Africa. (Cheers.) Its influence on the mercantile relations of Great Britain are only realized when a sudden rupture of the ordinary flow of events impresses its value on us. Egypt proper, consisting of the Delta and the Nile valley up to the first cataract, covers 216,000 square miles, or about the same superficies as the German Empire. It contains five and a-half million natives, and ninety thousand Europeans. This population is confined to nine or ten thousand square miles, the other being desert. On this space the inhabitants are very densely packed. In Belgium, there are 486 persons to the square mile, and in Great Britain there are 291; but in the Egyptian Delta there are 598 persons per square mile, or about one per acre. This does not include the floating population, of which, in times of peace, there is nearly half-a-million more. The country is agricultural and not manufacturing. It has no adventitious supplies of gold or iron, of silver or petroleum, to depend on; yet, it is as rich in food as when Jacob sent his ten sons thither to buy corn. It exports, as the product of the soil and the fruit of its labours, £2 7s. 6d. per head of the population—a remarkable amount, proving not only the fertility of the land, but the industry of the people. Of the thirteen million pounds' worth of goods Egypt exported the year before the war, England took over nine millions; all the rest of the world taking only four. Of the six and three-quarter million pounds' worth of foreign goods Egypt bought, England sold her three and a-quarter millions, and India and Australia one and a-quarter millions; all the rest of the world selling her only two and a-half millions. Putting the import and export trades together, England does sixty-two per cent. of it; India and the colonies seven per cent.—in all sixty-nine per cent.; while France does thirteen per cent., Austria six per cent., Italy seven, and Russia five per cent. There are no data to show what amount of English money is invested in Egypt, nor what share of the loans is held by English capitalists. But the sums are considerable; and these, taken together with our trade, give us a paramount interest in the country. (Cheers.) But large though these interests undeniably are, their being imperilled would not supply sufficient warrant for war. When our merchants and money-lenders speculate, they do so at their own risk. Although the Government are bound to ensure them justice, and prevent them being robbed, they are not bound to fight to make good the losses that come to them in the ordinary course of commerce. We did not occupy the territory of the South American Republics when they became insolvent, and we would not interfere in Holland if our large business with that country were damaged by internal disturbances. Our position in Egypt, it is true, is peculiar, as we are largely responsible for the form of Government that exists there. It is mainly our creation. But although our share in the reconstitution of Egypt, under the rule of Mehemet Ali, has often been cited as a pretext for our subsequent interference, neither it, nor our trading connection, justifies intervention by arms, though both may be rightly regarded as buttressing our other interests. (Hear, hear.) The first of these other interests is the Suez Canal, of which we own half the shares, and contribute 80 per cent. of the traffic. (Cheers.) On Thursday, I showed, or at least tried to show, how essential to our Indian Empire was the maintenance of our command of the Canal. It is the great toll-gate between the East and the West; and it is imperative, for both trading and strategical reasons, that we should have control over it. (Renewed cheers.) Comparing it with the Cape route to Bombay, nearly five thousand miles are saved—an all-important consideration in the event of a disturbance in India. Egypt supplied the land through which it was cut; France cut it; and England sustains it. (Hear, hear.) If it were not for our trade, it would relapse into the abandoned state which destroyed the ancient channels of the Pharaohs and the Caliphs. We are the carriers of the world. More than half the tonnage of the globe is owned by England. Our carrying trade is the backbone of the maritime supremacy upon which we depend for our prosperity, our power, if not our existence, as an independent nation. (Cheers.) If we had not a single colony, we should have an interest in the Canal superior to that of any other Power, or rather superior to that of all the other Powers put together. But, in addition to this, England is the centre of a vast empire, most of whose possessions lie in the Eastern seas, to which the Canal gives access. (Hear, hear.) Our material and political interests in the East are so overwhelmingly predominant, that they give us a right to a position distinct from, and superior to, that of any other nation. (Cheers.) It is unnecessary, after what I have already said, to enlarge further on this head. All the facts I have stated, and others equally cogent, can be verified by reference to maps, histories, and trade-registers. These are the trade and personal interests. They are weighty, but not so weighty as the military and national. We are as much concerned to prevent Egypt passing under the dominion of France as we are to prevent Afghanistan passing under the dominion of Russia. If France or any great State were in possession of Egypt, it would constitute a menace to India, and a danger to our Indian colonies. (Hear, hear.) Conceive what power France would have, if, in addition to her existing authority in the Mediterranean, she held Egypt, occupied Mecca, and controlled the Red Sea. She would drop the portcullis on our armies, as well as on our ships. (Hear, hear.) The same objection there is to Russia becoming master of Constantinople, controlling the Straits, and converting the Euxine into a naval dockyard, arsenal, and harbour of refuge, applies to France becoming master of Egypt, controlling the Canal, and seizing the Red, as the Russians would seize the Black, Sea. (Hear, hear.) France, in such a position, could make descents on India with a compact force of Frenchmen and Arabs ; and her cruisers, using the Red Sea as a shelter, could imperil our Eastern commerce, or make its safety dependent on the caprice of Boulevard Chauvinists. Russia, on our Indian borders, will force us into a heavy military expenditure ; France, in Egypt, would force us into equally great naval expenditure. (Hear, hear.) If this took place, we should never have any true peace with the French, any more than we have with the Russians. There would be an armed truce on both sides. There is one difference between the two Powers. Russia cannot invade us at home ; France can. We no more want Egypt than we want Afghanistan, or we want Constantinople—(hear, hear);—but we do want all these places in the possession of the native populations—Afghans, Egyptians, and Turks respectively. (Loud cheers.) Our interests in Egypt, as investors and traders, and as owners of an Eastern Empire, combined to induce our Government to enter into the Dual Control, as they combined to induce it, half-a-century ago, to limit the powers of Mehemet Ali, and to re-impose the authority of the Porte. If the intervention of 1882 is the productof the Control, the Control is the product of the intervention of 1840, as that was, in its turn, the outcome of the invasion of 1801, when we drove out the French and restored the rule of the Sultan. Partizan criticism has obscured, rather than explained, British policy in Egypt. (Hear, hear.) But, although occasionally erratic, this policy has had but one object throughout—Egypt for the natives or the Turks, or the two jointly, but not for us or any great Power. (Hear, hear.) Disorder injures trade. Anarchy destroys it. Being so closely identified with Egypt, as an outlet for British capital, a field for British enterprise, as a road to British possessions, and a possible base of hostile operations against us, our Governments have always busied themselves in its administration—often by advice, sometimes by command. This explains why the late Khedive, when his finances got into confusion in 1875, sought counsel from England. At his request, the late Mr. Cave was sent to examine into the position of the country. Mr. Cave reported that there had been great waste and systematic extravagance; that great works had been undertaken with insufficient means; that there had been heavy losses by Colonial adventures; and excessive military expenditure. He recommended the intervention of a superior Power to restore credit, and restrain expenditure. This report led up to the scheme of liquidation, which Mr. Goschen for the English, and M. Joubert for the French creditors, after some delay, and much difficulty, succeeded in organizing, and which was ultimately put into operation under the joint control of France and England.

Before this was accomplished, Ismail had to sell his shares in the Canal, and the English Government bought them for under four million pounds—a most profitable purchase. (Loud cheers.) But these and other personal sacrifices were not sufficient to restore confidence in Ismail, who, on the recommendation of the great Powers, was deposed by the Sultan; and Tewfik, whom his father describes as being without head, heart, or courage—(laughter)—with limited income and restricted powers, was appointed Khedive in his place. Although Ismail was extravagant, he was able. (Hear, hear.) He found the Egyptian debt fifteen millions, and he left it seventy-seven. But he also found the revenue four and a-half millions, and left it nine. He found the tilled area four million acres, and he left it five and a-half million acres. He found the trade five and a-half million pounds, and he left it nineteen millions. He attempted too much, but he was, nevertheless, the ablest Mahometan ruler there has been since Mehemet Ali. (Hear, hear.) Egypt was robbed. There is no other word which correctly describes what was done by the money-lenders and their agents. Out of sixty-nine millions borrowed, in eleven years, Egypt got only forty-three millions; twenty-six millions having been illicitly abstracted in its passage to the Egyptian treasury. ("Shame.") Interest had to be paid for what was really never received. By the scheme of liquidation, the debt was fixed at eighty millions. The revenue was estimated at £8,400,000. Of this amount, £3,565,000 was set aside for the payment of the debt annuities, and £4,825,000 was left for the expenses of government, for the Suez Canal interest, and other liabilities. It was over this arrangement that all the trouble arose. It was to upset it that Arabi and his countrymen rebelled. (Cheers.) The scheme itself was not opposed. It was only fair that Egypt should pay her debts, and the people made no objection to that; but they did object, ultimately with arms, to the manner in which the scheme was carried out. (Hear, hear.) Instead of entrusting the natives with some share of the work, every branch of the service was crammed with Europeans, many of whom were sinecurists. In 1881, there were 1,324 Europeans in various posts, drawing in salaries an aggregate of £373,700 a-year, or 4 per cent. on the gross revenues of the country. This was even too much for the long-suffering fellaheen. (Hear, hear.) It was against this flagrantly unjust arrangement, and not against the honest payment of all liabilities, that Arabi rose; and without approving of all he did, the motive that prompted him and his countrymen was commendable—(cheers)—and such as Englishmen, in like circumstances, would have been moved by. (Hear, hear.) His plan of reform was that subsequently adopted by Lord Dufferin, and to the enactment of which the late Government were pledged. It was at this juncture that, in my judgment, the Liberal Cabinet made their fatal and irredeemable error. (Hear, hear.) I agree with them as to our special and preponderating interest in Egypt. I agree that it was our duty to ensure its maintenance. I disagree with their meddling in a legitimate effort, on the part of the Egyptian people, to collect and administer their own revenue, when the conditions of the liquidation were complied with, the interest paid, and the stipulated sum for the redemption of the debt honestly apportioned for that purpose. (Loud cheers.) When this was done, all was done that we could rightfully ask for; and that it was done we have the statements of members of the late Ministry, notably that made by the late Premier himself, at Leeds, in the autumn of 1881. What was it to us whether Arabi was, or was not, president of the Khedive's Council, so long as the Government were sustained and their bargains kept? (Cheers.) The main difference between Arabi and the others was that Arabi was an honest soldier, and they were either puppets or speculators, to whose fingers many of the missing millions had stuck. (Loud laughter and cheers.) It is notorious that some of our *protegés*, from being very poor men, became very rich ones during their years of office under Ismail. (Laughter.) Arabi, on the other hand, had the power to enrich himself, and he did not do so. (Loud cheers.) We had a right to insist on compliance with the conditions of the liquidation. We had no right to allow personal prejudice against Arabi to prevent his becoming president. (Hear, hear.) But if there was a rebellion—and there would not have been if Arabi and his friends had been allowed to retain office—(hear, hear)—we should have called upon the Sultan, as suzerain, to repress it. It was no part of our duty to bombard Alexandria, because our nominee as president was not selected. (Hear, hear.) I have dwelt at length on the inception of the intervention, as in it is to be found the key to what followed. The principle is there. The rest is a matter of administration, or rather mal-administration. (Laughter.) Once started, events follow each other in natural order. Along with the French, we lodged an ultimatum against Arabi, but it was disregarded. Then the two Powers put themselves into fighting attitude, and prepared to enforce their demands. The French threatened and retired, but we fired. The Government were warned, by a battalion of authorities, that there would be an outburst of religious resentment; and they were pressed to send a force on shore to protect the European quarter of Alexandria. They treated the demand with disdain. What they were told would occur, did occur. (Hear, hear.) Alexandria was burned, and many Europeans killed. Then we sent soldiers, but it was too late. The insurrection had got head. While a company of marines could easily have kept order, it took an army to restore it. (Hear, hear.) We destroyed the Egyptian troops at Tel-el-Kebir, and we destroyed with them the country's defence. When we vanquished Arabi, we opened a way for the Mahdi. Egypt had an India as well as England—a fact that our politicians did not then know. The Egyptian army having been annihilated, a hastily organized, undisciplined, and ill-provisioned force was despatched to the Soudan, and slaughtered. Again they were told of the risk they were running, and again they discarded the advice. ("Shame.") They refused either to restrain the expedition or to strengthen it; and the gallant Hicks marched to his doom. Death rode on every passing breeze. Then we realized the situation. But it was once more too late. (Hear, hear.) We sent Gordon alone to stem the rushing wave of Moslem fury. He did his work nobly, but he failed, as every sane man outside of the Cabinet, who had ever thought on the subject seriously, knew he would. We repeated, with Baker, the blunder we made with Hicks, and with like disastrous consequences. Then we sent General Graham to relieve the garrisons which Baker never reached. Again too late! (Hear, hear.) The garrisons were massacred before he got there. After lengthened hesitation, we attempted to rescue one of the most heroic servants any nation ever possessed, but we were once more too late. The Nile demonstration demonstrated nothing but the courage of our soldiers and the culpable vacillation of our statesmen. (Cheers.) When Gordon was killed, we proclaimed a retaliatory campaign, and sent General Graham to Suakim with a composite army of navvies and soldiers to build a railway to Berber. Lord Wolseley proclaimed to the natives that we would go to Khartoum if it took us one hundred years; and, on the strength of this proclamation, he got the aid of friendly Arabs. But it was all bounce. (Laughter.) We did not go to Khartoum, and we never laid the railway. We sent the ships with the railway plant back to Chatham—(renewed laughter)—and we sent our native allies to their fate. And such a fate! ("Shame.") There is not, in all the chequered record of modern military adventure, a more melancholy and humiliating chapter than that which chronicles the recklessness and timidity, the vacillation and weakness, the blunders and incapacity, of the British Government in Egypt. (Cheers.) No language, however severe, can adequately describe the misery and chaos that their agglomeration of dissimilar aims and irreconcilable elements have produced. (Hear, hear.) In no single instance did the Government show even ordinary skill. Their policy, both in the Council chamber and in the field, has been one unrelieved and colossal failure—a succession of responsibilities shirked, duties neglected, and opportunities missed. (Hear, hear.) Millions have been squandered, thousands of people have been slaughtered, tens of thousands have been ruined, and no human being has been benefited by all the bloodshed and waste. (Hear, hear.) They stamped out the national rising and gave the country nothing in its place. They neither shut the door nor opened it, neither evacuated the country, nor ruled it. (Cheers.) It is a small satisfaction to me to say that I have had neither art nor part in the business. I opposed it from start to finish. I have re-told the dreary tale, not for the purpose of proving that I was right when other and abler men were wrong, nor with the expectation that its repetition will have the remotest influence on current politics. The country has condoned the blunders, and Parliament has endorsed them. Recriminations, therefore, are purposeless. But I wish to emphasise the necessity of the English people bestowing more attention on foreign questions when in the embryonic stage, and not allowing them to become the arena for party strife. (Cheers.) Liberals declaim against bloodshed; yet, they originated a war in which there have been more persons slain than in any other English war this generation. ("Shame.") They advocate economy; yet, they have buried in the sands of the Soudan more millions than they will save for the next fifty years. And all because the men who disapproved of the enterprise had not the courage to state their objection and vote against their party! (Hear, hear.) And for the future—what can be said? We have added nine millions to the already all but unbearable Egyptian debt. That is the cost of our bombardment. It ought to have been paid by the men who ordered, and the men who sanctioned, the outrage. It is doubtful whether, with all the legal thumbscrews they can construct, the bondholders will be able to wring the increased taxes out of the hard-earned income of the long suffering peasantry. If Egypt had difficulties in paying her way before, how can she pay it now with a heavier debt, with her society dislocated, her land ravished, her provinces in rebellion, and her frontiers open to invasion? (Hear, hear.) There was some stirring of the old fire in the depressed inheritors of the most ancient, and, at one time, a brilliant civilization, but we have quenched it. As the rising sun imbues with the charms of vocal utterance the statue of Memnon, so it was hoped that the victim of oppression who toils at its base would be penetrated by the rays of Western enlightenment, and would once more assume his place among the free peoples of the earth. (Cheers.) But these hopes are now dashed; and the unhappy Egyptian, pendulum-like, is doomed to oscillate between the exactions of local pashas, and the enactments of alien tax-gatherers. And thus we spoiled the Egyptians. (Hear, hear.) Why the African continent, which is not far short of a fourth of the world, should have remained so long closed to modern enterprise, is an enigma not easy of solution. It is now, however, being exploited on all sides. It is no longer the lost continent. Successive explorers have worked their way, with infinite hardships, through untravelled wilds, and tracked the courses of the Nile and the Niger, of the Congo and the Zambesi, as our fathers tracked the Potomac and the Hudson. They have lifted the veil that has hitherto enveloped the land in impenetrable mystery; and before the end of the century, it will take its place in the orbit of the world's civilization. (Hear, hear.) We now know what we before did not—that the interior is not all desert, and the inhabitants not all savages. There are fertile lands, teeming with industrious populations, desirous of exchanging their raw products for our manufactured goods. European nations are competing for this hidden commerce, much in the same way as they competed for the commerce of America after its discovery. The French are operating through Algiers, Tunis, and Senegal. They contemplate submerging the Sahara, which is supposed to be 140 feet below the sea. The entrance is to be from the Mediterranean, near the site of ancient Carthage. There is also an English scheme for letting the Atlantic into the vast arid basin by way of the river Belta. This latter project, which would only require a cutting of about twenty-five miles, embraces also a junction with the Niger. After the achievements at Suez and Panama, there is nothing unreasonable in supposing that, within another generation, we may see a waterway constructed into the interior of Africa, which would have greater civilizing, commercial, and climatic consequences than any engineering enterprise heretofore attempted. (Cheers.) Mehemet Ali appreciated the importance of this internal trade, and he and his successors pushed the boundaries of Egypt southward to the Equator, eastward to the Indian Ocean, and westward to Darfour. His ambition was to found a great Arab empire. He brought peoples and countries, before excluded from the world's history, into direct communication with superior and more civilized races. This greater Egypt is 2,000 miles long, and of the same breadth. After passing the Libyan Desert, there is a dense population, who are in possession of nearly everything which contributes to the exuberance of life. The country is replete with untouched natural treasures. "If you tickle the soil with a hoe it will laugh with a harvest." (Laughter.) Agriculture is rendered easy by the recurrence of the rainy season, by irrigation, by the rising of the river, and by an atmosphere ordinarily so clouded as to moderate the radiance of the sun. The valley of the Nile, from the lakes to the Mediterranean, presents a field from which England may draw needful produce, and, in return, fill with her manufactures. When the facilities for transit were much more defective than they were at the commencement of the war, about £2,000,000 worth of goods percolated by caravan through the desert to Cairo and Suakim. Some idea of the difficulty that trade laboured under may be formed when I state that the cost of carriage from Berber to Suakim alone was from £8 to £12 a-ton, and that nothing weighing over 500 lbs. could be carried in one parcel. It takes weeks for a boat to pass from Berber to Assouan; and yet, about 100,000 tons of merchandise finds its way annually by that route to Alexandria. The late Khedive commenced to make a railway from Berber to Suakim; but it was abandoned by the Liquidation. It will be made some day soon. One of the many blunders committed by the late Government in Egypt was in not leaving the railway plant at Suakim when they had it there. The line is certain to be constructed, either by the Government or by a private company. There would be no opposition to a railway from the Arabs, if they knew that it was intended only for trade purposes. (Hear, hear.) The Hadendowas, the tribe through whose country it would pass, have keen trade instincts, and they know it would bring them cheaper goods and grain, and get them better prices for their skins and oil and ivory. But, even if they were at first unfriendly, the road could still be made, as the Western and Pacific Railways have been, through countries of fierce and daring warriors, possessed of what the Arabs have not—arms of precision. There were, before the Mahdi's victories, telegraphic and postal services all the way to El Obeid, and a network of forts up to and beyond Gondokora. These have been destroyed, and it will be years before they are restored, and till the baleful effects of war are erased. (Hear, hear.) But the gradual establishment of a regular Government, and the opening of easier and more rapid means of communication to profitable markets, will gradually stimulate trade, and, in time, it is to be hoped, obliterate the bitter recollections of the war. (Hear, hear.) England may abandon the Soudan, but Egypt cannot. When resigning his Governorship, General Gordon told the Khedive that, although Lower Egypt was the head and chest of his kingdom, the Soudan was the belly. And his remark is true. (Hear, hear.) While the French are active in the North, the Germans are busying themselves in the West and East of Africa. Whoever else doubts the wisdom of a nation possessing colonies, Prince Bismarck does not. He is running round the world in search of islands and inlets to continents. Unless he belies his reputation, we will have trouble with him about the Zambesi as well as about the Cameroons. The Italians covet Tripoli, and the Spaniards Morocco; while the Portuguese are re-asserting claims which they have long allowed to lie in abeyance on the Congo and the Zambesi. One of the most interesting colonial experiments in Africa is that originated by Mr. Stanley, and espoused so warmly by the King of the Belgians. (Cheers.) It is a private association, with civilizing, but neither aggressive nor mercenary, objects. It seeks to promote unrestricted intercourse between whites and blacks, and unqualified free trade. It has already established five stations upon 278 miles of river and coast line. There is a regular means of communication between these stations ; and the trade already done by them is worth three millions a-year. Mr. Stanley calculates that when the Congo is fairly opened out, and the projects of the association are completely developed, there will be a trade with it of £50,000,000 a-year. (Hear, hear.) The amount is astounding, if not romantic ; but the calculation seems warranted by what has already been achieved. He believes there will, in a few years, be 150 steamers and 240 sailing vessels plying between the Congo and Europe. (Cheers.) In this trade, Englishmen are especially interested. Our old customers are leaving us. Some are getting supplied elsewhere, and others are turning manufacturers themselves. In India, for example, they are learning to make their own cottons very fast. Last year, India exported £16,000,000 worth of her own manufactures. She still is our best customer, but if her factories and coal mines develop, and English capital is invested in them, her demand for our soft goods will certainly not increase. Our cotton exports are nearly stationary. If the trade is to be sustained and developed, we must find other outlets for it. (Hear, hear.) When Lord Palmerston forced the opening of some of the China ports, the Lancashire manufacturers threw up their hats, and exclaimed, "Let every one of the 300 millions of Chinamen buy a cotton night-cap and our machines will be in full work." (Laughter.) I do not know whether all the Chinese did this or not ; but Mr. Stanley, with more justification, calculates that if all the millions of inhabitants living in the Congo basin, who are now naked, were to supply themselves with loin cloths—(loud laughter)—at the moderate price of 2d. per yard, it would create for the Lancashire people a trade amounting to £26,000,000 a-year. (Cheers.) This would be over one-third of our entire exports. But the natives want other things besides cotton. They will barter their tropical products for all kinds of cutlery and hardware, as well as clothing. (Hear, hear.) Such intercourse will banish the curse of Africa—the slave trade. (Cheers.) It is calculated that about one million negroes, in a year, are driven into slavery from the district lying between the Red and Arabian Seas and the Atlantic. Dr. Livingstone calculated that not more than one slave in five arrived at his destination, and, on some routes, not more than one in nine. ("Shame.") The others died on the road, from hardship and ill-treatment. This iniquitous and inhuman system cannot live alongside of British commerce. (Hear.) The efforts of all the explorers and trading organizations, from whichever side they start, converge on the territory known by the general name of the Soudan, which has a population roughly and variously estimated at from 80 to 180 million people. It is for contact with this vast region, where no good influence is superfluous, and where no co-operation should be disdained, that the natives of Europe are competing. They seek to serve a double purpose—to benefit themselves by business, and benefit the people who have hitherto been outside civilization. (Hear, hear.) The British possessions on the West Coast of Africa are amongst the oldest we own. We have held Gambia for 250, the Gold Coast for 220, and Sierra Leone for over 100 years. In 1860, we got Lagos, and last year we assumed the protectorate of the basin of the Niger. The climate is not favourable for Europeans. The old nick-name of Sierra Leone was the "white man's grave." But there is more prejudice than truth in the popular opinion as to its unhealthiness. The question of climate is one of carefulness and willingness to adapt yourself to circumstances. Englishmen once died off rapidly in tropical districts, because they ate, drank, and clothed themselves, in much the same way as they did at home. But wiser practices are now followed; and even along the low-lying coast of the Gulf of Guinea, our countrymen can and do live for years in excellent health. Our Settlements there would be more correctly described as trading stations than colonies. They are planted at the entrance, or along the banks, of rivers. We have treaties with the neighbouring chiefs, with whom our merchants exchange British manufactures for native produce. About £1,000,000 worth of British goods are sent to these Settlements yearly, and their cost to the British Exchequer for government is about £50,000 a-year. The North African Company, which is doing for English trade on the Niger much the same work that the East India Company did in India, and the Hudson Bay Company did in Canada, has stations nearly 500 miles inland. The Company's steamers ply regularly on the vast waterway with which the name of Mungo Park is so indissolubly associated. The land is rich and well cultivated. There are towns in the river valley with populations of from 10,000 to 60,000 people. Many of the native traders are wealthy; some possessing in coin and goods from £50,000 to £60,000. They have primitive but not ineffective methods of manufacture and agriculture, and they live in a class of dwellings very superior to those usually occupied by savages. They are favourably disposed to intercourse with the English, and, when treated as free people, possessing the inherent right to dispose of their own destinies, are willing to co-operate in the development of all measures needful for extending British influence into the interior. (Cheers.) The British possessions in South Africa, unlike those in the west, are veritable colonies. The climate is salubrious and invigorating. The physical features are very diversified. In some parts, Nature has distributed her gifts in profusion, and the landscape is as fair and picturesque as a realm in fairyland. In others, it is weird and desert-like. Corn and fruit are the chief objects of cultivation in the neighbourhood of the Cape, while further north there is a magnificent grazing ground. There are rich deposits of copper, coal, and diamonds. Lead, gold, and silver, too, are found to an unknown extent. The Cape colonies are amongst the most thriving and valuable we have. Our trade with them is large, and it is steadily and rapidly developing. In 1862, we sent them goods to the value of £1,900,000 ; in 1872, we exported them £3,700,000 ; and in 1882, £7,500,000. In twenty years, our Cape exports, therefore, have really quadrupled. (Hear, hear.) Our exports to Australia and to India, in the same time, have doubled, and to Canada they have increased three-fold. (Hear, hear.) With no colony or foreign country, have they risen so rapidly as to South Africa. We import goods nearly to the same amount as we export them—our total trade amounting to £14,360,000. This gives full employment for five lines of steamers, besides a number of sailing ships. Directly and indirectly, this tonnage employs a capital of £100,000,000 sterling. Our South African trade is capable of almost indefinite extension. (Hear, hear.) There is a large exportation of wool, and there will be, in time, an equally large exportation of cereals. But although profitable, the South African have been troublesome colonies. We have had two opponents to deal with—the Boers and the Kaffirs. They are both, like ourselves, aliens, although they each have been longer in the land than we have been. The Boers are descendants of the Dutchmen who landed at the Cape about 230 years ago. The Kaffirs are descendants of the warlike negroes, who found their way to the south, from the Equatorial regions, about the same time as the Dutch did from Europe. Between the two, the Aborigines have been all but exterminated. During the French war, in 1795, The Cape was taken by the English. It was afterwards restored to Holland, but finally ceded to this country at the Congress of Vienna, in 1814. The Boers never took kindly to British rule. They held upwards of 35,000 slaves, and a large number of Hottentots in a state of quasi-slavery. In 1835, in order to avoid compliance with the Slave Emancipation Act, and the restraints of British law, the Boers abandoned the Cape, and withdrew beyond its borders. Some settled in Natal, some on the Orange River, and some, subsequently, in the Transvaal. Wherever the Boers went, troubles followed like a shadow. Their career was marked by the massacre and spoliation of the native tribes, the slaughter of men and women alike, and the enslavement of children, their commanders being wanting in none of those ruthless features which characterized the slave-hunts of the Arab traders in the Soudan. Our differences with them were compromised in 1852. We annexed Natal, but we recognized the independence of the Orange River and the Transvaal Settlements. The Boers agreed to sundry conditions, the chief being the abolition of slavery. The Orange Free State has kept the treaty made at the Sand River; and our relations with it, under the enlightened rule of President Brand, have been agreeable and mutually advantageous. (Cheers.) The Transvaal Republic has not, and its breach of bargain has involved its citizens, and natives, and ourselves in troubles the end of which cannot be foreseen. The territory of the Republic is about half the size of France, and it contains a white population of 40,000—not many more than there are in Elswick Ward. The natives number about 800,000. Although the Boers bound themselves to abandon slavery, they did so only nominally. They call their slaves black ivory—(laughter)—and their forced labour apprenticeship. By the fundamental law of the Republic, no native can purchase or hold land in his own name. There is no marriage law for the blacks, and equality of persons of colour is not allowed either in Church or State. The natives can work in, but are not allowed to reside in, towns. They are compelled to herd in what are called locations, where not only the virtues, but the decencies, of civilization are over-ridden. To these locations they are called by a curfew-bell, and natives found outside their boundaries after nine at night are imprisoned. For these encampments they are required to pay a heavy hut-tax. Such laws and treatment do not commend Boers' rule to the natives within the boundaries of the Republic; while the filibustering organized by Transvaal desperadoes, if not with the sanction, at least without the disapproval, of the Government, brought them into open conflict with the neighbouring tribes. Gangs of men, armed with deadly weapons, organize themselves in buccaneering expeditions, make raids on the native kraals, burn their huts, shoot their adults, carry away captive the young people, seize the cattle, grain, and other stores of the unsuspecting and unoffending villagers, and then march home, singing songs of triumph, in which are blasphemous ascriptions of praise to God for success in their diabolical enterprises. Occasionally, some of the raiders stay on the sites of the demolished kraals, and occupy the farms of the murdered natives. Such proceedings provoke reprisals. It would not be reasonable to suppose that a million of brave blacks would submit, without resistance, to such aggression and violence. The enraged tribes made a formidable attack on the Boers in 1875 and 1876, and beat them. The commerce of the Republic was well nigh destroyed; the Government was bankrupt; and the Boers, discontented and divided, threatened with internal discord and external attacks, appealed to the British Government for aid. It was given, and the territory was taken over in 1877. For three years, it was held and administered by the British. During those three years, the military despotism of Cetewayo, and the power of formidable chiefs like

Seco-cœni* was broken. The Boers, freed by the action of this country from the fear of attack, then demanded to be relieved from British control. We refused the request, and the late Government went to war to keep the country; but, after our defeat at Majuba Hill, terms of peace were settled, by which self-government was restored to the Transvaal, so far as regards internal affairs; the control and management of its external affairs being reserved to the Queen as suzerain. The terms of this Convention have been violated repeatedly by the Boers. Wanton and brutal attacks have been made on the native chiefs who aided us. With a view of seeing justice done to our native allies, the late Government sent Sir Charles Warren with a powerful force to Bechuanaland. (Cheers.) He has restored peace, asserted the rights of the natives, vindicated the claims of justice, and done much to prevent unjust aggression and robbery hereafter. (Hear, hear.) Alarmed at our Commissioner's decision and promptitude, the Boers abandoned their buccaneering *protegés*, and readily accepted the arrangement we required. We will see whether they will keep it. The Boers profess to be republican. Yet, they have not the faintest idea of liberty. (Hear, hear.) Intellectually, they are barren, and they are destitute of all tenderness and enthusiasm. They are uncultured and unprogressive. They are domestic but not gregarious. A Boer's idea is to have a farm so large that he will need to get on a tower, and use a telescope, to see his neighbour's house. (Laughter.) He is stubborn and very pious. But he does not display much of the spirit of Christ in any of his dealings, especially with those dependent on him. Sir Charles Warren, at the instance of the late Government, assumed the protectorate of the territory known as Bechuanaland. It is larger than Spain. This was done with

* Pronounced "Sickakuni."

the sanction of all, and in some instances at the request, of the native chiefs. Heretofore, the freebooters have first harried, then preyed upon, and then demoralized, the natives. (Hear, hear.) We have taken measures which, if carried out, will prevent such proceedings. There will be room for European settlers, and they will be welcomed, but they will not be allowed to despoil the natives. The country abounds in minerals, gold being especially abundant. The Boers say it is the best land in Africa ; and, to vindicate their opinion, they named one of their robber republics, Goshen, the land of fertility and flesh-pots. (Laughter.) Grass, and patches of arable land, are interspersed with belts of well-grown timber. Water is abundant, and there are ample facilities for irrigation. It is situated on the great backbone of Africa, and is, for the most part, a plateau of from 4,000 to 6,000 feet above the sea level, and extremely healthy for Europeans. Khama, the Kaffir King, and his chiefs, who have throughout their negotiations with Sir Charles Warren, shown a shrewdness and discretion that would do credit to European negotiators, and who trust England, besought our Commissioner to extend our protectorate to the Zambesi, which Khama says is the boundary of his dominions. He has set apart a piece of country for himself and people, and has placed the rest of the land at the disposal of English emigrants. The only condition that he stipulates for—and it ought to entitle him to be made a vice-president of the United Kingdom Alliance—(laughter)—is a law prohibiting the importation of strong drink into his country. (Cheers.) This last addition to our Colonial Empire is the largest made for many years. It is of exceptional interest, and likely to be of exceptional value. It will keep open the great trade route to the centre of Africa ; and, if the reports as to its riches are to be trusted, it may turn out a second California or Victoria. (Cheers.) The filibusters, driven from Bechuanaland, are now commencing their depredations in Zululand. They foment native disputes; they help one section against another; and end by dispossessing both sides, and taking the lands themselves. We have assumed the protectorate of St. Lucia Bay and the Zulu coast; and it requires not much foresight to see that we shall be driven to extend it to the entire country. The Transvaal is made a base for these operations. Although the Boer Government may not support them, they do not, or they cannot, stop them. While the Orange State is free of debt, and peaceful and prosperous, the Transvaal, for the second time, is insolvent, and almost as disturbed as before the annexation in 1877. This is to be regretted, as the country has great natural resources. Coal and gold, and silver and iron, have all been found, and require only settled Government to enable them to be worked. The Eastern boundary of the Republic is not more than fifty miles from Delagoa Bay, one of the finest harbours in the world, and the natural depôt for all the trade of Central-Eastern Africa. A railway between Pretoria and Delagoa Bay has been projected, and concessions securing a monopoly of traffic for ninety-nine years have been obtained. The primary, and by far the most pressing, question in South Africa, is how to deal with the natives. There will be a good deal of pushing and shouldering between the Dutch and ourselves; but, in the end, each party will fall into his proper place. But with the natives, the problem is different and more difficult. (Hear, hear.) There are, in round numbers, about 2,000,000 natives in our colonies. How many more we shall be brought into immediate relation with, in consequence of the responsibilities we have assumed in Bechuanaland, I do not know; but it is a moderate calculation to put them at a million. The tribes, both within and beyond our boundary, do not melt away as the American Indians do, before the presence of white men, nor do they show signs of decadence like the Maoris. The primitive races, it is true, are about extinct; but the Kaffirs, who are divisible into various branches, are extremely prolific. In half-a-century, they will number from eight to ten millions at least. How are we to make them members of a civilized community? That is the problem we have to solve. The Zulus have much of the ferocity of savages; but they have many faculties which, under kind and considerate management, might become virtues. The Fingoes, the Galekoes, and Basutos are gradually acclimatising themselves to civilized ways. So, too, are the Bechuanas—Dr. Livingstone's favourites. But the process of changing the character of ignorant and semi-savage races is but slow and difficult. The most effective factors in the work of civilization have been individual ownership in land, independent personal liberty, and the acceptance of Christianity as a rule of life. (Loud cheers.) Although our progress has not been rapid, it has been decidedly encouraging. We must persevere. What may ultimately be evolved out of the ferment of adverse races and nationalities, it would be rash to predict; but, if the sovereign rule of England be withdrawn, there will be a scramble, in which the strongest, but not the best or wisest, will become masters. (Hear, hear.) If we neglect the neighbourly duties and responsibilities incumbent on a rich, enlightened, and powerful nation towards poor, barbarous border tribes; if we allow peoples capable of permanent advancement and civilization to grow in numbers, while they fester in barbarism, we lay the foundation for inevitable wars. If we shut our eyes, and turn our backs on their wants and defects; leave them to themselves; endeavour to see and know as little of them, and let them know and see as little of us as possible, we need not be surprised to find that they grow aggressive and dangerous. (Cheers.) The late Government incurred a great, but honourable responsibility, when they took over the civil and military administration of Bechuanaland. (Hear, hear.) The responsibility we have accepted must be fulfilled. It would be mean and humiliating to evade our duties; and, unless we are prepared to abandon the colonies altogether, it would be ruinous. (Cheers.) We cannot be indifferent to what is going on around us. Sir Charles Warren's expedition has cost more than a million pounds. If we had acted promptly, it would not have cost £50,000. (Cheers.) We should have a Minister charged with the direction of native affairs, empowered to deal with frontier difficulties as they arise, and before they work themselves into a knot that can only be cut by the sword. (Cheers.) We might, in this way, save such costly enterprises as we have too often had in South Africa. What is going on in Africa to-day is the counterpart of what went on in North America two centuries ago, and it will bring forth similar results. (Hear, hear.) Our overflowing vitality will not allow a vast country, rich in beautiful scenery and natural resources, with a salubrious climate and fertile soil, with great navigable rivers and inland lakes, to be left in the control of tawny lions, long-eared elephants, and negro fetish worshippers. (Loud laughter and cheers.) The African continent will, in time, be occupied by a mighty nation of English descent, and covered with populous cities, flourishing farms, with railways, and telegraphs, and all the other devices of civilization. The burthen of the argument that runs through this, as through all my other addresses, is that there is a promise of almost illimitable usefulness and grandeur lying before our colonists, and ourselves in unison with them—(cheers);—and that their possession has imposed upon us duties which we cannot neglect or ignore without suffering the penalties which would form the fitting punishment of selfishness and indifference. No empire ever treated its dependencies with the same consideration and liberty as England does hers. (Cheers.) We have granted absolute self-goverment to every colony in which the elements of self-government exist. We help them much, and control them very little. If we are true to the position and privileges we possess, we have before us the glorious destiny of working from an unapproachable vantage-ground for the regeneration of human kind in every quarter of the globe, and of indefinitely extending the dominion of freedom and the boundaries of civilization. (Loud and prolonged cheering, the audience rising and vociferating enthusiastically.)

## SECOND "HECKLING" MEETING.

**HELD IN THE JUBILEE SCHOOLS, TUESDAY, NOVEMBER 24, 1885.**

CHAIRMAN:—MR. ELIJAH COPLAND.

Mr. COWEN, on rising, was received with demonstrative cheering, in the course of which a working man in the front shouted out, amid great laughter, "Wor idol, wor pet, and wor pride," whereupon the cheering was again and again renewed. After its subsidence, Mr. Cowen said: Mr. Chairman, ladies, and gentlemen,—I have been bewildered by the questions I have got. They have come upon me thick and fast, or rather thicker and faster. (Laughter.) I have endeavoured to sort them and group them, but I have found it all but impossible to do so satisfactorily. The mere reading of the questions, without answering them, would take more than four hours; to answer them would take four times four. (Laughter.) The number would go to show that there is a large amount of political activity and intellectual inquisitiveness amongst the electors of Newcastle—both very desirable attributes, although they may be pushed too far. (Hear, hear, cheers, and laughter.) Before proceeding to reply to the questions *serialim*, I have one observation to make. My object, during this election, has been to lift politics as much as possible out of the rut of parochialism and personalities. (Cheers.) I have tried to discuss great national questions in a national, and, if I may be permitted to use the term, in a philosophic sense. (Hear, hear.) The common charge against democracy is that it is mean, petty, and mercenary. It is my ambition and desire to rebut this accusation, and to vindicate the intelligence and public spirit of my fellow-citizens. (Hear, hear.) As far as the contest has enabled me to come to a conclusion, I think this end has been partially gained. Several representative bodies have sent me inquiries. Some of these I have answered affirmatively, and some in a negative sense; and it is right to say that, on the whole, they have received my replies in a liberal and considerate spirit. (Hear, hear.) But there are one or two sections, or representatives of sections, who have displayed another spirit, and not only given audible expression to their discontent, but menaced me with consequences. I wish to tell these gentlemen that no attempt to threaten me with loss of support will induce me to alter an opinion deliberately formed. (Loud cheers.) It is impossible for any man to be master of the multifarious details of every branch of legislation and expenditure. I certainly do not profess to have a larger amount of information on these subjects than an average intelligent member of Parliament. The opinions I have given on some questions may require revision when I get more knowledge. I am open to receive information, and to revise my views on any question if I see cause for it. But I will not be intimidated. (Cheers.)

I am asked if a representative electoral body is not much better than a self-elected meeting in an intriguing lawyer's office. (Laughter.) I quite admit that a representative body is more entitled to respect than a self-appointed one. But is the Caucus representative? (Voices: "No," "Down with them," and cheers and laughter.) On that the whole question hinges. I deny that it is. (Hear, hear.) There is no man who, having any respect for fairness or intelligence, will contend that it is. The whole business of the meetings, which are supposed to represent all the electors, is planned by the committee or the officials, or, if you chose to call them so, a clique. (Hear, hear.) These meetings often elect more members than there are present. (Laughter.) Very often one hundred men have been chosen by fifty. The whole arrangements are so manipulated that the entire authority rests with half-a-dozen persons. (Hear, hear.) There was a meeting held recently in one of the Newcastle wards, at which a dozen persons elected about three dozen. At the Newcastle branch of the Tyneside Caucus only eleven gentlemen attended. Of these, only seven voted, and four did not vote all, so that seven men sent twenty-three representatives to the central meeting. (Laughter.) Yet, that is what is called a representative body. Now, I deny that the product of this arrangement is entitled to any more respect than the product of a meeting in a party lawyer's office. (Hear, hear.) For many years, the Liberal party adjusted their business in the office of the late Mr. R. P. Philipson. Before that, they did so in Mr. Charnley's back-shop. Now, the men who met at these places were no more or less representative than the men who now meet in the Caucus committee-rooms. I don't deny the right of any body to meet and do what it pleases; but I *do* deny their right to meet and speak in the name of the people of Newcastle. The people of Newcastle have no more to do with them than they have to do with the six Tooley Street tailors. (Cheers and laughter.)

"Did not we lend the Transvaal some money, and how much have they repaid?"

We lent them £400,000. A portion has been repaid, but I believe £380,000 is still due. (Cheers.)

A gentleman who was at the meeting last night at Byker Board School, reminds me that I made no reference to the Slaghter Nek incident, and he wishes to infer that that was a grievance against the English. I know that occurrence rankles in the Boer's mind. It was recalled in the Boer Proclamation of 1881; but, although the occurrence was attended with regretable severity, the English were in the right. They were defending the natives against the Boers. The affair took place so long ago as 1815. A Boer had brutally ill-treated a Hottentot servant, and he was summoned to appear before the Circuit Court to answer for his misdeeds. He refused to do so, and a troop of military was sent to arrest him. The Boer fired upon the English soldiers, and they, in return, fired upon him and killed him. The Boers took up the cause of their killed neighbour, and rose in arms against the English. A struggle took place, and the Boers were defeated and dispersed. The leaders were captured, tried, found guilty, and fifty of them were hung. The gallows broke down when they were half-hanged, but it was afterwards repaired, and they were all re-hung. The circumstances of their deaths were no doubt sad, but the Boers were to blame. They would have killed the English soldiers if the English had not been the victors. And, originally, the Boers had ill-treated the Hottentot. This is the Slaghter Nek incident, to which my correspondent calls attention. (Cheers.)

"Are you in favour of settling national quarrels by arbitration?"

When it can be done. (Hear, hear.) But that is not always, nor indeed often, possible. Force is, unfortunately, stronger than justice. When the world grows wiser, we shall have nations acknowledging the reasonableness of peaceably settling their quarrels as individuals now do, by a high judicial tribunal. (Hear, hear.) Over three thousand years ago, Amphictyon formed a council of virtuous men, at Thermopylæ, for the management of the affairs of Greece. But wise and humane though their objects were, whenever they actively interfered in public affairs, they were more powerful for evil than for good. They were the cause of wars, which were carried on with unparalleled exasperation for over twenty years. Last century, Abbé of St. Pierre and Mably, the publicists, projected an International Council. This was the forerunner of our Peace Society. Their projects were, like those of the Amphictyons—the substitution of the sovereignty of reason for the sovereignty of force. (Hear, hear.) But the world won't be ruled by reason. (Laughter.) Three years after the nations of Europe held a peace re-union in London, we had the Crimean War. Perhaps, the world may become wiser in time; and when it does we shall no longer suffer its happiness to be weighed in that scale in which the Brennuses of all countries, and the insolent of all ages. have thrown the weight of their swords. (Loud cheers.)

"Will you aid the civil servants of the Custóms in obtaining compensation for the loss they have sustained by the Treasury depriving them of the Bill of Entry?"

This is a hard case, but one the public knows nothing of. Certain officers in the Customs have, by great care and labour over a number of years, created a publishing business for collecting statistics, and supplying them to merchants, Chambers of Commerce, and private firms, with information about exports and imports. The officials have thus created an equitable copyright in their publication. The Treasury have forcibly taken it away from them, and are now making a profit of £10,000 a-year by the business established by others, and have refused to give the projectors and owners compensation. We have recently passed an Act for giving a tenant compensation for unexhausted improvements if he is ejected from his farm; but the men who have promoted this legislation evict, without consideration, the civil servants of the country from the possession of property which they have by their labour called into being, and which if it had been possessed by a private firm, would not have been sold for less than £100,000. The Customs officials are powerless, for if they resist their employers they will lose their places. But the injustice is none the less manifest. (Cheers.)

"Will you aid the Civil Service writers in securing an improvement in their position?"

Yes. The grievances of the writers in the public departments are very galling and very tangible. There are fourteen hundred of them. They receive wages at the rate of tenpence an hour, or thirty shillings a-week. Their wages are inadequate for the work done, which is difficult and laborious. They are required to manipulate, and deal with, accounts covering hundreds of thousands of pounds of revenue in the course of the year; and there is no superannuation-allowance granted, as in other Government offices. The writers want improved pay, and the chance of promotion for all. Their demands have been admitted as reasonable by a special committee of the House of Commons, presided over by Sir Arthur Otway, and by a Royal Commission, presided over by Sir Lyon Playfair, but the Treasury refused to comply with them—very unjustly, I think. (Cheers.)

Some one inquires whether I will oppose the granting of Royal dowries.

I have always done so. (Cheers.) But there are no more now to grant. All the Queen's children are married and settled; and the request that the members who opposed the grants made, and made in vain, has been conceded. A committee is to be appointed to inquire into the future fiscal relations of Parliament to the Royal Family. That inquiry may lead to fixing the amount, and readjusting the methods by which such payments are to be made in future. (Cheers.)

I am asked if the Panama Canal won't injure the Suez Canal, and alter our estimate of the value of Egypt to India?

This is a speculative question. It would be merely guessing to say how far the Panama route to India may affect the Suez Canal. It is probable that it may affect it greatly. (Hear, hear.) The Panama Canal is being rapidly made, and, like that of Suez, is being made with French money, and at French risk. England has taken no part in the project, although it may seriously influence her commerce and her politics. About one-half of the works has been completed, and the company calculate that they will get a tonnage of six millions to begin with. This is not far short of the tonnage of the Suez Canal now; and it is thrice what it was when the canal was first opened. (Hear, hear.) The construction of this American Bosphorus has been more difficult; and it may be a more important enterprise than its Egyptian forerunner. (Hear, hear.)

"Are all the lives lost at sea lost by ships being wrecked?"

No. The average number of men lost at sea is about 3,000 a-year, but they are not all lost through wrecks. A return was recently issued by the Board of Trade, showing that in one year—I think 1881—over 1,100 British sailors lost their lives by drowning otherwise than by wreck, and that nearly 300 were killed by accidents, and not by drowning.

"Are there many Acts, like the Employers' Liability Act, of a temporary character?"

There are fifty. The duration of some temporary laws is certain, and some uncertain. The Irish Coercion Act was passed for three years; the Irish Arms Act for four. The first terminated this year; the second will terminate next. The Bank Acts, the Election Act, the Mutiny Acts, and others are renewed year by year.

"Was there ever an instance, in modern times, of such popularity as that achieved by Mr. Gladstone?"

(Loud laughter.) It is not easy to institute a comparison,

but I think Mr. Pitt was longer and more widely popular. Mr. Pitt died when he was 47, and he had been Premier for nineteen years. His influence with the King was as great as that of Villiers had been. His dominion over Parliament was more absolute than Walpole's, and his favour with the populace as high as Wilkes's. Lord Brougham, too, sat high in the people's hearts. He was, for a season, the popular idol. After his election for Yorkshire, he was not only the representative of that county, but really of all England. No man of his time possessed the power he then wielded. These are cases that occur to my mind at the moment. There may be others. For the last six years, Mr. Gladstone's popularity has been phenomenal. (Hear, hear.) Under any other leadership, the late Government would have broken down long before it did. (Hear, hear.) Mr. Gladstone's overreaching personality alone sustained it through its accumulated misfortunes and mismanagement. (Hear, hear, and laughter.) But, like many others, Mr. Gladstone has had his reverses, and none more undeserving than that which he experienced in 1874. (Hear, hear.) There are few things more fickle than popular applause. (Hear, hear.) Shakespeare never wrote a truer line than when he made Othello say that "reputation is oft got without merit, and lost without deserving." (Cheers.)

"What was the cost of your two elections in 1874?"

(Laughter.) I don't remember. Indeed, I never knew. The first election was very expensive, but as Parliament was dissolved before I took my seat, no return was published, and I did not examine the accounts. (Laughter.) The second election, in 1874, cost over £2,000, which has been the average expenditure of the contests in which I have been concerned since 1865. If the money I have paid for election expenses for myself and others were capitalized, I could live handsomely upon the interest. (Laughter and cheers.)

"Are trades unions not inconsistent with the principles of political economy?"

Strictly speaking, they are. The pivot on which the doctrines of political economy turn is freedom of contract, liberty to buy in the cheapest market and sell in the dearest, power for the employer and employed to make their bargains without the interference of any middle-man. Trades unions infringe this theory. They try to regulate wages. Employers and workmen alike delegate their rights to separate or joint combinations, who alone can speak and act in their names. In doing this, they unduly violate the principles of political economy as laid down by the leading professors of that creed. (Hear, hear.) But the principles of political economy are being ignored or overridden in all directions, and in no way more flagrantly than by their former friends. In the case of trades unions, the violation has been an advantage. As the unions are at present managed, they often prevent strikes, and still more often mitigate their severity. (Cheers.)

"Why not tax tea?"

Why? Because it has now become a necessary of life, and all taxes on such articles are doubly injurious—injurious to the trade and to the public. (Hear, hear.) It is only between 200 and 250 years since it was first drunk in this country. There are now imported into London alone 220 million pounds' weight. In India, some 300,000 acres of land are under tea cultivation. To trammel such a trade, by the imposing of an additional duty, would be an especial injury to India, and a disadvantage to the poor people of this country, who are universal consumers of tea. (Loud cheers.)

I am asked to explain how money is voted.

For the State service, I presume, it is meant. It is somewhat difficult to do so satisfactorily. But briefly stated, the process is this. Early in the session, the Chancellor of the Exchequer submits an estimate for the sum required for the army, navy, and civil-service, and the means by which he proposes to raise it. The money required is voted or refused in Committee of Ways and Means. If granted, the manner in which it is to be applied is discussed, item by item, in committee of supply. In these committees, members can speak as often as they choose, and ask as many questions as they like as to the application of each vote, provided their speeches and their questions are relevant. There are, in all, about two hundred votes granted in the year, and they cover the whole expenditure of the nation. The resolutions in Committee of Ways and Means are embodied in a bill called the Budget Bill; and the resolutions passed in Committee of Supply are embodied in what is called the Appropriation Bill. That is, the votes are appropriated for the use of her Majesty in the different departments. The House of Lords may reject, but they cannot alter, a Money Bill. All propositions for taxing the people must be addressed to the representatives by Ministers of the Crown; and before any money is given, the Commons have, or rather had—for by the new rules they have been curtailed—(laughter)—the privilege of presenting grievances for redress. But I regret to add that, while the House of Commons has thus nominally absolute control over the national purse, its members display little vigilance in scrutinising the accounts. The money is voted on strictly party lines. I have never seen a single estimate reduced since I have been in Parliament. (Cheers.)

"Did you oppose the making of parks on the Moor?"

No. I did, however, prefer another park scheme to the one adopted. There were two projects before the Council—one to make two ornamental parks of 35 acres each, and another to make the whole Moor a park. Mr. John Hancock—(hear, hear)—prepared plans for the latter scheme, which contemplated planting clumps of trees and making walks and roads, and otherwise embellishing the whole 1,200 acres. This was to be done gradually—so much every year, until the Moor became like the Phœnix Park in Dublin or the Bois de Boulogne in Paris. (Hear, hear.) But the planting was not agreed to. Another scheme was projected by my friend, Mr. Hamond, and it has been a great and gratifying success; and Mr. Hamond is entitled to all honour for it. But some day I suspect Mr. Hancock's scheme, which I supported, will be carried out. It would benefit the herbage as well as beautify the expanse. I was always in favour of having parks, and, when they could not be got, having open spaces and playgrounds in populous districts. Along with others, I helped to secure Elswick Park for that purpose. (Cheers.) Munificently aided by Sir William Armstrong—(cheers)—the people of Newcastle, during the last dozen years, have done much to ornament this city. They will be amply repaid in the improved health and manners of the population. (Loud cheers.)

"How do you explain opposing the Cattle Plague Bill in 1878, and supporting it in 1884?"

Nonsense! The man who asks the question knows nothing about the subject. There was an attempt made in 1878 to pass a Bill, which would have operated generally to restrain the importation of cattle. The clauses in the Bill that were likely to have that effect, I, along with others, opposed, and they were altered. (Hear, hear.) The Act has worked fairly well, but it did not, as it was expected it would do, give the Privy Council authority to stop the importation of live cattle from countries in which disease was prevalent. Cattle afflicted with foot-and-mouth disease were sent from France to Deptford. From that place the infection was carried to the London dairies, and thence disseminated throughout the country. There are records of over

14,000 outbreaks of disease all traceable to that source. The direct and indirect loss caused by these outbreaks to the farmers by loss of stock, and to the general public by the increased price of meat, is estimated at millions. The Act of last year was designed to give the Privy Council power to prohibit the importation of all cattle from infected countries. It was to keep out disease, not to keep out meat, and it has effected its object. (Cheers.) Knowing the increased power and watchfulness of the Privy Council, the authorities in exporting countries have tightened their regulations, and become much more careful. There have been only two or three cases of foot-and-mouth disease this year. The country has not, for years, been freer from disease. There has, at the same time, been an increase of over six per cent. in the weight of dead meat imported; while prices, instead of having risen, have fallen. (Cheers.) We have, therefore, got quit of the disease, and with that, increased home-consumption, larger imports, and, as a consequence, lower prices. Every effort should be made to foster the breeding and rearing of English cattle; and that cannot be done if farmers are to have their herds decimated by the importation of disease. (Hear, hear.) The meat got from abroad is an important adjunct to our food-supplies, and every legitimate encouragement should be given to the trade. But it is not generally known that, out of every hundred pounds of flesh-meat consumed, only seven pounds is imported. (Cheers.)

"Have we not to pay to Russia £53,000 a-year until 1916, and how much have we already paid them?"

This inqniry refers to the Russo-Dutch Loan. England guaranteed in 1815 to pay to Holland, or rather to the agents of Russia in Holland, a debt that Holland then owed. There was some equivalent supposed to have been rendered by Russia to the allies in the war with Napoleon for this payment. It was, however, of a very shadowy kind. But why England had to pay is a question that has many times been asked, and never yet satisfactorily answered. This, however, is certain—that the conditions which both Russia and Holland agreed to when the loan was granted have not been kept, although England's part of the bond has been fulfilled. It has often been argued that, as the terms of the treaty under which the loan was got have been violated, England should refuse to pay the money. The late Mr. Joseph Hume, and the late Lord Dudley Stuart, proposed that this should be done, but it was not done. We have paid about six millions; and we shall have to pay about two millions more before our liability is discharged. It is a species of black-mail. We are under no moral, whatever legal obligations we are under to pay it. (Cheers.)

"Is there any way by which Germany can be compelled to fulfil her Treaty engagements to the people of North Schleswig?"

I pressed upon the Government of Lord Beaconsfield the desirability of raising the question at the Congress of Berlin in 1878. But Denmark is weak, and no one cares to espouse her cause. Lord Palmerston once said there were only two men in Europe who knew all the intricacies in the Schleswig-Holstein question—himself and another, and the other man was then dead. (Laughter.) The ignorance of, and the interest in, that subject are denser now than they were thirty years ago, when the remark was made. But the material facts are, that the Treaty of Prague provided that the people of North Schleswig were to have the liberty of saying whether they would be under Danish or German rule. The permission to give this decision was never granted, and the Danes in North Schleswig have been forcibly incorporated with Germany. This, I suppose, is but preliminary to the incorporation of Jutland, and the Germanization of the Baltic—a catastrophe which every friend of liberty will lament, but which I fear no nation will have the courage to contest. (Cheers.) We ought to be, but I fear we are not, specially interested in Schleswig, for it was the cradle of our race. Angelu, a little district on the Baltic coast of that State, was the original home of the people who have spread themselves over every land, and carried civilization to the remotest corners of the earth. I own my heart warms to the old Danish calf-yard; and if we had been something more than idly indignant, and had fought for the Danes in 1864—(hear, hear),—the course of events in Europe would have been very different from what it has been this last generation. (Cheers.)

"What was the cost of the abortive Berber Railway?"

I cannot tell the exact sum that was spent. It was mixed up with the general military charges in Egypt, and no details of it were furnished to Parliament; but a return has been recently printed showing the number of ships that took railway plant to Suakim and brought it back again. (Laughter.) According to this return, it would appear that there were forty ships engaged by the Government to take out the plant for the intended railway to Suakim; that the freight of these vessels was £133,677; and that, in addition, there was paid as dues, stowage, and other expenses, £70,000. In all, there was paid, as freight for goods that were never unshipped, but sent back to Chatham, £203,677. (Laughter.)

"Will you help the crofters?"

Yes, cheerfully—(cheers),—but I am not sure that I can do so. The late Government appointed a Commission to inquire into their condition. It took much evidence, and produced an able and comprehensive report, but the Government would not act upon the recommendations of their own Commissioners. The bill introduced by Sir William Harcourt was good enough as far as it went, but it did not go far. It left untouched the very question out of which all the strife had arisen. It satisfied neither the landlords nor the crofters. But as it was an advance, although a slight one, upon the present state of things, I regret it was not passed. The delay, however, may lead to the production of a more drastic measure. (Hear, hear.) I have no sympathy with those who wish to improve the Highlands by exterminating the population, and effacing the traditions and records of centuries. (Hear, hear.) I don't look approvingly upon the extinction in the Celtic mind of his pride of race, attachment to the place of his birth, and of his ancient manners and customs. Rearing game may be a very pleasant and profitable pursuit; but rearing men is both better and higher. (Cheers.) The time may come when the Highland lairds may rue the day when they exchanged a larger rent-roll with their palaces, and all the luxury that wealth can purchase for

So many hill plaids,
  And true hearts that wear them;
So many steel blades,
  And strong hands that bear them.

(Cheers.) By all means, let us have material improvements, but not at the sacrifice of the elements of national strength—hardihood, activity, power of endurance, and love of locality and country. (Cheers.)

"Are you in favour of abolishing imprisonment for debt?"

Yes—for debt, but not for fraud. (Hear, hear.) Insolvency—inability to pay—may arise from misfortune, and to imprison a man for that is to inflict punishment without an offence. But if fraud is committed in contracting a debt—if the property of others obtained by loan is dishonestly risked, it becomes a crime, which should be punishable either by the temporary forfeiture of the right to trade, or by imprisonment. I was associated with the late Mr. Bass in introducing a bill to abolish imprisonment for debt. We did not, however, get much support for it. (Hear, hear.)

"How would it do to increase the tax on dogs—(loud laughter)—and lessen the nuisance of so many of these animals, which are kept by people who cannot afford to feed them?"

It would not do at all. It is an indisputable canon in finance, that when a thing is taxed too high, it offers inducements for evasion, and lessens, rather than raises, the revenue. The tax on dogs has been raised as high as it can judiciously be. But why such an objection to a man keeping a dog? It is a pleasant companion, and the poor have none too many pleasures. (Hear, hear.) I have sympathy with the pitman who, when reproached for always being accompanied by a dog, apologetically answered, "Ye knaa a man luiks se nyaked like when he hessent a dog." (Roars of laughter.)

"Is the London coal-tax to expire next year, and will you help to prevent its re-imposition? What is the amount of the tax?"

The Corporation of the City of London and the Metropolitan Board of Works levy a duty of 3d. per ton on every ton of coal consumed in the metropolitan district—that is over an area of twelve miles from the city. The Act conferring this power expires in 1888. The London authorities want to renew it, so as to enable them to provide security for a new loan for executing a series of street improvements. They asked the late Government if they might calculate on their support if such a bill were submitted to Parliament, but Mr. Childers would not promise it. What the present or the next Government may do, I don't know. The tax is mainly a matter for the people of London. They have to pay 10 per cent. on the price of the coal put free on board in the Tyne, and 7½ per cent. on its price delivered over the ship's side in the Pool. The tax, too, is inequitable, as coals, whose first price is 3s. to 4s., and those which are 10s. per ton pay the same duty. But out of the five millions of people in the metropolitan district who pay this tax, not half-a-million of them know they pay it. If they did so, they would not pay it. We are indirectly concerned in the tax in this district, as an impost that raises the price of coal limits its consumption. If an attempt be made to renew it, I, for one, shall oppose it. (Cheers.) Let the London people, if they want to beautify their streets, do as we do—levy a tax on the owners and occupiers. (Renewed cheers.)

"Why do you call the Chairman of the House of Commons Mr. Speaker, when he never speaks ?"

(Laughter.) There is a reason for most things, and there is for this seeming inconsistency. In former times, the House of Commons had closer and more frequent contact with the Sovereign than it has now. All the members could not address the King, and so they, at the beginning of each Parliament, chose one of their number to preside over the proceedings, and to be their spokesman to the Monarch. The member thus chosen to perform the duties of this office was named the Speaker of the House of Commons. (Hear, hear.)

"What is paid for pensions in this country; and does not every change of Government entail great additions to the pension-list ?"

Not necessarily. And the amount thus affected is insignificant. There is much misconception abroad with respect to the granting of pensions. The facts, put in a few sentences, are these. By an Act passed shortly after the Queen came to the throne, she was empowered to give away £1,200 every year, in small pensions, to poor and disabled men or women who had done the State service in literature, art, or science. This money is dispensed in small allowances of from £50 to £200 a-year. The capitalized value of the sum is about £20,000. It is well spent. No liberal or intelligent man grudges it. (Hear, hear.) Although given nominally by the Queen, the pensions are really given by the Prime Minister for the time-being. There is a small number of permanent pensions paid for Court, military, or other services. They are the remnants of a corrupt time; and the interest of the recipients is gradually being bought out. It is in this list that the heirs of the Duke of Schomberg, the heirs of William Penn, and the descendants of sundry illegitimate children of Charles the Second are to be found. There are, however, only about a dozen of such pensions left; and the total sum paid under this head does not amount to that number of thousands of pounds. The Penn pension amounts to £4,000; the descendants of Lord Amherst, a favourite of George the Third, receives £3,000; Lord Bath, a descendant of a favourite of William the Third, receives £1,200. Then, there are the military and naval pensions. It was the practice formerly, not only to settle a pension on great and successful commanders, but on their heirs for ever. This was the case of the Duke of Marlborough, Lord Rodney, Lord Nelson, and others. There are about a dozen of these pensions now. The custom of granting perpetual pensions ceased about fifty years ago. The pensions conferred after that were for two or three lives. There are seven or eight pensions of this class. Amongst them, the earliest is the Duke of Wellington, and the last, Lord Napier of Magdala. The rule now is not to grant pensions at all, but to pay a lump sum, as was done in the cases of Lord Wolseley and Lord Alcester in the Egyptian campaign. (Hear, hear.) But by far the largest, both in amount and number, of the pensions paid are really the superannuation-allowances made to men who have passed a given number of years in the public service. These men take smaller salaries than they would be entitled to; and, in consideration, they receive, at the end of a specified term, an annual allowance. It is unfair to call these payments pensions. They are really deferred salaries. As for political pensions, these are now very few and small compared with what they were. There was, in the pre-reform days, gross corruption in this department; but in 1834 an Act was passed which regulated the granting of such pensions. Under it, the number of pensioners was limited and the amount reduced. A scale was fixed, and no man could get a pension unless he revealed all his sources of income, and made a declaration that he could not sustain the dignity of an ex-Minister without aid from the State. There are only three persons receiving pensions under this Act; and the total sum they get amounts to less than £4,000. In 1869, a further and more stringent Act was passed, which divided political pensions into three classes. Men who are poor, and who have for four years held offices bringing them in £5,000 a-year, can receive a pension of £2,000 a-year, but only four pensioners of this class can be paid at the same time. Men who have held office for six years, to which a salary of £2,000 is attached, can have a pension of £1,200 a-year; and men who have held office for ten years, bringing in a salary under £2,000, can have a pension of £800 a-year. The only persons receiving the first-class pension of £2,000 a-year are Mr. Walpole, formerly Home-Secretary for the Conservatives, and Mr. Childers. But as Mr. Childers has a pension of £866 from the colony of Victoria, he gets only £1,134 from the Treasury. Mr. C. P. Villiers, Mr. George Lefevre, and Lord John Manners have each second-class pensions of £1,200 a-year. But when they are in office, their pensions cease. The list of political pensioners, therefore, is neither long nor heavy ; and in each case it is well deserved. The idea that pensions are always given to ex-Lords-Chancellor is incorrect. When a man becomes Lord-Chancellor, he has to abandon his profession as a barrister. When he is in office, he gets £10,000 a-year, £5,000 for presiding over the House of Lords, and £5,000 as a judge. He loses his salary as President of the Peers when he leaves office ; but he continues to receive his salary as judge, and sits regularly in the highest court—the Court of Appeal. There is only one ex-Lord Chancellor now living—Lord Selborne. The Speaker of the House of Commons, when he retires, gets a pension of £4,000 a-year. (Cheers.)

"What are the regulations for getting into the House of Commons ?"

Very absurd, and very troublesome. (Laughter.) All the galleries put together won't hold more than 120 persons. Members formerly could give one order a-day each. That power has been taken from them, and admissions now can be got only from the Speaker's secretary or the Serjeant-at-Arms. Seats in the ladies' gallery are secured by ballot. The House is too little. It seats only about 250 on the floor, and 130 in the gallery ; while, as for the public, there is not accommodation for a fourth of the number who seek admission.

"Can a member speak when presenting a petition ?"

In the pre-reform days, a member could speak and move a resolution when presenting a petition. He cannot do so now, but he can state the prayer of the petition, and briefly summarise its contents.

A gentleman asks if I can tell him whether it was Mr. Bright or Mr. Gladstone who first justified the slow progress of legislation, by saying that two omnibuses could not go abreast through Temple Bar. It was neither of them. The simile is one of

General Thompson's, who used it in one of his letters to his constituents. Mr. Bright used it afterwards, but whether he got it from General Thompson or not, I don't know. There is nothing more common than for a man speaking and writing to unconsciously make use of expressions or illustrations that have been used by some one else. (Hear, hear.) We all use expressions and sentences from the Bible, or Shakespeare, from Pope, or Byron, without knowing that we do so. There is a tale told of a local mayor who had been invited to patronise the theatre. It so happened that "Hamlet" was being played. He knew nothing of Shakespeare, and had never been at the playhouse before. Before the performance was half-through, he got up in disgust and went away, because the actors, when professing to speak of Shakespeare, were only repeating remarks that everyone knew in common conversation. (Loud laughter.) Macaulay's reference to the New Zealander standing on the broken arch of London Bridge and sketching the ruins of St. Paul's, is to be found in Volney, Horace Walpole, in Kirke White, and in Shelley. When Lord Beaconsfield described all the Liberal Ministers in the Parliament of 1868 as "a row of extinct volcanoes"—(laughter)—he used a simile from Thomas Hope's "Anastasius;" and when he described certain High Church practices as "mass in masquerade," he was unconsciously quoting from "Don Juan." When Mr. Gladstone spoke of Irish eviction being "a sentence of death," he was quoting from Dr. Nulty, the patriotic Bishop of Meath—(hear, hear);—and when he said that the Soudanese were "struggling to be free," he was using an expression to be found in Wordsworth's sketches. This always has been, and always will be, the case. There is really nothing original in essence. All that can be is originality in form. The architect has the merit of the conception and erection of an edifice, yet he does not create the materials. He does, however, create the design. The materials are found for him, but the idea on which his plan is projected is his. It is so in literary work. Books are very often an epitome of other people's thoughts, but the merit of subordinating them to a general scheme, and shaping them for new utility requires no mean skill. (Cheers.)

I am asked to explain how it comes that I, who have been connected with various organizations—political and otherwise—should so strongly object to political organizations. I am asked if the modern caucuses have not similar objects in view to the old Chartists. The gentleman who sends this inquiry entirely misconceives my position. I had thought, after the repeated explanations I have given, that it was unnecessary to say more. I have never objected to societies being organized for definite political objects. (Hear, hear.) They have a distinct end in view, and, by their organization, they contribute to secure it. They educate the public mind, and bring the force of opinion to bear upon the Legislature. (Hear, hear.) This is not only legitimate, but honourable, desirable, and necessary. But that is a different thing from an electoral organization which has no principles, and simply strives to accomplish personal objects—the getting of a certain set of men into Parliament, or a certain set of men into office. (Cheers.) All organizations of this kind, in my opinion, will drift inevitably into cliques and corruption. (Hear, hear.) I was a member of the National Charter Association, which was quite different from the Caucus. It had a definite purpose, which was to secure the enactment of six proposed reforms—universal suffrage, vote by ballot, shorter Parliaments, payment of members, abolition of property qualifications, and equal electoral districts. The promoters of this measure sought to secure that end, and they were accomplishing a useful educational work, as well as seeking political justice for the people. (Cheers.) I knew several of the men who drew the charter—Mr. Roebuck, Mr. James Watson, Mr. Richard Moore, and others. All of them, however, are now dead. I was on terms of intimacy with many of the Chartist leaders—Mr. Bronterre O'Brien, Mr. Ernest Jones, and several of their colleagues—(hear, hear);—but as far as I know there are only two prominent members of the Chartist body now living. Mr. Geo. Julian Harney—(hear, hear)—is the only member of the first Chartist Convention, I believe, who is alive. I know Mr. Harney intimately. He represented Winlaton in the Convention. He was editor of the *Northern Star*. After it ceased, he lived for some time in Jersey; then he went to America, where his home still is. He is, however, at present on a visit to this country. I know his opinion on political matters well, and I know that the views I have expressed with respect to the caucus are his views. The only difference between Mr. Harney and myself is that his antagonism to caucus organizations is very much stronger than mine. (Cheers.) There is another Chartist living, who is not unknown in this neighbourhood—my old friend Mr. Thomas Cooper, the author of "The Purgatory of Suicides." As showing the views of an old Chartist on the position I have taken generally, and in this contest especially, I may be permitted to read a letter I got from him the other day. Although considerably over eighty years of age, Mr. Cooper's caligraphy is as clear as letterpress. He retains, in spite of all his troubles and his sufferings, his lively interest in public matters and his remarkable capacity for elegant and forcible literary expression. (Hear, hear.)

"LINCOLN, Nov. 17, 1885.

"MY DEAR FRIEND,—I am delighted to see your noble determination to have no committee and to defy the hateful caucus. (Loud cheers and laughter.) Here my heart grieves to see what they have done. Fifty years I worked and wrote with Charles Seely to lay broader and better foundations for the Liberal cause, and he has been returned seven times for his native city. At 81, his faculties are as fine and active as they were 20 years ago, and he doated on the idea of being returned again. But a new man, Ruston, who has large iron works, was ambitious of being M.P.; and the caucus, where some vociferous employés of his are foremost, backed up Ruston. (Laughter.) My friend 'sacrificed himself,' to use his own expression, and retired rather than divide the cause for which he had spent his life. His case is more lamentable, for he is now lonely, having recently lost the light of his life—whom I always deemed the most perfect woman in the world. She was a Hilton of your Newcastle, and, for goodness, beauty, and devoted love to her husband, was peerless. I grieve for him, for our friendship of 50 years has never been broken. I try to comfort him by writing to him as much as I can. Go on, my dear friend, keep your noble and independent way, and may you conquer every foe. (Cheers.) Alas! for the poor 'workies,' they *do* so fail in gratitude. But we must not heed that. They are *ours*, my friend. We are sworn to their cause, let the sacrifice be what it will—only we will not be their *slaves*. God bless you!—Your loving friend, THOMAS COOPER."

I am asked whether, if two or more persons enter into partnership to conduct a manufacturing, wholesale, or retail business, the profits of which do not produce the partnership a clear profit of £150 each per annum, I am prepared to vote for the alteration of the income-tax so that the Acts should apply to the total yearly profit made by the firm. I am further asked—

"Are you prepared to bring in a bill for the taxation of all incomes under £150 a-year?"

The gentleman who sends this question evidently does not know the rules of Parliament. No private member can bring in a bill to impose a tax. That can be done only by a Minister of the Crown. A private member may move an abstract resolution in favour of reducing a tax, but he cannot propose to impose one. Therefore, even if I felt disposed, it would not be within my power to make such a proposition in Parliament. But apart from that, I am altogether opposed, as I have said once or twice, to reducing the amount upon which income-tax is levied. (Hear, hear.) I don't profess to know the difficulties in the way of levying income-tax, or how its imposition on co-operative stores would alter their management. I believe it is because it would do that, more than from any objection on the part of the stores to pay their legitmate share of taxation, that they are opposed to any change in the present arrangement. I have only to add to what I have already said, that I object to the stores, or any tradesmen, or any class or section of the community, having advantages over the other. (Hear, hear.) I am for equality of taxation as of political opportunity. I certainly am opposed to putting a penalty on thrift—(hear, hear);—but at the same time I cannot but think that the tradesmen's complaint that the wealthy co-operators should be permitted to escape taxation while the tradesmen are so heavily mulcted in every impost, both national and local, is a just one. (Hear, hear.) I have not gone into the question in detail, and there may be points on it that I am not master of. I am quite willing to receive any information on the subject; but the broad doctrine I am contending for is the equality of individual tradesmen with co-operators. I cannot conceive that anyone, in justice, can object to that. It would be absolutely illegal to subject a man to income-tax when his income is not £150 a-year. (Hear, hear.) That can be easily understood and seen. There is no likelihood of any immediate alteration, and I should be very glad to exchange views on the question with anyone who is interested in it. But as for taking any action myself in Parliament, that is, for the reason I have given, impossible. (Cheers.)

I am asked about free-trade. I am a free-trader, and always have been. I have no superstitious regard for the principles of political economy, however; and if circumstances justified any alteration being made, I am not so fanatical as to stick to them against experience and knowledge. (Hear, hear.) When democratic countries like America, autocratic countries like Germany, and opportunist countries like France, are against free-trade, it might necessitate a revision of the arguments for and against the proposal; but there is no evidence at the present time to justify, or to warrant, any such change, as far as I know. (Cheers.)

Here is a question about the representation of Newcastle. I believe Newcastle is entitled to another member—(cheers);—and it could have had one by a re-arrangement of the county divisions, without any injustice either to Morpeth or any other borough. This is the largest constituency under the new arrangement, and it would have been desirable to have it divided. There are 30,000 electors, and this large number would have made a division very desirable. The old democratic doctrine of one man one vote, and one representative, would have been preferable to the confusion that must exist under the present system. The Government would have been willing to make a change in this direction, and my colleague, Mr. Morley, was equally favourable to it; but there was some influence, which I could never understand, that prevented it. (Mr. Cowen resumed his seat, amidst loud cheers.)

# IRELAND AND HOME-RULE.

---

DELIVERED IN ST. PETER'S BOARD SCHOOL, ON WEDNESDAY, NOVEMBER 25, 1885.

---

CHAIRMAN—MR. JOHN GLOVER.

---

Mr. COWEN, who was received with great cheering, said: Mr. Chairman, ladies, and gentlemen,—There are two methods of philosophizing. One is to form a theory, and then twist the facts to fit it. (Laughter.) The other is to collate the facts, and draw conclusions from a comparison of them. (Hear, hear.) The former method is that commonly adopted when Englishmen discuss Irish questions. They know what they desire, and they reason as if they wished it were. (Hear, hear.) This is a very easy, but a very deceptive process. Suppose we follow, to-night, the opposite plan, and instead of making the facts square with a preconceived hypothesis, we try to formulate a theory from the facts. (Hear, hear.) It is a slow procedure, but it is effectual. Political vivisection—(laughter)—is an operation from which the sensitive shrink. But it is as indispensable to the statesman as morbid anatomy is to the surgeon. (Hear, hear.) I want to establish my conclusions by arguments as strong as adamant. (Hear, hear.) And, to do so, it is necessary to unfold the tragic record of Irish wrongs, sufferings, and misfortunes. It is a painful tale. I will only tell so much of it as stands in the relation of causes to effects. To prescribe remedies, without studying the seat of the disease and the habit of the patient, is empiricism and quackery. (Cheers.) It is seven hundred years since we conquered Ireland. We have held Dublin nearly as long again as the Turks have held Constantinople. When we took it, Russia was a limited Dukedom; Germany but a historical; and Italy but a geographical expression. The English Kings still claimed supremacy over the greater part of France, and the Moors exercised it over Spain. In that interval, between the landing of Strongbow and the present time, Holland has risen to be the first of maritime Powers, and has sunk again into insignificance. The United States have been discovered and colonized, have won their independence, and have grown to be one of the greatest nations upon the earth. (Cheers.) There has been time, then, sufficient for English institutions to take root in Ireland. Have they done so—(a Voice: "No," and hear, hear),—and what is the fruit they have grown? Ireland is inferior to no other country in Europe in the gifts of Nature. It is blessed with a temperate climate and a productive soil; intersected by great rivers; indented with noble harbours; endowed with valuable minerals; possessed of prolific fisheries—(hear, hear),—and furnished with water-power capable of turning the machinery of the world. Yet, its agriculture is stationary, and a couple of bad harvests bring the peasants to the verge of starvation. (Hear, hear.) Its fisheries are resting, its minerals unworked, its water-power unused, its commerce languishing, its manufactures, except in one district, extinct, its population poverty-stricken, dwindling, and discontented. ("Shame.") The people are disarmed, forbidden to drill, and refused permission to volunteer, while the country swarms with regular and irregular troops. (Hear, hear.) This is the plain unvarnished truth. "When the herd degenerates, the herdsman is to blame," is a maxim as old as Socrates. (Hear, hear.) Ireland has degenerated under English rule. Is England to blame? Largely, I think. (Hear, hear.) Scotland is prosperous, contented, and loyal. How comes it that our union with her has been such a success, and with Ireland such a failure? Because the first was a union, and the second a conquest. (Cheers.) The Scotch Commissioners treated the English Government on terms of equality for a junction of commercial interests—a federal connection, which should regulate the trade and foreign relations of the two countries, but which left the laws and institutions of each untouched. The bargain was struck on those terms; but under it the Scotch people have displayed a civic genius unsurpassed since the days of Pericles. (Hear, hear.) They have transformed a barren soil into a garden, raised up arts and manufactures as by the wand of a magician, and metamorphosed one of the poorest countries in the world into one of the wealthiest. (Hear, hear.) The Scotch have thriven because we have allowed them to work out their own destiny in their own way. (Hear, hear.) They have retained their own law-courts and legal methods, their own church, their own system of education, their own forms of local administration, and their own land and land-tenure. (Hear, hear.) We have shown no such respect for Irish ways, wishes, and susceptibilities. We absorbed their laws and uprooted their courts. We established a religion which was repugnant to them, and forced them to support it. ("Shame.") We trampled out every vestige of local government, and centralized all power in an alien camarilla entrenched in Dublin Castle. (Cheers.) We confiscated their land, abolished their system of tenure, and cleared out the peasantry, as in a wild country they clear out the forests, to plant it with English adventurers. The different treatments explain the different results. We have sown dragon's teeth, and they have sprung up rebels. (Cheers.) To-day is the child of yesterday. No man can pronounce an intelligent opinion on the state of Ireland, or propound any acceptable scheme for its amelioration, unless he has studied the past and understands the present. The fundamental facts of Irish history are unknown to the majority of Englishmen, who have been taught to apply different rules of conduct and canons of criticism to the two countries. Before English politicians denounce the Irish as ignorant and uncivilized, they should study the annals of those not remote times during which education in Ireland was felony by English law ; and before they proclaim Irish peasants to be a race of beggars and assassins, they should familiarize themselves with the history of Irish landlordism and Irish law. (Loud cheering.) It is not generally known, or, if known, overlooked, that Ireland, after the six centuries which followed the introduction of Christianity, was the seat of the industrial arts, and the school of the West. (Hear, hear.) Residence there was considered essential to establish a literary reputation ; and to her seminaries and universities students flocked from every part of Christendom. They were Irish missionaries who first presented to the illiterate Saxon the rudiments of literature, science, architecture, music, and even the means of shaping the letters used in writing the English language. (Cheers.) Irish monks were the workmen who built most of the early Christian edifices. Old St. Paul's in London, and the magnificent group that stands at Westminster Hall, were of Irish design. (Cheers.) At that time, Ireland was the Christian Greece—the centre of scholastic enlightenment and enterprise. In the zenith of its reputation, it was ravaged and plundered by Pagan marauders, who desolated the country and disorganized its institutions. Intermittent wars, prolonged through centuries, demoralized the civilization which had been a beacon in the midst of darkness. (Hear, hear.) A loose confederacy of princes and chiefs was substituted for the republican monarchy which had so long prevailed with acceptance and success. Each sub-king fought for his own hand.

Their reckless contests, combined with their dynastic jealousies, afforded an opening for filibustering Normans, who sought, and soon found, a footing in the country. (Hear, hear.) The Irish chieftains were dispossessed of their lands, and driven into the west. The invaders pitched on certain towns, and constructed around them rudely fortified camps, called the Pale, whose boundaries were shifted according to circumstances. Within the sweep of their forces, the Anglo-Normans established their own government, and imposed their own law. Beyond the Pale, the native prince ruled his Principality, and the native chief ruled his clan. Fitfully, though gradually, the strangers pushed their power; but it was not until more than four hundred years after the first landing that the struggle of native Irish sovereignty against English rule closed by the tacit surrender of James the First. The Normans commonly respected the customs of a conquered race, and speedily incorporated them into their dominion. They did not do so in Ireland, and from that circumstance have flown centuries of mischief and misery. ("Shame.") The adventurer who got Irish estates returned to England to enjoy the plunder. The Norman nobles who had fiefs in France or in England were compelled to elect where they would reside, and perform the duties for which the fief was created. In Ireland, the practice of holding the land, and not performing the duties, continues to this day. Absenteeism, therefore, is the legacy of the Pale, and an accursed legacy it has been. (Cheers.) The Reformation imported a new element of antagonism into the conflict. Religious animosity was added to race hatred and national hostility. Henry the Eighth changed his church—he could not change his religion, as he never had any—(loud laughter)—and the English people changed with him. What the English had done, the King insisted the Irish should do. But they refused. Rather than do so, they rebelled again and again. (Cheers.)

Whole provinces were depopulated, and the people perished in thousands for their faith. (Hear, hear.) Unable to force them to leave their church, we have punished them for remaining in it. Catholics were excluded from Parliament, from all municipal corporations, the magistracy, from the bench, the bar, from the jury, and from the franchise. ("Shame.") Their bishops were banished, and the ordination of priests forbidden. They were not allowed to carry arms, and were forbidden to purchase or inherit land, to receive it as a gift, or to hold it on lease. They could not possess a horse of greater value than £5. (Loud laughter.) Children were encouraged to become informers against their parents, by a right of succession being granted to any child who conformed to the State Church. To satirize the spirit of the times, Dean Swift ironically advised the clergyman, whose church had been dilapidated, to give it to the Catholics; and, when they had repaired it, he might take it back again. (Loud laughter.) But three centuries of persecution only confirmed the Irish in their Catholicity. There is no nation now where the priests are more beloved and their flocks more faithful. (Cheers.) The Establishment, happily, is gone; but the animosity which religious ascendency created, unhappily, survives. The object aimed at by England was to make the Irish Protestant in creed and English in sentiment. All education, unless contributing to these ends, was at one time prohibited, and at all times discountenanced. To become a teacher in a Catholic school, or a tutor in a Catholic family, was a crime. Until within the memory of those present, all the endowed schools and universities, with scholarships, fellowships, Church patronage, and dazzling prizes, were at the service of the Protestant youths, but denied to the Catholic, who constituted four-fifths of the population. ("Shame.") Can you wonder that a people who thus had the eye of their mind extinguished, and intellectual blindness, as well as the habits and tastes of barbarism, forced upon them by law, should grow up in ignorance? ("No.") The reproaches for such a condition should be passed upon the gaolers, and not upon the prisoners. (Hear, hear.) Those who endeavour to master the intricacies of the Irish educational controversy, should keep this bitter history before them. They will find in it a clue to many contradictions—a key that will unlock many seeming mysteries. (Hear, hear.) Desperate though the efforts of the English monarchs were to eradicate Irish nationality and faith, they were feeble in comparison with those made to secure possession of the land. There were four great confiscations, each of which was preceded and attended by scenes of unparalleled cruelty. Spenser, the author of the "Faerie Queene," who was one of the Munster planters, tells us how all means of human subsistence were destroyed, and attempts made to starve the natives into submission. They crawled out of woods and glens, on their hands and knees, because their legs would not bear them. They looked like anatomies of death, and spoke like ghosts crying out of their graves. So says Spenser. The English armies left neither corn, nor barn, nor house unburnt. They killed, indiscriminately, blind and feeble; men, women, boys, and girls; sick, aged, and idiotic; and some of the Elizabethan chroniclers—not Spenser, however—gloat with the grim enjoyment of Mohawks over the tales of horror. ("Shame.") They were tyrants by creed, and torturers by text. (Laughter.) Cromwell's conquest was as coldly merciless. He caused one thousand poor boys to be sold as slaves, and one thousand innocent girls to be sent to Jamaica, to a fate which, as Sir Charles Duffy said, could not be adequately avenged if he spent an eternity in the place to which the Cavaliers' toasts consigned him. (Hear, hear, and laughter.) William's Irish wars were equally brutal; and they were accompanied by an act of treachery as great as the partition of Poland, and as inhuman as the massacre of Glencoe. English history does not record a more damning transaction than the violation of the Treaty of Limerick. And, yet, men who can tell us all about the bigotry that revoked the Edict of Nantes, and drove an army of skilled artizans out of France, have never heard how we drove 150,000 Irishmen into the Continental armies. (Cheers.) If the exiled Huguenots changed the course of trade in this country, the exiled Irish soldiers changed the course of history at Fontenoy and Austerlitz. (Renewed cheers.) Such of the peasantry as survived successive settlements, as they were mildly called, were driven to the bogs and mountains. In the productive valleys and undulating meadows, the camp-followers of the conqueror were planted. The strangers took all that was worth having—the rest was left to the natives. The descendants of those strangers hold the same lands to-day, but they don't live on them. They are neither in the country nor of it—aliens alike in creed and social sympathy. The descendants of the dispossessed moodily brood over their fate, which has deprived them of the

> Fertile plain, the softened vale,
> Which were once the birthright of the Gael.

(Hear, hear.) The perversity that keeps these confiscations in mind is censured by complacent English critics. It is ancient history, they say, and should be forgotten. But defeated nations always dwell on the memories of old losses, even when traces of them are being gradually effaced. (Cheers.) England, we are reminded, has been conquered more than once. That is true, but the conquerors absorbed the natives, or were absorbed by them. That has not happened in Ireland. We treated them as enemies to be extirpated, not as subjects to be conciliated. For any English settler to speak the native tongue, use an Irish name, wear the Irish apparel, adopt any of the customs of the country, was punishable by loss of his land; while for him to marry an Irishwoman, to trust his children to an Irish nurse, or to give them Irish sponsors at baptism, constituted high treason. The racial barriers then erected have, unfortunately, not yet been overthrown; and both we and the Irish suffer in consequence. (Hear, hear.) It is nearly a thousand years since the Normans parcelled out the English land; it is not three hundred since the English parcelled out the Irish. If Irish kings had planted Catholic settlements in choice English counties, as late as the time of the Commonwealth, and driven the Protestant English to the hills and fells, it would have been found that, even to this day, we would not have patiently acquiesced in the transfer. (Cheers.) Those memories are painful; but who can blot them out? As long as Englishmen gloat with patriotic pride over the records of great deeds done by their ancestors at Agincourt or at Waterloo, so long will Irishmen, as Sir Gavan Duffy eloquently says, be disturbed by agony and wrath over the desolation of Desmond, the spoliation of Ulster, and the brutalities of Carhampton. (Hear, hear.) England, too, is different from Ireland. Here we have many other occupations besides agricultural; Ireland has none. Hence the earnestness with which her people bemoan the loss of their land. The race-resentments are traceable to the Pale; the religiou antipathies, engendered by our attempts to coerce the people to Protestantism; the agrarian rancour comes down from the planters; the national distrust from the penal laws, which, Mr. Burke says, were as elaborate a contrivance for the oppression, impoverishment, and degradation of the people, and the debasement of human nature, as ever proceeded from the perfidy and ingenuity of man. (Cheers.) But although this generation suffers so severely from it, it is not responsible for the past. We cannot annul it, and we need not make party politics of it—(hear, hear), but if we wish to legislate in relief of the evil bequeathed to us, we must keep it before us. When we declaim against Irish ignorance, we should remember that, for generations, we prohibited education—that the penal laws left over four millions of persons unable to read. (Hear, hear.) When we reproach the Irish with want of manufactures, we should recollect that we deliberately injured theirs in the interest of our own, and that one of William the Third's most solemn pledges to Parliament was, that he would do all that in him lay to destroy them. (Hear, hear.) He kept this pledge, although he broke the one he made at Limerick. (Laughter.) But no living Englishman has anything more to do with the enactment of the penal laws, or with the iniquity of the imposition of fatal restrictions on Irish trade, than any living Englishman has to do with the massacre of 1641. (Hear, hear.) For the last fifty years, they have struggled to atone for former wrongs; and because their efforts have not been more effusively acknowledged, the Irish are accused of ingratitude. It is not easy to define what measure of gratitude is due for tardy acts of justice. (Loud cheers.) The English concessions have been shorn of their grace and merit by being so long delayed, and by being yielded to pressure rather than conviction and sympathy. (Hear, hear.) We deny to reason what we render to fear. (Hear, hear.) Many of the concessions have been carried out by hostile agents; others have been allowed to remain inoperative, or have been administered in a recalcitrant spirit. The American War stimulated our English sense of justice. In the hope of averting an Irish rebellion, we gave Ireland a Parliament; and, as usual, we sweetened the gift by a general admission of past transgressions. Mr. Pitt summed up the history of the connection of the two countries in a pregnant sentence. England, he declared, had deprived Ireland of the use of her own remedies, and rendered her subservient to English interests and opulence. The Parliament was to rectify past errors, and redress her wrongs; but no sooner did the danger, which it was called into existence to prevent, disappear, than it was corruptly and fraudulently destroyed. Catholic emancipation was promised as a *solatium* for the loss, but it was not granted until thirty years after the Union, and then only under compulsion. (Hear, hear, and laughter.) The Duke of Wellington, when urging the measure on his brother-Peers, did not do so that justice might be accomplished, and the long delayed debt paid, but because it was no longer safe to resist it. (Cheers.) "We have," he said, "to choose between emancipation and rebellion; and I prefer the former as the less evil of the two." (Laughter.) No one can wonder that the gratitude of Irishmen was not touched by such questionable generosity. (Hear, hear, and laughter.) The glaring injustice of maintaining a Protestant Church at the cost of the Catholic people was admitted by all; but it was maintained for generations, and, according to the acknowledgment of the author of the Act, was only finally disestablished because the Fenians blew down a gaol in Clerkenwell, and burst open a police-van in Manchester. (Hear, hear, and cheers.) It was fear, not justice, that secured that reform. A like indifference to agrarian evils was displayed until they were driven upon our consideration. In the copious election programmes of both great parties, in 1880, there was no reference to the reiterated demand of Irish peasants for a redress of their grievances. When they were spoken of, by isolated English "Philistines"—(laughter)—it was to sneer at, or jest about, them; but when the Land League paralysed the Castle and its constables, a very different tone was taken. (Cheers.) Then the necessity for an Irish

Land Act was discovered, and one was passed in hot haste. (Laughter.) When well-meaning Englishmen are chagrined, and perplexed, that their efforts at reparative justice are not more warmly reciprocated, and do not strike a responsive chord in Irish hearts, they may find in retrospect a reason. (Hear, hear.) It is not the deed, but the time when, and the temper in which, it is done, that captivates the recipient. (Cheers.) Acts, too, good and wise in themselves, have failed from defective and adverse administration. We made the Catholics eligible for office, but we admitted none of them to it. (Laughter.) We opened the door, but not a soul was permitted to pass. During the debates on the Emancipation Bill, Sir Robert Peel said, "Catholics are eligible, but because they are eligible they are not entitled to office. Whether they are admitted or not is in the discretion of the Crown." In other words, the legal ban was lifted, but the social one was retained. And it is so to this day! In the county of Cork, where there are ten Catholics for one Protestant, there were, a few years ago, in offices of honour and emolument in connection with the Government, the magistracy, the poor-law, and the police, 1,190 Protestants and 185 Catholics. In the report published since Parliament rose, it is shown that whilst there are 227 Protestants, there are only 45 Catholic officers in the Irish Constabulary. It is an advantage to have the Constitution broadened, but the benefit is neutralized, if, when Catholics seek admission, they are told there is no room for them; and that all the places are filled by Protestants, who secure an entrance in right of confiscated land and penal laws. This class and sectarian exclusiveness—the spawn of prejudice and injustice—applies to every department, from the Castle to the petty police-barracks. (Hear, hear.) From 1700 to 1800, only one Irishman filled the office of Lord-Lieutenant. Since 1800, only two—and these were Tory Irish noblemen—have been Viceroys.

The Chief-Secretary and Under-Secretary are Englishmen and Protestants; and out of the twenty-nine officials in the Castle, all are Protestants but two. In the Customs, Inland-Revenue, and in the offices of the Board of Works, all the chief places are filled by Protestants. ("Shame.") The minor ones are given to Catholics. And this is half-a-century after emancipation, and amongst a population where only one in five is Protestant. It is impossible to conceive that there are not a large number of Irish Catholics eligible for these places, and that they were excluded either through a latent distrust, or a desire to maintain the old ascendency. In Eastern rivers, you trace, by their colour, the waters that rise in different geological strata. Their courses are distinguishable from the source to the sea. The streams of Irish discontent, springing from different well-heads, are quite as broadly marked. Angry and venomous currents, racial, religious, and agrarian, have guttered into, and undermined, its national life. The Irish policy of the Plantagenets was oppression and hostility; of the Tudors, the sword and the penal statute; of Cromwell, the sword, penalty, and wholesale confiscation; of William and Anne, the sword, repression, renewed confiscation, and laws against trade. They all failed. (Cheers.) The Hanoverians initiated a more humane policy. The sword was temporarily returned to the scabbard. Proselytism, accompanied by restraints and disabilities, was tried. They were to be taught to fear, that they might be taught to love. This failed too. A new departure was taken at the emancipation. A policy of alternate coercion and concession—the lash and lollipops—was started. (Laughter.) It has failed also. Our measures are never thorough. They are always clogged with reservations. We have always a splinter in the wound. And we stand now, eighty-five years after the Union, in the presence of as intense and widespread disaffection, as ever moved the Irish people this century. (Cheers.) We have attempted all forms of rule but one. We have never trusted Irishmen. (Cheers.) Why not try that? Give them—and by them I mean all classes, irrespective of creeds and origin—the management of their own affairs. What they want, is the right to domestic legislation. (Hear, hear.) The Imperial Parliament would then, as now, have the exclusive power of dealing with all questions affecting the Crown; of legislating for the colonies and dependencies; of regulating our relations with foreign States; of providing and controlling the supplies for national defences; of upholding the integrity and stability of the Empire. (Hear, hear.) Amongst the attributes of sovereignty would be the right of coining money, carrying the mail, of regulating the Customs, granting patents, copyrights, and making wars. The Irish Parliament would deal exclusively with Irish affairs. (Hear, hear.) Its Constitution would be a counterpart of the Imperial. Irish Ministers would be responsible to their Parliament, as their Parliament, in turn, would be responsible to the people. (Cheers.) While they constitutionally exercised jurisdiction over all purely Irish business, they would be required cordially to unite with England in proceedings which concerned the two islands in common. (Hear, hear.) The Imperial Parliament would act for the Empire, and the Irish Parliament for Ireland. Each, within its sphere, would be supreme. Is there anything unreasonable, or impracticable, or revolutionary in such an arrangement? (Cries of "No," and cheers.) It was because we refused to adopt it for our American colonies that we lost them. (Hear, hear.) It is because we have adopted it in our other large colonies that we retain them. (Hear, hear.) Federalism is but the application to national life, of the principle that we act upon in domestic and civil life. Each family regulates its domestic affairs; each municipality manages its own business; because they can do so with more knowledge, and will do so with more zeal, than any outside individual, or any distant governing body. (Cheers.) But as regards matters of general concern in the State, the members of the municipality respectively act in unison. The fullest growth, and the widest range of action, both in the individual and in the city, as well as in the country, is compatible with fidelity to the State. Fidelity and independence, in the centre, can be maintained without sacrificing either in the different parts. Every member of the body politic would have free and healthy play, and the life of the whole would be the life of every section. (Hear, hear.) That procedure I would apply to the political relations between England and Ireland. The earliest forms of political union rest, not upon territorial contiguity, but upon blood relationship. In the lowest savagery, as well as in the highest civilization—in the old plan as in the new nationality—this is the primary, as it is the strongest, ground, for sustained common action amongst groups of men. (Hear, hear.) But we have not yet reached that condition of positive knowledge, and perhaps we never shall, when we can say, with an assurance of correctness, how much of the progress is due to innate race qualities, and how much to early and later environments. It is, however, certain, that running all through political phenomena there is a general course of events, in view of which it can be affirmed that the order of events has been from the individual to the tribe or city; their fusion and expansion to the nation and to federation. The chief problem of civilization has always been how to secure concentrated action amongst men, on a large scale, without sacrificing local independence, or doing violence to national sentiment. History says it is not possible to solve this problem without the aid of the principle of representation. Apply it equally to the different communities in the same State, and to the different citizens of the same community. This association of equal men and equal peoples, mutually aiding one another, each profiting by the resources which the other possesses, and marching onward, free from all fetters, to the realization of their destiny—indicated by their aspirations, by the locality of their birth, by their tradition and idioms—is the highest form of political organization which human experience has evolved; and it is specially adapted to the pecular relations between England and Ireland. (Cheers.) It is in accordance, too, with Anglo-Saxon sentiments and sympathies. They were the only race that came out of the mediæval crucible with their conceptions of local Government intact. England itself was a confederation of States rather than a united kingdom. The federation was not only of shire and shire, province and province, but of realm and realm. All the groups were subordinate, but all were free. They all acknowledged an imperial supremacy. Yet, for all local and administrative purposes they were independent. Over the confederated States presided a king, and round him stood the Council of Wise Men. It was out of this organization that our Empire grew, and by it it is still guarded. The genius and training of the English people, then, as well as their political and social structures, are all in harmony with the federalists' idea. Centralization, the Roman idea, is despotic; federation, the Teutonic idea, is democratic. (Hear, hear.) It was the community that embraced the latter conception of governing the Dutch, the Swiss, and the Scandinavians, that led to the terrible battle for freedom with which the drama of modern history was ushered in; and it is through it we have shown a capacity for the completest form of local self-govermnent, combined with federal union. In their mountain fastnesses, the Swiss have preserved, in its present form, the rustic democracy of their forefathers. Yet, modern

Switzerland is made up of more discordant and unmanageable elements than are to be found in Great Britain and Ireland. Four languages—German, French, Italian, and Rhœtian—are spoken within the limits of the Confederacy; while, on religion, the Cantons are as sharply divided as ever Orangemen or Catholics were, or could be. But deeper down than even the deep-seated differences of speech and creed, lie the patriotic feelings generated by the common possession of political freedom. (Cheers.) Complete local independence, and adequate federal representation, give a more intense national cohesion than any centralized Government, however cunningly devised, could secure. (Cheers.) Identical results, in very different circumstances, and under very different conditions, have been secured in democratic Scandinavia, and autocratic Austria. There are no two countries in Europe whose course has been freer from domestic discord, or more steadily prosperous, than Norway and Sweden since their confederation; and when Austria ceased to be the master, and became the partner with Hungary in the Austro-Hungarian Empire, chronic discontent was transformed into settled contentment. (Loud cheers.) But the happiest illustration of dual government—the most conclusive proof that concentrated action can be secured without sacrifice of independent action—is furnished by the United States. When it was proposed, it was laughed at and derided in much the same way as Home-Rule is to-day. It was declared to be impossible that thirteen colonies, with a population of five millions, would overcome their mutual jealousies so far as to unite in a single political body. Yet, not thirteen, but thirty-nine, free States—stretching over more than three millions of square miles of territory, and containing not five, but fifty, millions of people, as unlike as Connecticut and California, or as Louisiana and Massachusetts—have been united, and are held together in bonds as firm as they are free. (Cheers.) It is in the flexibility of the union, in the complete independence that is preserved by each State, except when that conflicts with the federal principle, that lies the surest guarantee for this masterpiece of political wisdom. (Hear, hear.) But in the British Empire itself, we have an example of federation in another, but equally successful, form. We have accorded to all our large colonies the full power of self-government, and we are gradually evolving a comprehensive federation which will secure to each all the local rights they now enjoy; while it will bind them, both by interest and good-will, still more tightly to the Imperial community. (Loud cheers.) It is impossible to cite more conclusive evidence of the success of Home-Rule than that presented by Canada. (Hear, hear.) For the first forty years of the century, that colony was either in rebellion or preparing for rebellion. It is two thousand miles from our shores, or forty times the distance of Ireland; it is close to a great and friendly State, which is certainly not unwilling to incorporate it; it has two provinces, and the people of each differ in race, religion, language, and law. Those in one province are French and Catholic, alienated by memories of recent conquests and harsh legislation. The population of the other—Scotch and Irish settlers—had carried with them inveterate race feuds and religious animosities. It is not easy to conceive of a country where, or a population amongst whom, Home-Rule could have been less auspiciously attempted. (Hear, hear.) The two provinces were united in the one Parliament, with all the elements of distraction, disaffection, and danger. Has the Empire been disintegrated? Has the Dominion joined, or does it now ever talk of joining, the United States? Is it torn by domestic dissension? Has not Home-Rule transformed the rebellious and languishing colony into one of the most loyal, contented, and prosperous that Great Britain possesses? (Cheers.) Provinces that were against each other, in seemingly hopeless discord and antagonism, are now united. French Catholic and Irish Orangemen, English Catholic and Scotch Presbyterians, meet in one Parliament, and subordinate their strifes and rivalries to the common interest of the country they control, and the Empire of which they form a part. (Hear, hear.) It is the practice of party politicians to complicate what is simple, and to make inextricable what is not complex; but it is not conceivable that intelligent Englishmen can, or will, permit themselves to be permanently prejudiced against a system of rule, the merits of which they have not fully investigated. I have no faith in my powers of advocacy, but I feel satisfied that if I had twelve of my countrymen—of any class, or creed, or party—in the jury-box; and if they allowed me, like Dean Swift, to plead the case under another name, they would pronounce the Irish grievances proven, and decide that their scheme for self-government was in principle sound, and would, in practice, be workable. (Loud cheers.) In Ireland's chequered history, there was a brief period of prosperity. The American War brought England trouble, but brought Ireland liberty. This was the first time, since the invasion of Henry II., that she had had free-trade and a free Parliament. In the twenty years that followed the restoration of her independence, she made great strides in prosperity. Freedom brought her trade, and revived her manufactures. Lord Clare, in 1798, said, "There is not a nation on the globe that has advanced in cultivation and commerce, in agriculture and manufactures, with the same rapidity in the same period." (Cheers.) All classes of the community—Protestant and Catholic, peer and peasant, rich and poor—were united in one bond of sympathy, and one common sentiment of triumph, at the legislative independence of the country. But that Parliament was destroyed by a combination of perfidy and corruption, such as the British annals furnish no parallel to. (Hear, hear.) Since the Union, Irish history has been a record of repression and turbulence—repression on account of turbulence, and turbulence on account of repression. (Hear, hear.) There have been, in the eighty-five years, nearly fifty Coercion Bills; and there have not been, over that long period, three successive years in which the Constitution has not been suspended. The population has steadily decreased. It is four millions less than it was in 1847. There have been three positive famines, and repeated periods when distress bordered on famine. Trade has declined; manufactures have all but expired; and agriculture has retrograded. Only two things have increased—pauperism and discontent. Discontent flows from injustice as surely as heat from fire. How long has this state of affairs to continue? How long is Ireland to be a menace and a danger, instead of a source of strength and security, to the Empire? (Hear, hear.) Can any valid reason be given why we cannot give her the liberty we so fraudulently deprived her of eighty-five years ago? She was prosperous under her own rule; she is miserable under ours. (Hear, hear.) It is marvellous to see liberal-minded and intelligent Englishmen ignoring the fact, written in blood over the chronicles of twenty generations, that Ireland will never be contented until she is ruled by Irishmen as uniformly as England is by Englishmen. (Cheers.) Her national sentiment is an anvil that will wear out many hammers; her history, a forced long battle for this end. All her heroes are men who have fought for her; all her poetry is filled with legends of their struggles; and we can only extinguish the idea by extinguishing the population. It will dissolve the Empire to give Irishmen Home-Rule, say some. Those who say so must have forgotten that already there are fifteen Parliaments in the British dominions ; and it cannot be seriously contended that the making of one more will make the difference between unity and dismemberment. (Cheers.) But Hóme-Rule, I hold, will consolidate and strengthen, not weaken, the Empire. (Hear, hear.) Whatever Irish policy may be propounded, all parties are agreed that it is disaffected. We may disagree as to the cause, and as to the cure for the disaffection ; but as to the disaffection itself, there can be no doubt. A war with a great Power, or a rebellion in India, would convert a vague sentiment into a purpose and a passion. No captain can safely lead his ship into action, unless he feels confident in the fidelity of his crew. There could be no confidence in an Irish crew, in their present temper, if the country were to get into trouble. Our difficulty would be Ireland's opportunity. (Hear, hear.) Her slumbering disloyalty would be militant, and another Paul Jones might make a descent on Mayo—(laughter)—or another Hoche might attempt, and, this time, succeed, in landing at Bantry Bay. Both would find sympathisers on shore. (Hear, hear.) Most of us have forgotten that, so late as 1840, the French Government consulted the Irish rebel soldiers as to the feasibility of a military expedition to Ireland ; and the Prince de Joinville, son of Louis Philippe, published a pamphlet to show how easily it could be accomplished. During our strained relations with the United States, at the time of the Tyler and Polk Presidency, schemes for invading Ireland and attacking Canada with Irish help, were openly discussed. Sir Robert Peel justified his attempt to conciliate the Irish Catholics, by establishing a national system of education, by partially endowing Maynooth, and in establishing Queen's Scholarships, on the ground that war was possible both with America and France, and that until Ireland was contented, our diplomacy was hampered, and our powers of resistance paralysed. What has been, may be. (Hear,

hear.) We are very wisely constructing additional coaling stations abroad, and fortifying our harbours at home; but forts, docks, arsenals, and battlements, mounds and artillery, are of little avail unless they have fervent and stalwart men to defend them. (Cheers.) We can, by a simple act of justice, turn four millions of lukewarm or hostile Irishmen, into active friends, and build around their section of the kingdom a patriotic and puissant rampart, which will as far excel all artificial batteries as men excel brutes, or brutes excel material nature. (Hear, hear.) Why don't we do it? Because, whisper nervous politicians, "If we left the rival factions to themselves, they would tear each other to pieces, and, in the wrangle, the interests of the Protestants and property minority would be endangered." I do not believe it. (Cheers.) There is no justification for such fears. Religion ought not to divide a nation, and the Catholic majority need not alarm Protestant Irishmen. Why should it? Belgium is a Catholic country; and the religious liberty of Protestants is as secure there as it is in England. There are keener clerical controversies in Switzerland than in Ireland, yet the freedom of all is recognized and respected. (Hear, hear.) Churches, like monarchs, are apt to be tempted into persecuting practices when they possess uncontrolled power. It is a fact, however, to be cited to the honour of Irish Catholics that on two occasions, during the reigns of Queen Mary and James, they had the opportunity of retaliating, and refrained from doing so. (Hear, hear.) Their fathers had been mercilessly treated by Cromwell; but, notwithstanding that, James's Irish Parliament displayed unique moderation and forbearance. They inflicted no penalties for religious opinions. They ordered the tithes paid by Protestant farmers to be paid to Protestants, and the tithes paid by Catholic farmers to be paid to the Catholic clergy. They did not deprive the

Protestants of arms, or the franchise; or impose upon them the penal laws which had been relentlessly levied against them, their religion, their property, their family peace, their political and civil rights as subjects. On the other hand, many of the influential Irish Nationalists have been Protestants. (Hear, hear.) The volunteers, whose action secured the Parliament of 1782, met in the Protestant Church of Dungannon, and their chiefs were of that faith. The Constitutional leaders—Grattan and his colleagues—and the leaders of the United Irishmen—Wolfe Tone, Orr, and their associates—were Protestants. So, too, were prominent men among the Young Irelanders—Smith, O'Brien, Mitchel, Davis, and Martin; while all the Parliamentary leaders the Home-Rule party have had—Mr. Butt, Mr. Shaw, and Mr. Parnell—have been Protestants. (Hear, hear.) In any scheme for an Irish Parliament, the rights of the Protestants will have to be guaranteed. But there would be no more difficulty in doing that than there has been in assuring the rights of the Catholic minority in Canada. Christianity belongs exclusively to no sect, and patriotism to no religion. (Cheers.) Irishmen are asked to point to the measures that an Irish Parliament would pass, and that an Imperial Parliament won't. This is the cant of despotism. (Cheers.) It is what Austria told the Lombards, what the Germans told the Alsatians, and what the Czar tells the Poles. The Austrians and the Russians and the Germans may mean to rule their conquered provinces for their good—I do not say they do so—but the Poles and the Alsatians prefer to rule themselves, even though they may not do so cleverly. (Hear, hear.) That is the reply of Irishmen too. They say, "We don't deny the competency of the British Parliament, but it has enough work of its own to do; it cannot do what we want, however able or however willing it may be. Leave us to attend to our business, and you will have more time to attend to yours. (Cheers.) We are a smaller people and poorer ; but we have interests that you don't understand, and wants that you do not know of, or, if you do, that you cannot legislate for. We know where the shoe pinches ; we require a new pair that will fit our feet ; and we want to make them ourselves." (Hear, hear, and laughter.) That is the Irish contention. Is it not a reasonable one ? It is not true, however, that Irish measures are promptly passed in the British Parliament. They are passed in earnest only when they become the instruments of party warfare ; or when popular discontent developes into insurrection, and the noblest spirits become rebels. (Cheers.) But their complaint is not so much about specific measures as it is against the whole system of Government. It crushes the energy, wastes the strength, destroys the spirit, neglects the interest, and contravenes the sentiments, of the people. (Cheers.) A nation is a moral essence, and its feelings are facts. The sense of national pride, the inherited tendencies of generations, the recollections of former grievances ; the fame they wish to enhance ; the independence they wish to guard, are as much realities as wealth or national power. (Hear, hear.) They make up the soul and spirit of the nation. It is futile to attribute, as some do, the perennial movement in Ireland to agitators who transmit from one to another the inheritance of subversive ideas. They might as well attribute the conquest of the world, by Christianity, to the underground labour of the secret society. I have reasoned out my conclusions without reference to pending party controversy. (Hear, hear.) Some of these may modify, and others exaggerate, the situation ; but they are distinct from the mastering contention that controls all Irish agitations—that, while forming part of the British Empire and relegating all questions of Imperial interest to the Imperial Parliament, they would manage their own affairs in their own way. (Hear, hear.) It is this principle that has given such boundless vitality to colonial enterprise; and however conciliation may lure us, or coercion may threaten, there will be no peace in Ireland until it is granted. (Cheers.) During the late Government's term of office, Ireland passed through the old sad drama—starvation, conspiracy, murder, arrest, and trial. It opened as surely with the razed cabin, and closed with the penal cell and the gallows' drop. The Ministers, as usual, stuck a plaster on the raw sore, and affected astonishment that the patient winced under the infliction. (Hear, hear, and laughter.) The Land Act reduces rents, but does not stop eviction. Over 60,000 peasants have been turned out of their homes and holdings since it was passed. ("Shame.") This year, the evicted persons number nearly 18,000. The Act benefited a section of the better class farmers, but it never touched the most necessitous—(hear, hear);—whilst Coercion Acts have done more to embitter Irish feeling against England than any Act of the British Legislature of this country. (A Voice: "That's true," and cheers.) It is a lowering of the argument I have been upholding to impart into it personal considerations; but, in view of recent apologies and recantations, I may be pardoned if I remind you that what some are saying now, I said years ago. (Hear, hear.) The secretary of the Newcastle Liberal Club, in the name of its members, wrote to me in February, '81, and here is my reply:—

"I am favoured with your letter of the 7th inst. You send me a copy of a resolution passed at a meeting of the Junior Liberal Club, desiring me to 'support the Irish policy of the Government.' I understand that this resolution was passed at a meeting consisting of 32 persons, 23 of whom voted in its favour, and 9 against it.

"I shall give the best consideration I am able to the promised Land Bill. The question is as difficult as it is old. It is impossible for the Government to treat it in any other way than by a compromise. Until their scheme is laid before the House, I cannot pledge myself to any absolute course of action. (Cheers.) The indefinite expression, 'a good Land Bill,' may mean a great deal, or it may mean very little. All I can say is, that, recognizing the difficulties of the situation, I will give cordial aid to any proposal that essays to deal, in a liberal and comprehensive way, with so complicated a subject. (Cheers.)

"On the 'coercive policy of the Government' I can speak more definitely, as I know what they intend doing. I do not wish you and your friends to have any doubt as to my intentions. I mean to oppose the Coercion Bill on every occasion, and at every point, by all the resources in my power. (Hear, hear.) When all opportunity of defeating the bill is gone, I will strive to delay its operation by every honourable, fair, and legitimate process. When that resource is exhausted, I will assist in mitigating the harshness of its clauses, and minimizing the despotic powers that the Government are seeking to obtain. (Cheers.) I never felt more convinced in my mind on any subject than I do upon this. It is my emphatic belief that the repressive course the Ministry is pursuing will embitter the relations between England and Ireland. (Cheers.) It may create a temporary lull in the present agitation; but it will certainly further weaken the faith of the Irish people in the equity and sacredness of English-made law. I regard the bill as cruel, unjust, and impolitic; and, so regarding it, I conceive that I am acting not only strictly within my right, but doing my duty, in availing myself of every instrumentality that the forms of Parliament permit, to oppose its enactment. (Cheers.) I am quite aware that many Liberals view the subject in an entirely different way; and, of course, they are equally justified in supporting the measures of the Ministry. But a man must act up to his convictions. (Hear, hear.) I regret that I feel myself compelled to assume such an unqualified attitude of opposition to a Ministry with whose policy, in the main, I sympathise." (Loud cheers.)

I kept my promise, and was Boycotted in consequence. (Hear, hear, and laughter.) My predictions have turned out true. (Loud cheers.) And the men who were mistaken are angry and resentful! The Irish cause, which is a subject for a sneer to the political "Philistines"—(laughter)—has always had for me an irresistible fascination. The Irish Celt, whom English caricaturists usually picture either as a gorilla or a baboon, has noble qualities. He loves the scenes where he was born, and the roof which sheltered him from birth. He is a dutiful son, a faithful husband, and a kind father. (Hear, hear.) If his dwellings are unclean, his affections are pure. (Cheers.) He is patient in suffering, and unwavering in trust, when trust is given. Like Ixion at his wheel, he eternally traces the same circle of woes. He tills a few sad acres for bare life, wears a few poor rags for bare warmth, and he softens the hard leaven of his lot with the dews of a simple faith in heaven. (Cheers.) The chivalry, the romance, the tenderness, and faithfulness of his nature, have often captivated his conquerors, and turned the descendants of English planters into the foremost of Irish patriots; and it has made one member, at least, of the British Parliament as faithful a friend of there cause as ever the green flag fluttered over. (Loud and prolonged cheering.)

The CHAIRMAN: A gentleman has sent up this question: "A few words as to why Ireland lost her Parliament would please the meeting."

Mr. COWEN said Ireland lost her Parliament because the English Government spent about two millions of money in buying the votes of corrupt representatives, and dispensed a large number of peerages—something like 200, he believed. In this way, they corrupted the representatives, and secured the extinction of a Parliament which, with many defects, had nevertheless been a great benefit to the country. It was an exclusive Parliament—there were no Catholics in it. If they would turn to the memoirs of Lord Castlereagh and Lord Colchester they would find it to be one of the most painful periods of English history. ("Bravo!" and cheers.) He was also asked, "Is it true, as stated by Mr. Hamond, that you and he, when members for Newcastle, always consulted each other before voting?" In all matters affecting the district, Mr. Hamond and himself always consulted together. They were both connected with the Corporation, and understood the requirements of the district. At the same time, they were on opposite sides of politics, and to political matters, of course, the answer did not apply. (Cheers.) He was asked if he would address a meeting at the Elswick factory on Thursday. He would have been extremely glad to do so; but he had been speaking every night that week; and he had to speak again on Friday night. He had made engagements for Thursday which it was impossible for him to break. He had intended going to the funeral of his old friend and colleague, Alderman Angus; and in addition to that there were other matters which had to be attended to before Saturday. He feared, therefore, that he would be prevented from speaking at Elswick factory; but if he had been at liberty, he should have been only too glad to do so. (Hear, hear.) A gentleman asked him if members of Parliament were free from Imperial taxation or income-tax? Certainly not. Mr. Coltman asked him if he would assist in facilitating the transfer of house property. He would heartily support any effort in that direction. Mr. Coltman also asked if he would support a proposal for giving the same facilities for performing marriage ceremonies in chapels as existed in the case of churches. He sympathised with the idea contained in the question. (Cheers.)

# CONCLUDING MEETING.

HELD IN THE TYNE THEATRE, ON FRIDAY EVENING, NOVEMBER 27TH.

CHAIRMAN—MR. R. O. LAMB.

Mr. COWEN, who was received with prolonged enthusiasm, said: Mr. Chairman, ladies, and gentlemen,—I must apologise for being the cause of calling so many of you here to-night, on this busy day of the week, and just on the eve of the day of the poll. ("No, no.") I have been busy during these last nine or ten days speaking to the people of Newcastle. During that time, I have talked in public over sixteen hours. If everything I have said were collected, it would make more than two three-volume novels. (Laughter.) That is an unconscionable amount of political disquisition to pour into one town in such a short space of time. (Laughter and cheers.) I feel this explanation is due to you for asking you to attend again to listen to what will be really a simple summary and condensation of what I have already been saying. I promise this, however, that I shall occupy your time for but a limited space, and, in that sense, shall make some atonement for the inconvenience I have put you to. ("No, no.") On entering the meeting to-night, I heard a friendly voice ask, "What is the order of the day?" (Cheers.) I answer, in the electric watchword of the French Convention, when the forces of the coalesced kings concentrated for their final spring upon the Republic, the order of the day is—"Victory!" (Loud and prolonged cheering.) Whether we are able to pass that order, whether we are vanquished or victorious, remains with the people of Newcastle to decide—(cheers, and a voice: "Top of the poll"),—at least I hope we can say that the fight we have fought has not been without its fruits. (Loud cheers.) The constituencies have been harrowed and cross-harrowed with political principles. The ploughshare of fact and argument has been driven through many a cherished prejudice, and over some fondled delusions. Trimmers scout a rigorous insistence on principles. They are too busy weighing interests and balancing probabilities to heed them. They are in favour of popularizing only so much truth as is convenient or opportune. Instead of approaching national questions from the high level of what should be, they approach them from the low level of what they are. (Hear, hear.) Principle is the source whence flow all the ideas that make up our political system, and constitute our rules of conduct. They are the quintessence of facts. To lay down a principle, to disengage from a series of facts the idea that rules and embraces them, to discover what is permanent in accidental phenomena, is contrary to the habit of the hand-to-mouth politicians. They prefer to deal with opinions which are shifty, and personalities which are piquant. (Cheers.) I am not allured by these evanescent disputations. (Hear, hear.) Men die, opinions fluctuate, but principles are immortal. I hold fast to them regardless of those by whom, or the circumstances in which, they are applied. They are the magnetic north to which, without deflection, all my arguments and aspirations inevitably point. (Hear, hear.) By teaching principles, our aims are raised, our views enlarged, our faith purified. To me politics are the science of mundane existence. Its starting point is the individual—free and self-centered. Every human being has a quality peculiar to himself, that distinguishes him from every other human being that has been, that is, or will be. (Hear,

hear.) Those distinctive qualities constitute his character and his life. To develop these attributes—moral, intellectual, and physical—is his mission. To accomplish this mission, he requires freedom, without which there can be no responsibility; and equality, without which liberty is a deception. (Hear, hear.) Upon these cardinal principles, my political creed rests. Upon them, all my hopes of human betterance hinge. If there be any sufficiently curious to examine, they will find, in these elementary ideas, the origin of my dislike of caucuses—(laughter and hear, hear)—my distrust of parties, my aversion to centralization, and my belief in the fullest forms of local liberty compatible with imperial integrity. (Cheers.) Liberty is not a placard to be read at the street-corners. (Laughter.) It is a living power, felt within and around us. It forbids all interference with individual action, provided such action does not infringe the liberty of others. (Hear, hear.) It abolishes privileges, removes monopolies, throws open all public services, prevents either creed, or birth, or social position, being a barrier to success. (Hear, hear, and cheers.) Health and wealth, industry and thrift, capacity and endurance, are irregularly distributed, and will favourably handicap those endowed with them in the race of life. These inequalities we cannot obliterate; but all artificial hindrances that stand in the way of individual effort, of free and full mental expansion, ought to be cleared away. (Cheers.) A fair field and no favour; honour always; and victory if possible for the best, the bravest, and the wisest. That is my ideal. (Cheers.) It was once the Liberal ideal. (Laughter and cheers.) It is not with everyone so still. (Laughter.) The popular cry now is for the State to over-ride the man—for legislation to supply the place of open competition and free personal action. This, in my judgment, is retrogression. (Hear, hear.) It is going back to the time when our intellectual life was regulated by censors, our legislative life by a governing caste, and our industrial life by revenue-officers. (Laughter.) We have, during the last sixty years, conquered liberty of conscience, political securities, freedom of the press, and unfettered commerce. During all that time we have been busy unfolding mediæval swathes and entanglements; and there are some amongst us who now seem bent on encircling us with others equally as anomalous, if not as oppressive. They are all for organization. If they don't take care, they will organize all spontaneity, intrepidity, and initiative out of the people. As has been well said by the foremost teacher of the faith I am preaching, their "organization is not of humanity, but of the kitchen of humanity." (Laughter and cheers.) Machinery and mammon are their motto. (Hear, hear.) The life of the stomach is their problem. (Renewed laughter.) They animalize man by concentrating excessive attention upon material interests, and by putting forward as an end that which is only a means. (Hear, hear.) Men cannot be regenerated by merely growing fat. (Hear, hear, and laughter.) Physical amelioration is the consequence of moral amelioration. The result of every attempt made to promote the well-being of mankind, by taking the management of their affairs out of their own control, has been to deteriorate, and not to improve, their condition. It is through the perpetual gymnastics of political life that national character is purified, elevated, and strengthened. The State is a growth, and not a machine. (Hear, hear.) It should have a free organic life. It is invested with authority to punish crime, and it cannot, with reason, be denied the power of preventing it. But this ought not to be a justification for meddlesome, inquisitorial, and enervating legislation, which aggravates the evil it is designed to cure. (Hear, hear.) Under its operation, society becomes stationary, torpid, and inactive. Uniformity produces monotony and stagnation. The State has no right to attempt to regulate the private actions of individuals, or to entrench upon their primary relations with each other. One man's wit become's another man's wisdom. One nation's experience ought to become another's guide. The competing principles of excessive dependency on, and a rational independence of, government, were never more appositely illustrated than in Sparta and Athens. All the mental tendencies of the two States, all their social usages, were devised to exhibit these two diverse doctrines. (Hear, hear.) The Spartan laws were devised to form the people in one uniform mould. Strength, craft, and hardihood, were the ends sought by their stern legislative maxims. They had no literature, no science, no money, no commerce, no colonies, no foreign policy, no luxuries. They improved nothing, and they cultivated but one art—that of self-defence. This is the normal condition of a country where the Government does everything. It is hostile to all advance and adventure. Sparta bequeathed the world no legacy, and she might have passed out of memory but for the records of her cultivated foes. The Athenians were the antithesis of this. They had liberty with law, and government without oppression. They encouraged the development of individual genius, and gave absolute freedom to it. They left the faculties of each to find their most congenial sphere of action. They bred men, not merely citizens. (Cheers.) The Spartans belonged to the Peloponnesus—the Athenians to the world. In war, the Athenians were at least equal to their rivals; while in the nobler arts of poetry, sculpture, architecture, oratory, philosophy, they have distanced all competitors, ancient and modern. The Athenians can never pass out of recollection. They made the earth their monument. The older the world grows, the more varied experience we get, the more comprehensive our survey of history becomes, the stronger our grasp upon the comparative methods of inquiry, the more surprising do the accomplishments of this marvellous community seem. (Hear, hear.) We have, in these two States, the two systems—collectivism and individualism—amply exemplified. If you take the first as the basis of your labour, if you take to settling humanity by line and rule, you will, sooner or later, secure the triumph of despotism—make the life of the nation repose on beliefs blindly accepted, and establish constraints as the sole method of life. This stereotyping men into systems—encasing them in legal armour, dangling before them material Utopias, making the fleshpots the pivot on which all their efforts turn—(hear, hear, and laughter)—is a prostitution of national aspirations, a violation of human liberty, an encroachment on individual life, and a barrier to progress. (Hear, hear.) I am opposed to it both by conviction and sympathy. I am against hiding the man under the sectarian, deadening the ceaseless vital impulses of the mind by prescript, and killing free intelligence by formulas. The Calmuck Tartars, according to Mr. Carlyle, pray by turning a rotary calabash, with written prayers on it. It would be easy to make a machine, at Birmingham or elsewhere—(loud laughter and cheers)—that would repeat, with precision, the political liturgies; but no such contrivance will bring ethical fire into the human soul, or quicken the national spirit out of darkness into life. (Hear, hear, and cheers.) I distrust all such mental mechanism. I would emancipate the individual from all trammels which crush his activity, or dwarf his intellect, and enable and encourage him to develop himself in the plenitude of all his faculties, free alike from the worn-out formularies of political castes, the subtle fetters of modern system-mongers—(laughter)—or the sophisms of the self-appointed interpreters of party ethics. (Laughter and cheers.) A question of more immediate, if not of more ultimate importance than that of State Socialism, is that of our imperial position. (Hear, hear.) Are we to maintain the Empire—(A voice : "Yes")—and are we prepared to make the sacrifices necessary to do so ? ("Yes," and cheers.) That is a question the new electorate must answer promptly and decisively. (Hear, hear.) We have now the largest share of the world's trade, and no small share of its surface. Do we mean to keep them ? ("Yes," and cheers.) Many Englishmen are possessed of the belief that we owe our pre-eminence to the operation of natural causes, as fixed and permanent as those which control the seasons or regulate the ebb and flow of the tide. This is a delusion. It arises from our habit of estimating the whole world by our own sensations. We talk of things, not as we know them, but as they seem to be, or as we like them to be. We are, no doubt, largely indebted to the advantages of geographical position and material products. We owe something to climatic conditions. A lotus-eating land, where every aspect charms the senses into rapture, where the body requires but little for its support, and that little is found readily supplied, repels enterprise. That is not the case with us. We have had to fight for our position. (Hear, hear.) Our difficulties have enhanced our energies. We have turned opposing forces into the tools with which we have achieved success. Our energies have given us the mastery of the seas, and created for us Settlements in every corner of the globe. (Hear, hear.) Our imperial supremacy has secured us mercantile supremacy. If one leave us, the other will follow ; and, if our trade be destroyed, the whole fabric of our prosperity will go by the run. (Hear, hear.) That, at least, is my opinion, and I have supplied reasons for entertaining it. It is not the opinion of all Liberals. The acknowledged and uncontested bias of many of them is sincerely hostile to the maintenance of the Empire. Some regard it is as a dangerous excrescence, to be cut off at the first favourable opportunity; others as a luxury which is kept for the exclusive advantage of a class. If it were a matter of choice, many might prefer that England should be a modern Athens rather than a modern Rome. But it is not a case of choice—(hear, hear),—it is a case of necessity. We cannot undo the past. We cannot separate the nation from its history, or surrender the pre-eminence which generations have placed us in. (Cheers.) It would be craven, insensate, and injurious to do so. We have the Empire, we must hold it; and, to do so, we must be prepared to defend its interests in council, and fight for them in the field or on the ocean. (Renewed cheers.) It is neither wise nor honest to deceive ourselves. Our position requires us always to be ready, and, when necessary, to be willing to fight. Doctrines are often taught by men of authority and influence, that are incompatible with these responsibilities. Hopes are raised that cannot be realized, and disappointment and discontent ensue. For politicians to promise what they cannot perform is to delude the people, and pave the way for inevitable reaction. (Hear, hear.) It was because of the well-meant attempt to combine the incompatible, and to reconcile the irreconcilable, that we saw Egypt turned into chaos—(loud cheers)—the Soudan into a Pandemonium, and that we have witnessed, during the last five years, pacific professions combined with war and lavish expenditure, with loss of territory, reputation, and authority. (Loud cheers.) The late Government began with what they thought was a concert in their favour, and they ended with something very like a coalition against them. (Hear, hear.) The reason for the change in the attitude of the Powers is patent. Our Ministry hesitated. First they would, and then they wouldn't. (Loud laughter and cheers.)

Aggressive and not over-scrupulous foreign statesmen became possessed of the belief that our decadence had begun, that we had lost our nerve, and that we had only to be menaced and coerced, and we would submit to any humiliation and condone any defeat. (Hear, hear.) That is the explanation of the unfriendliness of Germany and Austria, the fractiousness of France, and the unconcealed hostility of Russia. (Hear, hear.) We cannot afford to have illusions on this subject. It is too serious. We have drained the resources of half the world into our coffers. Enterprises abroad have laid the foundation of half our homes. Other nations are envious of our success, and they would seize a slice of our estate whenever they found us tripping. (Cheers.) They respect only one quality—strength. (Loud cheers.) They yield to only one influence—force. We need not be splenetic or unduly suspicious; but we shall require to be wary if we are to baffle the combination of rivals, and we shall require to be ready if we are to resist the attacks of enemies. (Hear, hear.) We should have an avowed and definite imperial policy. (Cheers.) We should make up our minds as to what we will and what we will not do. A policy is the withe that binds the sticks of the Empire into a bundle. Loosen it, and the sticks drop asunder. To sustain such a policy, we must lift the direction of foreign affairs, and of the army and navy out of the petty arena of party plans. (Cheers.) Our course must be consistent and straight, our language homogeneous and harmonious. We must not shift according to the emergencies of Ministers. (Hear, hear.) If our policy is to be at the mercy of varying, meddling, many-headed faction-mongers —(laughter);—if we undo to-morrow what we did yesterday; if we play a game of party see-saw with national interests—(laughter and hear, hear)—then, we may lay our account for alternate attacks and apologies, for successive displays of imperiousness and submission, until we have made enemies all round, and brought about our absolute isolation. (Great cheering.) No one will treat with, or trust, a nation whose policy is uncertain. (Hear, hear.) We cannot have a better illustration of the weakness I am describing than what is now going on in Afghanistan. The Russians are delaying the demarkation of the frontier, in the hope that the elections will secure them a more friendly Cabinet than the one now in office. This ought not to be. (Cheers.) When the integrity of the Empire is at issue, there should be no difference amongst our statesmen. And there would not be if we substituted a national for a partizan foreign policy, and we had an army and a navy adequate to sustain it. (Cheers.) We should then find our foreign troubles diminish, and our relations with other States less liable to friction. (Hear, hear.) Great States have their drawbacks, but they also have their advantages, and one of them consists in diminishing the amount of warfare and in narrowing its sphere. The United States, the greatest democracy in the world, and Russia, the greatest despotism, manipulate their foreign affairs with less friction and more consistency and success than we do. In the American Republic, external questions are dealt with by the President, and his Ministers and a committee of Senators. In this way, the authority of both the Executive and the Legislature is recognized and represented. The policy promulgated by Mr. Monroe, with the volume of traditions modifying and emphasising it, is the basis on which their diplomatic system is built. It has been steadily adhered to by all parties—by Democrats and Republicans, by Federalists and States-right men. (Cheers.) Given an international dispute, everyone is aware in advance how the United States will act. They will welcome all new States to the Union; they will exclude foreign nations from the sphere of their legitimate authority, and exact reparation for injuries done to the nation or its citizens. (Cheers.) But beyond this they will not go. That is their policy. The world knows it, and knows, too, that it will be stuck to, and can be defended. (Renewed cheers.) They have, in consequence, few external complications, and no dangers. (Hear, hear.) The Russian foreign policy is equally steady and well-defined, although it is radically dissimilar in purpose. The American is defensive; the Muscovite is aggressive. There is no art that the Russians cultivate with such diligence as diplomacy. It is the only field upon which they can display their political skill and activity. They have no Parliament, and the official class is limited. Educated Russians, therefore, concentrate on foreign affairs much thought and great effort. They thus get, in their diplomatic service, an acuteness and activity elsewhere unknown. They have a visible object in view, and an undeviating advance is made towards it. The end is never lost sight of, and every influence is utilized for the purpose of attaining it. By this means, the Russians' external policy is distinguished by unparalleled persistency and stability. From the days of Peter the First to the present, her efforts have been to secure fresh territory, and she has assailed, in succession, Sweden, Poland, Turkey, Persia, and every Asiatic Khan. When worsted in battle, her diplomatists have usually managed to recoup her in Congress. We have not that unity of conception and execution which characterizes both the American and the Russian policy. (Cheers.) The inefficiency of our diplomacy, with its vacillation and contradictions, contrasts strangely with the logical development of the Russians. This may be explained partly by the difference in the character of the two peoples. We distrust theories and principles, and allow ourselves to be absorbed in the interests of the moment, without troubling about remote consequences. The Russians look farther ahead. We have two rival parties who fight over the Empire, while the Russians have but one which fights for the nation. (Cheers.) The mischief done, and the impression produced abroad, by our inconsistencies are equally unfortunate. All parties are perplexed; the strong are irritated; and the weak always disappointed, and sometimes disgusted. (Hear, hear.) Formidable problems will meet the new Parliament on the threshold, but none so formidable as the two indicated. (Hear, hear.) It will be expected to adjust an aristocratic constitution to a democratic suffrage, to reconcile inequality of condition with equality of power. It will have also to determine whether England will adopt the huxterer's religion—(hear, hear, and laughter)—"Mind your own doors," or whether she will keep her Empire, and, as a consequence, continue to assert and maintain her position as an active and efficient member of the European Areopagus. (Cheers.) These are the questions that lie nearest to our legislators. They far transcend in importance more catching cries, many of which, indeed, are included in them; and a constituency has the right to know from its representative, without equivocation, trimming, flattery, or disguise—(loud laughter)—his matured conclusions upon them. During the last fortnight, I have tried to state mine, and to give the facts on which I base them and the arguments by which I sustain them. (Loud cheers.) Montaigne, in presenting an edition of his essays, says,—"I have gathered a nosegay of flowers, in which there is nothing of my own but the string which ties them." (Laughter.) I may apply the same simile to my addresses. The principles I have expounded are as old as civilization, and as universal as truth. But the method of applying them, and giving them proportion, place, and design, is my own. (Cheers.) I end, as I began, by re-affirming my faith in the Democracy. (Cheers.) It is freedom's fulcrum. I seek, however, no change but that which comes by evolution, and the consequent survival of the fittest. I disown no tradition of English worth, and would not ruthlessly destroy any institution, or wantonly undermine any custom, that links us to a vanished but glorious past. (Loud cheers.) But I would shrink from no reform which leads to an extension of English liberty and the elevation of English character. (Hear, hear.) The Democracy has its destiny in its own hands. I hope that it will not vibrate, as has been predicted, between servility and revolution; that it will do something more than monotonously revolve in a beaten circle, where, as Mr. Lowe said, "every ant's nest is made a mountain, and every thistle a forest tree"—(laughter);—and that it will turn its freedom to noble uses. Such, certainly, is my belief. (Hear, hear.) Gentlemen, my case is completed. I have performed my allotted labour. (Cheers.) You will to-morrow perform yours. (Renewed cheers, and a voice, "At the head of the poll.") It remains to be seen whether you will approve of the creed I have expounded, and of me as its exponent. (Cheers, and a voice: "We will.") I have arrived at no opinion as to the result. Whatever your verdict, it will not weaken my gratitude for the unvarying consideration, courtesy, and kindness, I have received at the hands of the people of Newcastle, over the somewhat extended period of time during which I have been associated with them in public work. (Loud and prolonged cheering.) As for my opponents, I have not intentionally said anything to give offence; and I hope I have not unintentionally said anything that has done so. (Hear, hear.) I have striven to be educational, and not retaliatory and imputative. I have expounded doctrines, and explained their application. I have appealed to your intelligence and your sympathies, and not to your prejudices or your passions. (Great cheering, again and again renewed.) If I have been candid, I expect I have not been captious. If I have been firm, I trust I have not been unconciliatory. If I have been critical, it has been for persuasion and warning, and not for recrimination. (Loud cheers.) A man may secure momentary applause, but not eventual success, by suborning his convictions to the low and harsh exigencies of party strife. (Hear, hear.) Several of my friends fear that, as I have not canvassed, and my competitors have, my chances of election have been greatly imperilled. (Loud cries of "No, no," "Never," and cheers.) Perhaps so. But if I am beaten—(a voice: "No, at the head of the poll")—because I did not canvass, I shall not complain. I dislike the system. If not contrary to the letter, it certainly is contrary to the spirit, of the law. (Cheers.) I am in favour of the ballot, and opposed to over-organization; and if I had shrunk from carrying into operation my own principles, I might have been reminded of the words of Montrose—

> He either fears his fate too much,
> Or his desert is small,
> Who dares not put it to the touch,
> To win or lose it all.

(Loud and continued cheering, the entire audience rising and continuing to cheer for some time.)

The CHAIRMAN, when the enthusiasm called forth by Mr. Cowen's address had subsided, said Mr. Cowen was prepared to answer any relevant question.

Mr. COWEN, who was again received with enthusiastic cheers, said: Now, I have received upwards of a thousand questions, covering all conceivable subjects, and it has been impossible to reply to the whole of such a mass. It has even been impossible to group them. A gentleman sends me a question, and says he has asked it three times without getting any reply. I am sorry for this; but it did not come specially under my notice before. The gentleman asks—

"Is Mr. Cowen prepared to defend constitutional rights by his voice as well as by his vote, as a privileged House of Commons prevented Mr. Bradlaugh from taking his seat in the late Parliament; and is it true that you walked out of the House on one division?"

The question is respectfully put, and is entitled to an answer. I wish, therefore, to say it is not correct that I ever left the House without voting when Mr. Bradlaugh's case was before it. (Cheers.) I voted on it every time I was there. (Hear, hear.) I remember, too, that instead of leaving the House and not voting, I voted in two or three divisions with only a handful of members. On one occasion, my late colleague, Mr. Dilke, was teller, and there were only three or four members behind him. As for speaking on the question, it is a matter of discretion and convenience. It is not always desirable to speak, and not always possible. I would be very glad to speak in support of Mr. Bradlaugh being allowed to take the oath, and lend him my Northumberland burr—(laughter and cheers)—if the opportunity occurred, and I could do so with advantage to his cause. (Cheers.) A gentleman asks me—

"Do not the Government get and use large sums of unclaimed money belonging to private persons?"

Yes. When a person dies intestate, and his heirs are not known, the property goes to the Crown, which holds it in trust till some claimant makes good his right to it. The Treasury has over £330,000 of money of this kind in hand. It also holds large amounts of undistributed assets and unclaimed dividends in bankruptcy; a class of funds classed "dormant" in Chancery; estates reverting to the Crown by reason of illegitimacy, and unclaimed prize-money and soldiers' unclaimed balances. These funds, together, run up to a very formidable amount. In addition to these, about £40,000,000 of suitors' money in Chancery was, by an Act of 1882, borrowed for National Debt purposes. The Courts of Justice at Temple Bar have been mainly built by the surplus interest of suitors' money. The Treasury, by the late Bankruptcy Act, has collected £5,000,000 of unclaimed assets and dividends. Altogether, the Crown gets in these ways substantial windfalls both in real and personal property. Information respecting these sums of money and property is published, but it is done in such an imperfect and unsatisfactory manner, that persons entitled to them have little chance of getting at it. Efforts have been made by private members to pass a Bill establishing a Government department for the collection and distribution of unclaimed funds and valuables. But success has not attended the attempt. Indeed, there has not been an opportunity got to discuss the subject in Parliament. It is well deserving of consideration. Individual certainly suffer, and the State gains by the existing arrangement.

"Why should not a working man be a Tory?" (Laughter.)

Many a man inherits his political opinions as he does his property. (Laughter.) Political faith is largely a matter of sentiment, disposition, and training. The working classes, up to a certain era in English history, were, as a rule, Conservative. They certainly were Conservative during Mr. Pitt's *regime.* Since then, they have been Liberal, and Liberal because the Conservatives refused to concede them political rights. (Cheers.) They have now got those political rights, and stand on the same level as other classes; and no doubt they will be Tory or Liberal, according to circumstances.

"Is compulsory education consistent with the doctrine of individual liberty?"

This is an important question, and it would take a long time to argue it out. I should be quite willing to do so, however, if time would allow, and circumstances were favourable to doing so. (Hear, hear.) My friend, Mr. Auberon Herbert, is in Newcastle just now, and he is a master of the subject, and can state the arguments for and against with much greater effect than I can; and I recommend my interrogator to put himself in communication with Mr. Herbert, and he will reply with some of the best arguments in favour of individualism and education. (Laughter and cheers.)

---

## CHARACTER OF THE MEETINGS.

This closed the programme which, shortly before the dissolution of Parliament, Mr. Cowen had himself arranged, and which he was able, satisfactorily and efficiently, to go through. At each of the meetings which he addressed, the candidate was received with the most decided manifestations of enthusiasm and approval; and such was the impossibility of accommodating all who were anxious to listen to the speeches, that in almost every instance an out-door overflow meeting was held. In each case, too, a resolution of confidence in the old member was submitted, and was carried, if not unanimously, with, at most, only a very few dissentients. For the purpose of elucidating the relations of Great Britain to her vast and extensive possessions abroad, Mr. Cowen had recourse to a series of large maps displayed on the walls at the places of meeting, at which the subjects were dealt with. These, on a sufficiently compressed scale, it was the intention of the Publisher to have introduced into their appropriate places in the present volume; but time not permitting, this feature of the work has had to be dispensed with. To those, however, who may desire it, the object will be answered by reference to any ordinary Atlas.

## THE POLLING AND THE RESULT.

The polling for two members took place on Saturday, the 28th of November, and the result was officially declared on the Monday afternoon following. It was as follows :—

| | |
|---|---|
| Mr. Cowen ... ... ... ... | 10,489 |
| Mr. Morley ... ... ... ... | 10,129 |
| Mr. Hamond ... ... ... ... | 9,500 |

The two old members were thus re-elected. With this verdict, Mr. Cowen, in an address, which he issued a few days afterwards, expressed himself abundantly satisfied, but intimated that, the "meanness, the implacability, the vindictiveness, and the personal rancour of local politicians" having become unbearable, he has resolved, notwithstanding that result, "not again to contest the city."

# INDEX.

www.ingramcontent.com/pod-product-compliance
Lightning Source LLC
Chambersburg PA
CBHW030645030726
47497CB00006B/1965

* 9 7 8 3 3 3 7 1 7 6 7 6 1 *